The Philippine Islands
Vol.-27

By

Ed. Emma Helen Blair and
James Alexander Robertson

The Philippine Islands
Vol.-27

by   Ed. Emma Helen Blair and James Alexander Robertson

ISBN: 978-93-59399-82-9

Published by

DOUBLE 9 BOOKS

2/13-B, Ansari Road, Daryaganj
New Delhi – 110002
info@double9books.com
www.double9books.com
Tel. 011-40042856

Preface

The principal topics treated in this volume (1636–37) are the commerce of the Philippine Islands (especially with Nueva España) and the punishment inflicted by Corcuera on the Moro pirates of Mindanao. The former is fully discussed by Juan Grau y Monfalcón, procurator of Filipinas at the Spanish court; the latter is related in various documents, written mainly by participants in the Mindanao campaign. Certain minor documents relate to the administration of the islands and to the religious orders there.

A letter from Corcuera (June 30, 1636) gives a brief account of the great ecclesiastical controversy of that year; we present it here, not so much for the new information contained in it (which is not extensive) as for its being evidently the direct expression of the governor's own opinions, and not (like some others of his reports) dictated more or less by other persons. Corcuera says that "the friars are lawless people, and he would rather fight the Dutch in Flandes than deal with them." He asks that the king will adjust these matters, or else send another governor to the islands, so that one of them may attend to ecclesiastical affairs and the other to temporal. Part of Cerezo's letter of August 10, 1634, to the king is answered by the latter (October 10, 1636) in his despatches to Corcuera; it relates to military affairs — approving Cerezo's action, and giving some directions to Corcuera.

A royal decree of August 14, 1636, commands the municipality of Manila to reimburse their procurator-general, Juan Grau y Monfalcón, for the time and money that he has spent in attending to their business at the Spanish court. Another document of this sort (November 6, 1636) gives Corcuera orders regarding certain matters which his predecessor Cerezo had laid before the Spanish government. A third document (of the same date) approves the proceedings of Pedro de Heredia as governor of Terrenate, and promises reënforcements for the Spanish fort there.

The noted Memorial informatorio (Madrid, 1637) of Juan Grau y Monfalcón, procurator-general for Manila and the Philippines at the Spanish court, is here presented; it concerns the important and long-debated question of the restrictions imposed on the trade of the Philippine Islands with Nueva España. Certain measures have been proposed to the Spanish government which the procurator regards as dangerous to the interests of the Philippines, and he hastens to urge against these proposals numerous forcible arguments. He claims that the adoption of the former must result in the ruin of the citizens. And thus the crown must either support the entire expense of the islands, or abandon its hold on them — the former a heavy tax on its means, the latter most damaging to its power and prestige. A royal commissioner has been sent to Acapulco to investigate the revenue frauds alleged there, which greatly disturbs those who are engaged in trade, both in Nueva España and in the islands. The proposal to abandon the islands has been revived; the procurator rehearses the arguments advanced for this, and vigorously attacks them, urging that the possession of Filipinas be maintained by the crown as is that of Flanders. He proceeds to represent the importance of the islands, adducing many arguments to show this: the dependence of the Malucos on Filipinas, the size and number of those islands, the greatness and importance of Manila, the mineral resources of the islands, and, above all, their commerce.

The procurator describes this commerce, both domestic and foreign. Under the former head he enumerates the chief products of the islands, the diverse peoples who inhabit them, and the number of Indians and foreigners paying tribute to the crown and to private persons. He emphasizes the importance of the central location of the islands, and the restraint and hindrance that they constitute to the schemes of the Dutch for gaining control of the Oriental trade. Considering next the foreign trade of Filipinas, he represents it as far the most valuable part of that commerce, and gives a historical sketch of Oriental trade in general, with an enumeration of the commodities and products obtained therein, and much valuable information regarding the origin, quality, and prices of many goods. He relates how the Dutch were driven from Maluco, but afterward regained much of the spice region, notwithstanding the efforts of the Philippine Spaniards to prevent this. A list of the Dutch forts and factories in the archipelago is presented. From these data the procurator draws forcible arguments for the retention and support of the Philippine colony by the crown. This is fully justified by the importance of the clove trade, which otherwise would be lost to Spain; and by that of the Chinese trade, of which Filipinas enjoys the greater part. The maintenance of the Philippines will result in preserving the missionary conquests in the Far East, securing the safety of India, depriving the Dutch of their trade, relieving the expenses needed to preserve the American Spanish colonies, and maintaining the prestige of the Spanish crown. The royal treasury alone cannot meet all the expenses of the islands, nor is it wise to allow them too much commerce with Nueva España; the king is therefore advised to combine these two methods of relief. For his guidance in this matter, valuable information is submitted by the procurator, regarding

ABOUT THE EDITOR

Emma Helen Blair (1869-1951) was an American historian and author known for her significant contributions to Philippine history and also scholarship. Born on July 19, 1869, in Ohio, she pursued her education at Ohio Wesleyan University and later at Columbia University. Blair's passion for history and research led her to collaborate with James Alexander Robertson, an esteemed scholar, in editing and compiling "The Philippine Islands, 1493-1898" series. This monumental project spanned fifty-five volumes and covered the colonial history of the Philippines from the 16th to the 19th century. The comprehensive series showcased her expertise in meticulously examining and also presenting historical documents and narratives. Her work significantly contributed to a deeper understanding of the Philippines' complex past and its interactions with various colonial powers. Her commitment to historical accuracy and attention to detail earned her a reputation as a meticulous and reliable historian. Beyond her contributions to Philippine history, and main thing that Emma Helen Blair also authored "The Philippine Policy of Secretary Taft" and co-wrote "A History of the Philippine Islands" with Robertson. Both of these works further demonstrated her dedication to scholarship and the exploration of the Philippines' political and social developments.

James Alexander Robertson was born in Corry, Pennsylvania, in 1873. He was the sixth of eight children born to Canadian parents who became naturalized citizens of the United States after moving to Corry in 1866. His father, John McGregor Robertson, was a builder from Verulam, Ontario, close to Peterborough. His mother, Elizabeth Borrowman Robertson, immigrated to Canada as a child from her native Scotland. When Robertson was seven years old, his mother died. After three years, he and his family relocated to Cleveland, Ohio, where James finished his secondary education. In 1892, he enrolled in Adelbert College at Western Reserve University for graduate study. He studied in Romance languages, majoring in Old French, and received his Bachelor of Philosophy degree from Western Reserve University in 1896.

CONTENTS

Preface

The principal topics treated in this volume (1636–37) are the commerce of the Philippine Islands (especially with Nueva España) and the punishment inflicted by Corcuera on the Moro pirates of Mindanao. The former is fully discussed by Juan Grau y Monfalcón, procurator of Filipinas at the Spanish court; the latter is related in various documents, written mainly by participants in the Mindanao campaign. Certain minor documents relate to the administration of the islands and to the religious orders there.

A letter from Corcuera (June 30, 1636) gives a brief account of the great ecclesiastical controversy of that year; we present it here, not so much for the new information contained in it (which is not extensive) as for its being evidently the direct expression of the governor's own opinions, and not (like some others of his reports) dictated more or less by other persons. Corcuera says that "the friars are lawless people, and he would rather fight the Dutch in Flandes than deal with them." He asks that the king will adjust these matters, or else send another governor to the islands, so that one of them may attend to ecclesiastical affairs and the other to temporal. Part of Cerezo's letter of August 10, 1634, to the king is answered by the latter (October 10, 1636) in his despatches to Corcuera; it relates to military affairs — approving Cerezo's action, and giving some directions to Corcuera.

A royal decree of August 14, 1636, commands the municipality of Manila to reimburse their procurator-general, Juan Grau y Monfalcón, for the time and money that he has spent in attending to their business at the Spanish court. Another document of this sort (November 6, 1636) gives Corcuera orders regarding certain matters which his predecessor Cerezo had laid before the Spanish government. A third document (of the same date) approves the proceedings of Pedro de Heredia as governor of Terrenate, and promises reënforcements for the Spanish fort there.

The noted Memorial informatorio (Madrid, 1637) of Juan Grau y Monfalcón, procurator-general for Manila and the Philippines at the Spanish court, is here presented; it concerns the important and long-debated question of the restrictions imposed on the trade of the Philippine Islands with Nueva España. Certain measures have been proposed to the Spanish government which the procurator regards as dangerous to the interests of the Philippines, and he hastens to urge against these proposals numerous forcible arguments. He claims that the adoption of the former must result in the ruin of the citizens. And thus the crown must either support the entire expense of the islands, or abandon its hold on them—the former a heavy tax on its means, the latter most damaging to its power and prestige. A royal commissioner has been sent to Acapulco to investigate the revenue frauds alleged there, which greatly disturbs those who are engaged in trade, both in Nueva España and in the islands. The proposal to abandon the islands has been revived; the procurator rehearses the arguments advanced for this, and vigorously attacks them, urging that the possession of Filipinas be maintained by the crown as is that of Flanders. He proceeds to represent the importance of the islands, adducing many arguments to show this: the dependence of the Malucos on Filipinas, the size and number of those islands, the greatness and importance of Manila, the mineral resources of the islands, and, above all, their commerce.

The procurator describes this commerce, both domestic and foreign. Under the former head he enumerates the chief products of the islands, the diverse peoples who inhabit them, and the number of Indians and foreigners paying tribute to the crown and to private persons. He emphasizes the importance of the central location of the islands, and the restraint and hindrance that they constitute to the schemes of the Dutch for gaining control of the Oriental trade. Considering next the foreign trade of Filipinas, he represents it as far the most valuable part of that commerce, and gives a historical sketch of Oriental trade in general, with an enumeration of the commodities and products obtained therein, and much valuable information regarding the origin, quality, and prices of many goods. He relates how the Dutch were driven from Maluco, but afterward regained much of the spice region, notwithstanding the efforts of the Philippine Spaniards to prevent this. A list of the Dutch forts and factories in the archipelago is presented. From these data the procurator draws forcible arguments for the retention and support of the Philippine colony by the crown. This is fully justified by the importance of the clove trade, which otherwise would be lost to Spain; and by that of the Chinese trade, of which Filipinas enjoys the greater part. The maintenance of the Philippines will result in preserving the missionary conquests in the Far East, securing the safety of India, depriving the Dutch of their trade, relieving the expenses needed to preserve the American Spanish colonies, and maintaining the prestige of the Spanish crown. The royal treasury alone cannot meet all the expenses of the islands, nor is it wise to allow them too much commerce with Nueva España; the king is therefore advised to combine these two methods of relief. For his guidance in this matter, valuable information is submitted by the procurator, regarding the expenses of maintaining and governing the Philippines (under eight different headings — civil, religious, and military — sufficiently itemized to give a clear outline of expenditures under each, and summarized at the end), the revenues of the colonial treasury, and the real nature of the deficit therein. He claims that the islands contribute more than what they cost, since they have to bear the great expenses of maintaining and defending Maluco against the Dutch (which includes more than one-third of all the expenses of Filipinas), and aid all public needs with their time, property, and lives, as volunteers — thus saving to the crown an enormous expense. The procurator asks that these services be duly rewarded by the crown, and recommends that for this purpose the magistracies in the islands be kept for rewarding such worthy citizens, and not sold, as heretofore, at auction. But chiefly he urges the importance to them of the trade with Nueva España which is chiefly based on that which Manila carries on with China and India. Efforts have been made in Spain to suppress the former commerce, as being detrimental to that of Spain and the Indias. He admits that this last is decreasing, but claims that Filipinas is not responsible therefor. The causes of that decline are, rather, the greatly lessened yield of the precious metals in America, the enormous decrease of the Indian population in the colonies, the smaller consumption of goods among the Spaniards therein, and the exorbitant imposts and duties levied on the merchants. To deprive Filipinas of its commerce would be a measure both unjust and useless. The writer briefly reviews the history of that commerce, which at present is in a declining and feeble condition, owing to the many restrictions that have been laid upon it; and discusses certain misrepresentations that are current regarding supposed violations of the royal ordinances in the trade of Filipinas and Peru. Some of these acts are greatly exaggerated, and others, being inevitable in all trade, must be overlooked. Several instances are cited to show that even in Sevilla violations of the royal ordinances are taken for granted, and sometimes condoned even when discovered; and the procurator urges that the Filipinas be not more severely treated than other parts of the royal domain. He admits that their cargoes, like those from other colonies, contain some unregistered goods; but declares that the amount of this has been greatly exaggerated, for which he adduces various arguments. He also explains that the products of the islands themselves go to Nueva España outside of the amount permitted, which has been incorrectly represented. He again presents for consideration the additional two per cent duty imposed on Philippine shipments, and with forcible arguments urges that it be abolished. The procurator even declares that the commerce of Filipinas pays higher duties than does any other, and that the citizens of Manila have lost in it more than they have gained — in proof of which he submits a list of shipwrecks, wars and military expeditions, insurrections, conflagrations, and other occasions of loss and damage since the foundation of Manila. He then enumerates the goods sent to Nueva España from Filipinas, which are necessary to the former country for supplying the needs of its people; compares these goods with those sent from Spain; and discusses the effect of this Chinese merchandise on the Spanish silks. The memorial closes with a brief summary of the considerations and arguments therein contained, and a request for leniency in the imposition of duties on goods from Filipinas.

During the summer and autumn of 1636, a Mindanao chief named Tagal harries the coasts of Cuyo and Calamianes. Returning homeward laden with booty and captives, these pirates are attacked (December 21) by a hastily-gathered Spanish force of ships and men, and in this battle Tagal and many of his followers are slain, and most of their plunder recovered. This victory is a great gain to the Spaniards in maintaining their stand against the hostile Moros, and many of the latter are rendered submissive for the time being. An account of these events is given in a letter unsigned and undated, but evidently written early in 1637, and probably by the Jesuit Pedro Gutierrez.

By order of the royal Council a compilation is made (February, 1637?) of all information in the government records pertaining to the office of auditor of accounts at Manila. The writer (some clerk in the government employ) gives a brief historical sketch of this office, its relations with the royal officials, the advantages and disadvantages connected with it, and the proceedings of the council regarding this office, up to 1637.

The Moro raids of 1636 arouse the Spaniards to the urgent necessity of subduing those fierce and treacherous pirates; and Corcuera organizes an expedition to Mindanao, led by himself, for their punishment. Several accounts of this campaign (which had far-reaching consequences) are presented—largely from Jesuit sources, since members of that order accompany the governor, and it is their missions which are most endangered by the hostility of the Moros in Mindanao.

One of these is a letter (June 2, 1637) from the celebrated martyr in the Japanese missions, Marcelo Francisco Mastrilli, who went to Mindanao with Corcuera. He relates with much detail the events of the expedition, which the devil strives from the start to hinder. The Spaniards capture the Moro forts at the mouth of the Rio Grande, killing several of Corralat's best officers, and seizing many vessels and military supplies; then they destroy many villages belonging to him. On March 18, the Spaniards storm a fortified height back of the port where they first entered. Corralat is driven from it, and flees to a little village in his territory; and in the conflict his wife and many of his followers are slain. Some Recollect fathers, held captive by the Moros, also perish—one of them slain by them, in anger at their defeat. Corralat's treasure is seized, and divided among the soldiers; and much booty obtained by the Moros in plundering the churches in their raids is recovered. After destroying all that can be found, Corcuera returns to Zamboanga; leaving troops behind to subdue another Moro ruler, named Moncay. The wounded Spaniards — many of whom were injured by poisoned arrows — are cared for at Zamboanga, so successfully that only two men out of eighty die, and these "because they would not let themselves be cured." Mastrilli ascribes this success not so much to the antidotes that had been furnished from Manila as to the virtues of a relic that he had, of St. Francis Xavier, and to the patients' faith therein. In due time, the detachment sent against Moncay return, bringing that chief's brother as envoy to offer his submission, and a promise to aid the Spaniards against Corralat, and to receive among his people Jesuit missionaries. Corcuera returns to Manila, after sending an expedition to reduce the villages on the western coast of the island, and arranging for opening a mission on the island of Basilan and securing for its people (who desire to maintain friendship with the Spaniards) the protection of the Spanish fort at Zamboanga. Other Moros along the southern coast offer to become the vassals of Spain, and the Joloans hasten to secure peace with the conqueror. All this opens a broad field for gospel work, and Mastrilli urges that Jesuit missionaries hasten to till it.

The usual Jesuit annals are continued by Juan Lopez (1636–1637). The archbishop is now on very friendly terms with the Jesuits. The noted martyr Mastrilli comes to the islands, and is regarded with much veneration by the people on account of certain miracles vouchsafed him; he departs from Manila on his way to Japan. Certain Dutchmen, prisoners at Manila, are converted; some of these, and some discontented Spaniards, undertake to escape from the islands, but most of the fugitives come to grief. The Dutch are at swords' points with the natives of Java and Amboyna. The Spanish relief ships sent to Ternate encounter the Dutch and gain some advantage over them. A chief in Celebes and another in Siao have sent their sons to be educated in the Jesuit college at Manila; and to the former have been sent some soldiers and a missionary. The Camucones pirates were unusually daring in the year 1636, and carried away many captives from Samar; but on their return to their own country many of them perished by storms or by enemies. The Mindanao raid of the same year, and Corcuera's Mindanao campaign, are briefly described. The ruler of Jolo is hostile, and Corcuera is going thither to humble the Moro's pride. In Japan, all persons having Portuguese or Castilian blood have been exiled to Macao.

Returning victorious from the Mindanao expedition, Corcuera makes a triumphant entry into Manila (May 24, 1637), which is described by the Jesuit Juan Lopez. The festivities, secular and religious, last during several weeks, and include processions, masquerades, illuminations, masses, music, and dancing—and, finally, a dramatic representation of the conquest of Mindanao. The Manila Jesuits appeal (in August of that year) to the king, through the governor of the islands, for a further grant, to aid in erecting their buildings. This request is endorsed by Archbishop Guerrero.

On August 20, Corcuera sends the king his own account of his recent campaigns against the Moros of Mindanao; he promises to undertake next year expeditions to Jolo and Borneo. He asks the king to confirm his grant of extra pay to wounded soldiers; he also complains of the illegal acts of Pedro de Heredia, who has long been governor at Terrenate, and asks that an official be sent from Spain to take Heredia's residencia.

The Editors

June, 1905.

Documents of 1636

Sources: The first document, and the first of the three decrees, are obtained from MSS. in the Archivo general de Indias, Sevilla; the rest, from the "Cedulario Indico," in the Archivo Historico Nacional, Madrid.

Translations: The first document is translated by Emma Helen Blair; the second, by Robert W. Haight; the third, by James A. Robertson.

Letter from Corcuera to Felipe IV

Sire:

Your Majesty was pleased to present for archbishop of this city Don Fray Hernando Guerrero, formerly bishop of Nueba Segobia. I avow to your Majesty, in all truth, that, [even] if I did not feel under obligation to give you an account of what is going on in these your islands, which are in my charge, I would not dare to inform any other person than my natural lord of the archbishop's harsh, unbending, and irritable disposition. By the galleons which arrived last year came his bulls, which, with the decrees of your Majesty, he presented in the royal Audiencia. He was admitted to his church, whose canons and dignitaries he had often threatened because they had not been willing to receive him before his bulls came. In the royal court of justice, before which he appeared to be presented [to his see], he swore upon the gospels not to interfere with your Majesty's jurisdiction, to respect your royal patronage, and to be always your royal vassal. All this he has violated, three or four times; and during the ten months while he has governed the church he has not failed in each of them to annoy me and disturb the peace. The first occasion was, that an artilleryman had killed a slave-girl belonging to the sargento-mayor; she had formerly belonged to the artilleryman, and he had maintained illicit relations with her. The said archbishop took her away from him, and made him sell her. [Then follows an account of the murder and the execution of justice on the criminal (the body of the latter "was borne to its burial by La Misericordia"), and of the early part of the controversy with the archbishop.] A fuller account of this will be given to your Majesty by the fathers Diego de Bobadilla and Simon

Cotta,1 who are persons of great truthfulness, and have much authority in their order; they are going, as its agents, to Rome. From this your Majesty may be assured that they will give you truthful information about whatever you may be pleased to know regarding these islands. I entreat your Majesty, with all respect, that you will be pleased to command that their affairs shall be promptly and favorably despatched; for this religious order merits such favor for the services that they render to your Majesty. They furnish chaplains for your galleons that sail to Therrenate, on which service no one likes to go, on account of the danger. The said fathers are also rendering the same service in the galleons which go to Castilla; they receive twelve pesos a month as pay, which has been assigned to them on account of the convenience of this service to your Majesty — although the said fathers would serve without pay, most willingly, in order to show better the affection with which they always engage in your Majesty's service.

The said religious order, to defend themselves from the flagrant injuries which the said archbishop was inflicting upon them — although they sought means, and those the mildest, for peace — could not avoid the appointment of a judge-conservator. He defended their rights, and compelled the archbishop to withdraw the acts [which he had issued against the Society], although the said judge-conservator allowed himself first to be excommunicated. Here there is occasion for making a long relation to your Majesty; but I will refrain from that, mindful that the said fathers will make a report to you. I made an offer to the archbishop to pay, out of my own purse, the four thousand ducados which the judge-conservator had sentenced him to pay for the crusade fund; and that I would take into my own charge his affairs, and the satisfactory settlement of them with the said judge-conservator. For this purpose I went to visit the archbishop at [the convent of] St. Francis, to which he had retired; and in the presence of the provincial and of another religious (an Augustinian, procurator for his order) I made him that offer — on the condition that he would detach himself from the religious orders, who, as I judged, were disturbing his mind with evil counsels. He would not accept my offer with that condition, preferring to remain [where he was] until affairs had gone through their proper course, and [thus] lowering himself from bad to worse. On the Friday before Christmas Eve, he came to my lodgings after evening prayer, and with much feeling asked that, since I would give a furlough the next day to the prisoners in the jail, I would also release him from the affliction that he was suffering, and adjust his affairs. He had been declared to be suspended [from his office] for four years. I was embarrassed at this, and doubted whether I could do him any service or accomplish anything for his aid. I called together the learned jurists and advocates of this royal Audiencia, that they might give me their opinions after having carefully studied the question whether I could demand that [relief for the archbishop] from the judge-conservator, and ask him to grant it for my sake. In this council were present the provincial and the rector of the Society of Jesus, the dean [of the cathedral] and other canonists, and the judge-conservator himself; and in it I asked this last, in virtue of the opinions rendered by the said lawyers, to restore the archbishop to his government, and to withdraw from him the pecuniary fines, which amounted to more than eight thousand pesos. I could not obtain a favorable answer then, nor indeed for more than a fortnight afterward — although I offered to the judge-conservator, and to his brothers and relatives, all the favors that I could show them not unworthily, in an official way. At this very time I am assigning a pension of two hundred pesos to a sister of his, a poor woman, the wife of Don Sebastian de Herbite — to whom your Majesty was pleased to grant, by one of your royal decrees, an encomienda of three hundred ducados. That decree has not yet been fulfilled, because he has not come from España; and this sum has been given to his wife to aid in her support until her husband shall return, and your Majesty's command regarding him can be carried out. To another officer (a brother-in-law of the said judge-conservator), who has ability, and deserves reward for his own sake and for the services of his father, I gave the office of alcalde-mayor for Laguna de Vay. I assure your Majesty that the settlement [of this affair] cost me much care and effort, besides a thousand pesos in cash from my own purse which I spent for various matters. Peace having been concluded, and the archbishop having been absolved and freed from the penalties, he went to his own house in my coach; and I conveyed him to the holy church, and even to the choir — where I knelt, in order to set a good example to all, to recognize his authority; and I went to my own seat, to hear mass.

We remained in entire harmony about a month and a half. But the royal chaplain of your Majesty for the seminary of Santa Potenciana rang the bell for the Gloria, on Holy Saturday, a quarter of an hour before the cathedral bells rang; and for this the archbishop — although he knew that that chaplain is in charge of your Majesty's seminary, and only removable by you, and that he has no authority to wreak his anger on him, as he does on the others, his own clergy — commanded that two pairs of fetters should be placed on the chaplain, at the house of his fiscal. I was informed of this by a memorial from the directress of the said seminary, saying that it was left without chaplain and without mass. I sent by my secretary a message to the said archbishop, entreating that he would have the kindness to command that the chaplain be released, on account of the deficiency which his absence caused in the seminary; but he began to reprimand my secretary, as if the latter were the one to blame. For that reason, I sent by an adjutant an order to the said chaplain to come to me, to give his account of the affair; and within one hour he was sent back to his prison. Although the archbishop knew this, he left his house, going through the streets with a great disturbance, and attended with tapers, to consult with the religious orders whether he could excommunicate me; for he asserted that I had broken into his prison and taken away his prisoners. His fiscal hastened to tell him that the chaplain was already in his prison, at which the archbishop became quiet and returned to his house. He would not allow the chaplain to appeal to the bishop of Camarines; so the latter appealed for royal aid against fuerza — the archbishop having detained him six or eight days in prison because he would not pay the twelve pesos which he had been fined for having rung the bells for the Gloria too early. The fine was paid by a friend of his; and thereupon he was allowed to leave the prison.

After that, the archdeacon, Don Francisco de Valdes (who had been presented for that dignity by Don Juan Cereso de Salamanca), finding that his health was impaired, and being offended at the abusive language that the archbishop used, whenever he felt so inclined, to him and the other members of the chapter, in the choir, handed to the prelate his resignation of the said dignity — as much because he could not fulfil its duties on account of his infirmities, as for the reason just stated. He also placed his resignation before the government. The archbishop replied that Don Francisco must aid in the church services until Holy Week and Easter were past. After that time had expired, the archdeacon again demanded that the archbishop accept his resignation, and allow him to go to his own house to recuperate; but the prelate refused to accept it. Don Francisco therefore memorialized the government, placing the said resignation in your Majesty's hands; and it was accepted from him in your royal name, for the reasons that he alleged therein. For this cause he again became disquieted, and displayed his former bad temper. The juris-consults had affirmed that the said prebend was vacant, and that the government could present another person in Don Francisco's place — as was done, by presenting Master Don Andres Arias Xiron, cura of La Hermitta (one of the best benefices outside the city walls), who was provisor of this archbishopric while the bishop of Cibú governed it, and has always given a good account of himself. The archbishop disliked Don Andres because he did hot resign his office as provisor before that prelate entered upon the government of his church, so that the latter might bestow that office on Don Pedro de Monroy — who caused so many disturbances in the time of Don Alfonso [sic] Faxardo, excommunicating the auditors, and constraining the Audiencia to exile him from the kingdoms. This man was made provisor when the archbishop began to govern, and he caused fresh disturbances when justice was executed on the artilleryman;

and during the term of the judge-conservator the office of provisor was taken away from Don Pedro. As he left the city, through fear of the said judge-conservator—the ecclesiastical cabildo ruling [the archdiocese] and its dean being provisor—I gave orders at the city gates that the guards should not allow Don Pedro to enter them, to cause more commotions in the city. One day, at evening prayer, [his friends] brought him within the walls by a gate opening toward the sea, clad in the garb of a Franciscan, walking between two religious of that order; and the Dominicans received him into their house. The religious of both those orders, forcing their way through the guard and overpowering its commander, who was holding Don Pedro, smuggled in the latter through a little postern gate which the said Dominican fathers had.

Through the hatred and ill-will which the said archbishop bears to the said Don Andres Xiron, he refused to accept the presentation of the latter [to the archdeanery]; and in regard to this subject he has had so many disputes with the Audiencia of your Majesty over the fuerza which he committed against the said Don Andres, that he went so far as to excommunicate Auditor Çapatta for having rendered the decision that it was fuerza. By this act he excommunicated the entire Audiencia, as Çapatta alone remained of the auditors—for the rest of them are dead; the last one was Don Albaro de Mesa y Lugo, who died about six weeks ago—although it is true that, according to the concordant opinion of lawyers, the Audiencia cannot be held as excommunicate. I called together the advocates in the Audiencia, and named three for the defense of the case, who should continue to act with the authority that was given to them by the ordinance and iterative decrees of your Majesty. The royal decree having been issued, the archbishop yielded, and absolved the said auditor, Marcos Çapatta. But as he continued his display of fuerza against Don Andres Arias Xiron, an act and an iterative decree were also issued against the archbishop, which he refused to obey in any case. In this stand he was aided by the friars—Dominicans, Franciscans, Recollects, and Augustinians—at the time when the alguazil-mayor of court proceeded to execute the royal decree which exiled the archbishop from the kingdoms and deprived him of the temporalities. A friar carried to his house the monstrance with the most holy sacrament; he was clad in his pontifical robes, and, holding the monstrance in his hands, the three religious orders being present, he awaited the said alguazil-mayor with the said royal decree. The latter, seeing this array, did not know what he ought to do. The Audiencia commanded him to drive the religious out of the archbishop's house by force, with the assistance that he had, and to serve the royal decree. They ordered him to remain there with his soldiers, with all devoutness and respect, before the archbishop, and to wait until he should lay down the most holy sacrament, before executing the decree; also that he should not allow the archbishop to eat or drink, nor permit any one else to enter his house to give him food. The friars refused to go away, until the soldiers had to carry them away bodily. Then, at eleven o'clock at night, they were going about the streets, and finally obliged me to take other measures, after I had sent, in the name of your Majesty, protests to the provincial of St. Dominic and the guardian of St. Francis—informing them that their religious were gathered at the gate of the archbishop's house in the manner of a [religious] community, with lighted candles in their hands. The religious refused to go away until I gave orders that the soldiers should carry them in their arms to the convents. Their intention was to stir up the community, and cause scandals and tumults in it; and in truth they would have succeeded in this if your Majesty had not here your armed troops. For in these Philipinas Islands these friars are lawless people; and I would rather fight the Dutch in Flandes than deal with these friars, or have occasion for trouble with them. I will write further particulars about them in a separate letter and information to your Majesty, in order that you may be pleased to command that some corrective be applied to these disorders; and so that the governor may be enabled to conduct the government and attend to the service of your Majesty without being hindered by them.

The archbishop remained in the island of Maribeles—to which place he allowed himself to be conveyed for his disobedience—more than a fortnight. During this time the royal Audiencia set affairs in order, after having written to the bishop of Cibú (to whom pertains the ecclesiastical government [in such cases]) that the bishop of Camarines—who is second in that succession, and was here in the city—was to govern the church. This he has done, removing the suspension of divine services, and absolving the excommunicated ad cautelam. The archbishop, before the alguazil-mayor of the court could arrive to notify him of your Majesty's royal decree, had declared excommunication against the auditor Çapatta and the governor of Filipinas—as your Majesty will see by the papers which I send, which were posted in the churches. However, all the matters that I have mentioned, and everything else, I will leave for the report which the said fathers of the Society, Diego de Bobadilla and Simon Cotta, will make to your Majesty, in your royal Council of the Indias; they will inform you of all the circumstances and details which here I omit.

The royal Audiencia, exercising the clemency, kindness, and affection with which your Majesty treats your vassals (especially the prelates and ecclesiastics), issued a new royal decree to restore the said archbishop to your Majesty's favor and to his archbishopric—all which has been carried out, for the sake of a good example to all the foreign peoples here; but making preëminent the authority of your Majesty's jurisdiction in what concerns him. But we always remain hopeless that the said archbishop will govern his church peaceably, without interfering with the said royal jurisdiction or with your Majesty's patronage; for he is instigated [by others], and cannot be obliged, on account of the extent of his authority, to punish the ecclesiastics and his cabildo. He unites himself, on every occasion, with the three religious orders aforesaid — who do not content themselves with giving opinions which are not for his good, but force him to carry out these. They act thus out of revenge for my being told, when I first came here, of their shortcomings by the said archbishop; and they cannot revenge themselves, for this in any other way than by driving him into the same uneasy disposition. In order that your Majesty may form some idea of the archbishop, I will tell you of what occurred on Holy Thursday. At half-past two in the afternoon, when he was in the choir to perform the ceremony of washing the feet of twelve priests, he began to put on his pontifical robes, and at the same time gave orders that the musicians should sing. The sub-chanter was not there, not having arrived at the church; and moreover the dignitaries (who do not have to put on their vestments with him) had not come. One of these was Don Francisco de Valdes, who resigned the archdeaconry; he had treated these ecclesiastics so badly with insulting language that, on the last occasion of that, the said archdeacon resolved that he would not serve in the church during the term of the archbishop. As he did not possess your Majesty's confirmation of his prebend, they all said that he could do so. At this time the singers came in, and began the offices; the archbishop became so angry (for he is exceedingly choleric) that he snatched the miter from his head and flung it on the floor. Thus he went on, throwing down the rest of his vestments, one after another; and when he had stripped off all of them he went to his own house, snorting with anger, and uttering a thousand insults against all the prebendaries, and leaving all the priests sitting, barefooted, on a bench. Such are the actions of the archbishop; and with his headlong tendencies, combined with the excellent counsels that the friars give him, I shall have plenty to do in keeping them all quiet, and endeavoring to live in peace. All these things demand from your Majesty suitable and efficacious correction.

For the honor of God and of your own service, will your Majesty be pleased to command that all these matters be amended, or else to send another governor, so that one shall take care of ecclesiastical affairs, and the other of the temporal, for one man alone cannot do both; for the hindrances which these religious orders put in his way are many, and he has no time left for the political government or military affairs, or for considering the general welfare of the provinces. May our Lord guard the Catholic person of your Majesty, as Christendom has need. Manila, on the last day of June in the year 1636. Sire, your Majesty's vassal kisses your feet.

Sevastian Hurtado de Corcuera

I, Alonso Vaeça del Rio, public notary, one of the number [allotted] to this city for the king our sovereign, attest and give truthful testimony to the persons who shall see the present, that today, Friday, which is reckoned the ninth of May in the year one thousand six hundred and thirty-six, at about eight o'clock at night, a little more or less, Christoval de Valderrama, notary of this archbishopric, stationed himself at the corner of the archbishop's house, near the dwelling of the master-of-camp, Don Lorenzo de Olasso, to read a document. This he did by the light of a taper, in loud and intelligible words; and at the noise I, the present secretary, and several other persons went to the windows in the house of Captain Luis Alonso de Roa (which forms half a square), on the side where the said notary was standing. Continuing his reading, he said that inasmuch as the most reverend prelate of these islands had been making his official visitation on Master Don Andres Arias Jiron, a beneficed cura for the district of La Hermita; and in order to interrupt him, so that he could not continue that visitation, Don Sevastian Hurtado de Corcuera, governor and captain-general of these islands, had nominated the said Don Andres for archdeacon of the cathedral of this city; and besides, in order that the archbishop should accept him and bestow upon him collation and canonical installation, had issued against the said archbishop a royal decree in which he commanded him to give Don Andres the said collation — which was contrary to the bull In cena Domini: [accordingly,] the said governor and the licentiate Don Marcos Çapata de Galves, auditor of this royal Audiencia, had rendered themselves liable to excommunication; and he therefore commanded them that, within half an hour, they should withdraw the said royal decree — under penalty of four thousand ducados of Castilla to be applied for the Holy Crusade, and of the major excommunication, late sententia, ipso facto incurrenda; and he would place them on the public list of excommunicated persons. The aforesaid statements — with another, that he would proclaim an interdict, and would today impose a wholesale suspension of divine services — are those which I could understand; and I came to give an account of it to the said governor. Being in the apartment of the royal court, his Lordship, having sent away all persons except me, commanded that I should make an official statement of the affair — with a solemn declaration (which I made) that this demand was made with no intention of proceeding against any ecclesiastic, but only for the purpose of rendering an account of this occurrence to his Majesty and to his royal Council of the Indias. By this command I give the present; and it is witnessed by Captain Lope Ossorio de Soto, Eugenio de Rui Saenz, Captain

Diego Diaz de Pliego, Captain Luis Alonso de Roa, and Alférez Francisco Mexia—who all were with me, the present notary, in the house of the said Captain Luis Alonso de Roa, when what I have related occurred; and they also heard it. And, as witnesses that I attest the present deposition, were present Don Pedro de Arredondo Aguero, Alonso de Çornoca, and Antonio Dias. This deposition is dated on this said day, at about nine o'clock at night, a little more or less; and I sign it, in testimony of the truth.

Alonço Vaeça del Rio, public notary.

[Then follows an attestation by other public notaries that the said deponent is an authorized notary, and worthy of trust.2]

1 "Costa" in Barrantes; but Sommervogel gives the name of no Jesuit, under either form, who could have gone from Manila in 1636.

2 The mass of contemporary material in Spanish archives on the contest between Corcuera (the civil arm of the government) and the Jesuits on one side, and the bishop and friars on the other, shows how important the matter was considered, and the virulence with which the fight was waged on both sides. The various documents relate the affair pro and con, and it is narrated in official, semi-official, and religious documents. The facts of the case are stated, somewhat succinctly, in a printed document, undated (although probably 1636 or 1637), signed by Licentiate Ruiz de la Vega, and addressed to the king, in which many of the letters between the various parties concerned (all given in this series) are given in full or extract, but nothing new is told. This document is in Archivo general de Indias, at Sevilla, in the patronato "Audiencia de Filipinas; cartas y espedientes del gobernador de Filipinas, vistos en el Consejo; est. 67, caj. 6, leg. 8."

Letter from Felipe IV to Corcuera

The King: To Don Sebastian Hurtado de Corcuera, knight of the Order of Alcantara, my governor and captain-general of my Filipinas Islands, and president of my royal Audiencia thereof. The letter written to me by Don Juan Zerezo Salamanca, governor of those islands by appointment of the Marqués de Cerralvo, my viceroy of Nueva España, upon the death of Don Juan Niño de Tavora, on the tenth of August, 634, which treats of military affairs, has been received and examined in my Council of War for the Yndias and is answered in this.

He says that the preservation of those islands depends upon not undertaking new enterprises, but keeping the indispensable garrisons well defended, and reducing those of less importance, whereby there will be troops in that camp sufficient to undertake large enterprises, as the governors did in other days. At present, on the contrary, for the reason given, they are contented with not losing anything that is in their charge. It has, therefore, seemed best to warn and charge you, as I do, to inform me very needfully in regard to this, and of what ought to be done for the greater efficiency of the government.

He likewise says that to withdraw the forces from the island of Hermosa would be a difficult thing, notwithstanding that it appears, by the explanation that he sends me in the letter which he writes me concerning affairs of government (a copy of which I send you with this), that this is expedient. Accordingly, the force there should be reduced to only two posts, doing away with the expense of rations for the others—although, in his opinion, all that is being done is superfluous. After considering the said clause of the letter, you will inform me of what occurs to you in this matter, and what is advisable to be decreed.

He declares that the fortress of that city is in a state of defense, although not with the completeness that was maintained in former times, and that the fortification of the city is a difficult task. The site of its settlement is admirable, because more than half of it stands on an arm of the sea, where it cannot be surrounded by any enemies, and another stretch of wall is bathed by the river. But the remaining side, toward the land, has some heights; and the ground is such that a trench can be opened up to the wall, which has no terreplein. The wall is seven palmos high; the redoubts are very small and irregular—on the contrary, being in the way of the casements. Of the three cavaliers which the wall has, the moat is so filled up that there is hardly a sign that there was one. Considering the great importance of that post, and the fact that building can be done very cheaply, at less cost than in any other part, he resolved to build a royal cavalier, by gathering up the remains of what stood there before to repair the fortifications, in modern fashion, at the weakest part of the wall. Without drawing from my royal treasury, he had commenced the work four months before, and hoped to have it finished in two more. The ditch was being opened effectively at the same time, and to reduce the number of posts for the defense of this city, and that it might be better fortified, all the redoubts which disturbed the communication between the cavaliers were to be destroyed, and the wall would consist of merely four bastions. You will inform me as to what has been done, and what you may judge should be done.

As for the careless storage of the powder; for [Don Juan says that] all there is on those islands is contained in a chamber of the fort of that city, and that in so prominent a place that it overlooks the wall; and that if by some accident (which may God avert!) this powder should explode, besides the risk to the city, there would remain no more powder in that whole country, nor material with which it could be made. To avoid so great a difficulty there would be built in some of the said four cavaliers two round towers, so that a large part of the powder could be divided and protected. Supposing that you realize how important it is that a part of the powder should be safe, and free from the accidents which might be brought about by any of it igniting, I charge you strictly to carry out this matter pertaining to the safety of the powder, that it may be more secure and suitably placed.

He says that one of the motives which led him to fortify the wall is that the religious orders have built churches close to it, so large that they are obstacles; and because one of the churches, which is called Minondo, is near the Parián where during the year there are settled twenty or thirty thousand Sangleys (who are the people that rebelled in times past); and through mild measures the people of the Parián have aided this work with four thousand pesos from the treasury of their common fund. This has appeared well to us, and you will take measures in it which you may judge most expedient, warning them that no height commanding the city must remain. If there is any difficulty, and the churches would receive loss, you will avert such injury; and will send a plan [of the building]; and for the future you will not consent that any work be built to the damage of the public.

He says that he had informed me that the galleys were of little importance, and that of Terrenate alone was worth maintaining; but that, having considered the matter further, he is of a different opinion. For they are necessary in order to reënforce with them Terrenate on occasions of danger, but in the port of Cabite, where they are lying, they are not so useful as they would be if they were taken to the province of Pintados, in Otón, or Cibu, within view of the domestic enemies in Mindanao, Joló, and Camocón—who are the ones who rob the natives. And he says that if he had only had twenty oared vessels that year in that region, the enemy would not have come out from their country, causing disturbances and terrorizing the provinces as they usually do. With the first relation which notified Don Juan Zerezo to carry out this plan, in the past year of 635, I ordered you that, since the galleys caused great expense, you should do away with them; and that, if you found difficulties in doing so, you should advise me of it. In order that a decision may be made in this matter, I order and command you to inform me very fully of what occurs to you in regard to it, so that, having examined this, I may order such measures to be taken as shall be most expedient.

He says that Pedro de Heredia, governor of Terrenate, had advised him that many soldiers of that garrison were about to mutiny, and that he was letting the matter pass as well as he could, hoping that aid would arrive. This had been caused by the fact that Father Immanuel Rivero, commissioner of the Holy Office, had published an edict which affected many of them, concerning the crime against nature, whereby he gave them two months' time to be absolved; and to this was added the fact that it was understood that the governor was instituting an investigation as to who were absolved, whence arose their despair. On this account, as well as because the Dutch had a very strong galleon in Malayo and were expecting others from Chacarta, it was necessary that the ordinary reënforcements should be much increased; for, if only the usual number came, they would infallibly be lost. At the time when this advice was received, two galleons and a patache were getting ready, for the affairs which he had mentioned gave him more anxiety than the enemy themselves. Several, in the council which they held, thought best that he should not take the risk or weaken his forces; and that this reënforcement should be sent in light vessels, and to the usual amount. But considering the condition and the danger of those forts, it was resolved to reënforce them creditably, sending the said two galleons manned with good infantry and first-class troops. He raised one company of volunteer soldiers from the camp, which was an important thing, and it is well that this should be done every year, so that no soldiers be forced to go; for, knowing that there will be many exchanged, they will go willingly. He appointed as commander Admiral Don Geronimo de Himonte [sic], who conducted himself extremely well, observing the orders which he carried, not to turn aside for other enterprises, but to place the reënforcements in Terrenate, and to defend himself from whomsoever attempted to hinder him. The two [Dutch] ships that the enemy were awaiting were on the way for this purpose: they were boarded and burned by Indians of the Votunes from the kingdom of Macasan, who found them anchored, with the troops on land, and killed those who remained on board. But the ship from Malayo, trusting to its strength and extreme lightness, attempted to attack the reënforcements all alone, taking this risk on account of the importance of the matter, knowing that the soldiers from the garrison of Terrenate were awaiting the outcome of this affair before resolving to kill the governor and higher officials, according as they had plotted. The said galleon fought with the ships which brought the reënforcements eight days [dias; sc. horas] and escaped dismantled, with great loss. In the ships with the reënforcements seven persons were killed, including the chief pilot. After this, the reënforcements arrived safely, at the time when Pedro de Heredia had arrested a hundred and fifty persons; he had burned or garroted eleven, a number had died in prison, and forty more were sent back in the same ships which brought the reënforcements. The case on the first hearing was brought before Don Lorenzo de Olasso, master-of-camp of the soldiery in those islands. Although the charges against them were not sufficiently substantiated, and some were of opinion that they should be leniently dealt with; yet, considering that if these forty soldiers were guilty they might infect the garrisons in which they were stationed, and as the affair was of such public importance and within sight of so many barbarians and particularly Sangleys—who are more than any other nation liable to this wretched practice, they ought to be proceeded against with much discretion and severity. The despatch of the reënforcements, and what was done in its execution and fulfilment, are approved. In regard, to removing the soldiers, I ordered you by my decree of the filth of November of 635 to send two companies to Terrenate in two galleons, so that two others might be brought back from there; and in this manner that garrison would be exchanged every three years, and all the companies of the troops there would divide the labor equally. Accordingly, I charge you to have the foregoing executed; and you will see to it that thanks are rendered to Don Juan Zerezo for the care with which he prepared the reënforcements which he sent. As for the delinquents arrested, you will do justice to them as is most fitting to the service of God our Lord and myself, proceeding very circumspectly.

He likewise informs us that Pedro de Heredia wrote to him that the natives of the islands of Terrenate, who hitherto recognized Cachil Varo as king of Tidore, have refused him obedience, and crowned in his place another Moro chief named Cachil Horotalo, saying that this one is the true heir of that kingdom and that Cachil Varo is an intruder. This makes him very anxious, because besides the fact that it is not his affair to disinherit kingdoms, the new one whom they pretend is the king has been hitherto retired in Malayo under the protection of the Dutch, fulfilling the duties of naval commander; and he had even sent him ambassadors, promising fidelity. Little dependence is to be put upon his words, and Cachil Varo is a very valiant Moro and my true servant, to whom hitherto presents have been given each year, and, before him, to his father. Besides having become hispanicized, and an ally of this crown, he has retired to his fort in Tidore, which is a more important one than those I hold, and he is obeyed by the people in general, with more than two thousand chiefs. This has appeared satisfactory; and I charge you particularly always to aid friendly kings with whom we have alliances and friendship.

He says there is nothing in that government so important as that the port of Cavite be well provided with the necessary naval supplies, and some person who is very competent and intelligent placed in charge of it. The other offices are given as favors, but for this one some person is sought who must be asked to accept it. Such has been the case with him who is stationed there as commander of the fort and river-master—namely, Captain Juan de Olaz, who attends to it in such manner that for many years the port has not been so abundantly supplied nor more faithfully administered—very different from the condition in which it was, lacking everything. You will give him many thanks on my behalf and let care be taken regarding his person, that favors may be bestowed on him when occasion offers.

He says that the rewards in these islands are scant, and particularly those which he has had to give, as he has not had authority to appoint to encomiendas; and that, as well on this account as owing to the events which have occurred in his time, he has promoted some worthy soldiers with commissions as infantry captains—considering that they are the ones who perform the labor which is most necessary; and that they have, aside from their pay, only their simple place as before. Several in consideration of this honor have settled down and become citizens, which is a thing much to be desired. The sons of principal men have been encouraged to enlist as soldiers, and have commenced to serve in the infantry, which was much run down. With especial care he has given none of these appointments to any servant of his—excepting his captain of the guard, as all the other governors did; and the offices of justice have been appointed from the veterans in service and the old settlers. In the foregoing cases you will observe the military ordinances.

The other clauses of the said letter have been examined and at present there is nothing to answer to them. Madrid, October 11, 1636.

I the King

By order of his Majesty:
Don Gabriel de Ocaña y Alarcon

Royal Decrees

Ordering the city of Manila to compensate Grau y Monfalcon

The King: To the council, justice, and magistracy of the city of Manila of the Philipinas Islands. Don Juan Grau y Monfalcon, your procurator-general, has reported to me that you had many serious matters of great importance pending in this my court, on which depended the conservation of that community. Seeing also that the persons who had charge of these did not conclude them, you appointed him as your procurator-general; and, besides him, a regidor of that city council [ayuntamiento], who might come here to confer about those affairs, giving him a salary of two thousand pesos. The latter, coming to these kingdoms, died in Eastern India. Consequently, you again made a new appointment, [conferring it] on Don Diego de Esqueta y Mechaca, a regidor of that city, who is coming to this my court in the first trading fleet. All the papers, records, and instructions, which you gave to the said regidors for the despatch of the business having reached the hands of the said Don Juan Grau, he has attended to its expedition with so great promptness, personal care, and interest, that he has indeed settled your affairs, so that when the said Don Diego de Esqueta arrives here he will find nothing for him to do. Don Juan has attended to it all at his own cost, and since the time of his appointment as such procurator-general — more than six years — you have not sent him any of his salary, or anything for the expenses that he has incurred. He has expended considerable money from his own funds — something which few would have done, especially in so hard times — as he desired to give you entire satisfaction in regard to the matters with which you had charged him. By that means the great expenses that you might have incurred, if the said procurators had remained here with salaries so considerable, have been avoided. He petitioned me, in view of this, to be pleased to grant him the favor of a decree of recommendation, so that you may consider him as well recommended, in order to give him a reward for his service, past and present, in the said negotiations; and that you may assign him some fixed salary for his service in the future, for so long as he shall hold powers of attorney from you. He petitioned that he be remunerated for what he has spent, and that you also assign him a certain accommodation of lading-space in the ships that sail to Nueva España. This matter having been examined in my royal Council of the Yndias, where the care taken by the said Don Juan Grau has been known and experienced; and after they had considered the aforesaid and the good account that he has given of the matters under his charge, with the diligence and carefulness of which you will have learned through the many despatches which he has sent and continues to send you; and because my will is that he receive in full the grace and favor which his care merits: I have considered it fitting to issue the present. By it I charge and order you that, since it is so just to make him compensation, you grant him that which he should have, in accordance with what you consider due him for his work, past and present, in your affairs and negotiations. You shall also pay him the sum which he shall have spent and what he shall spend from his own property in the said matters. What you shall thus determine, and what you think can be done for him, you shall give to the person who shall hold his power of attorney in that city. Thus is my will. Given in Madrid, August fourteen, one thousand six hundred and thirty-six.

I the King

By order of the king our sovereign:
Don Gabriel de Ocaña y Alarcon

Signed by the Council.

Orders given to Sebastian Hurtado de Corcuera

The King: To Don Sebastian Hurtado de Corcuera, knight of the Order of Alcántara, my governor and captain-general of the Filipinas Islands, and president of my royal Audiencia therein. A letter written to me by Don Juan Zerezo de Salamanca on August 10 of the former year, 1634, while he was governor ad interim of those islands, on matters pertaining to government and justice,1 has been received and examined in my royal Council of the Indias. On the points therein that have needed to be considered, you are hereby answered.

The said Don Juan Zerezo declares that Geronimo de Fuentes, an inhabitant of that city, bid for a magistracy at auction. The judges of the auction knocked it down to him, and made out his title for it. Some of the regidors opposed this, and appealed to the Audiencia. The latter, in order not to make a precedent, so that the alcaldes or judges of the provinces should attempt the same with their successors, had the possession [of the magistracy] given to him, and left the party his right safe and in force. That is approved.

By my decree of August 26, 633, I ordered that, in matters of government and the expenses of my royal treasury which should arise from the petition of litigants, my fiscal should be allowed to see all the enactments of my governors, so that he may take notice of what appears to [concern] him. I am informed that he is so doing; and that it would be advisable to order the said fiscal that, in disputes over jurisdiction with the Audiencia, he shall defend the decrees which pronounce in favor of the government's jurisdiction. Notwithstanding that I order that Audiencia to observe and obey those decrees with special care. I have deemed it advisable to charge you—as I do—that you shall do what pertains to you in your offices, and shall observe the decrees, laws, and ordinances which are given for the good government of those islands.

I have determined that the ships which are despatched to Nueva España shall sail without fail every year in the early part of June. Don Juan Zerezo tells me that it could not be established in the year of 634. I charge you straitly to attend to the execution and fulfilment of this, with the earnestness that I expect from your zeal.

As for the loan of sixty thousand pesos which the inhabitants of Macan made, as you have understood it, to my royal treasury of that city—the payment and reimbursement of which my fiscal afterward opposed, saying that the Portuguese were holding back considerable property of those citizens; and which was for that reason placed in a separate fund, where it is deposited—you shall order that those accounts be adjusted, and that what amount is theirs by right be paid to the parties, according to justice.

He mentions also that word was received from the kingdoms of Japon that the persecution of Christians was greater than ever in the year 633, and that more than twenty religious from all the orders were martyred; and that it would be advisable that no religious go to that kingdom for the present, because of the little good that they do, and that, on account of this, the intercourse and commerce of that kingdom with those islands has been closed. Since intercourse and friendship with them should not be lacking, and since you have understood how important this matter may be, you shall endeavor to attend to it with all the skill that is requisite; and you shall regulate yourself by the orders that are given, and in accordance with the needs of the church of Japon, and the benefit and utility which may accrue from the labors of the religious in those districts. Madrid,

November 6, 1636. I the King

By order of his Majesty:

Don Gabriel de Ocaña y Alarcon

On Terrenate matters

The King: To Pedro de Heredia, commandant of the port of the island of Terrenate and governor of the soldiers there, or the person or persons in whose charge it may be. Your letter of May 13, 634, has been received and examined in my Council of War of the Indias. In it you state what soldiers are in those forts, and how inadequately they are aided with what is needful and requisite for their sustenance; while the infantry reënforcements sent from Manila are of men who have no sense of duty (mestizos and other kinds of lineage), although men of courage should be sent; and that would be done, provided that one company of those who serve me in the camp of Manila should be sent annually to those islands. For more than one hundred and twenty of the soldiers [there] seeing that they could not leave it, and induced by their evil dispositions, conspired to seize that fort; and while they were awaiting an opportunity to accomplish their designs, one of them informed you of it, and that they had chosen a sargento-mayor, a captain, and all the other officers that belong to a company; and that the circumstances which you mention had been overlooked, in order to defer to a better opportunity the punishment that it was advisable to inflict. Desiring to get rid of this danger, you undertook their arrest, committing the matter to Sargento-mayor Juan Gonzalez de Casares Melon, a prominent officer; and he carried it out with great expedition and adroitness. Having arrested them, they made known the said conspiracy, and other abominable crimes, and that they had committed the sin against nature. Having proved the accusations, you executed justice on the leaders of the said conspiracy and sent the others to my governor of the Filipinas Islands. Although you had very few galleys in those forts, you sent the guard-galley of those forts to the island of Fafares — which is inhabited by hostile Moros, of the religion of Terrenate, and by the Dutch — with as many infantry as possible, accompanied by the king of Siao and the sargento-mayor, Juan Gonzalez de Casares Melon. They took such good measures that they defeated the enemy, killing four hundred Moros, with but little loss to our men, and captured about one hundred and fifty persons. The Spaniards took from them ten pieces of artillery, and many muskets, arquebuses, and other arms; and left their settlements destroyed and burned, and their fort razed. I thank you heartily for what you have done in my service. You shall always be regardful of what may be most to my service, and shall strive for the conservation of whatever belongs to us. You shall see that the enemy are checked, and that they do not become powerful with new forts. In my name, you shall give thanks to Sargento-mayor Juan Casares Melon for the good management displayed in what he has done; and tell him that account will be taken of his person in order to grant him reward. I have ordered my governor and captain-general of the Filipinas Islands to attend very particularly to all that concerns those forts. Because of the great importance to their conservation and condition of exchanging the soldiers in those forts, I have ordered two companies to be sent in two galleons, and two others that are there to be taken back; so that in this way the soldiers of that presidio shall be exchanged every three years, and all the companies of the army shall share in the work equally. I have thought best to advise you of this, so that having understood it, you may, on your part, secure, in what pertains to you, the fulfilment of it all. Madrid, November 6, 1636.

I the King

By order of his Majesty:

Gabriel de Ocaña y Alarcon

1 See Cerezo's letter of that date, in Vol. XXIV, p. 308.

Memorial Informatorio Al Rey

By Juan Grau y Monfalcón, Madrid, 1637.

Source: This document is obtained from a printed book in the Academia Real de la Historia, Madrid, collated with the MS. copy in the Biblioteca Nacional, Madrid.

Translation: This is made by James A. Robertson.

Grau y Monfalcon's Informatory Memorial of 1637

Informatory memorial [addressed] to the king our sovereign, in his royal and supreme Council of the Indias, in behalf of the distinguished and loyal city of Manila, capital of the Filipinas Islands, in regard to the claims of that city and of those islands and their inhabitants, and the commerce with Nueva España: by Don Juan Grau y Monfalcon, their procurator-general at this court. Madrid, in the royal printing office, 1637.1

Number 1. Intention of this memorial, in which are discussed all the principal matters of the Filipinas Islands.

Sire:

Don Juan Grau y Monfalcon, procurator-general of the distinguished and ever loyal city of Manila, capital of the Filipinas Islands, makes, by authority of that city, the following declaration. Since the preservation of the islands is the most efficient means for that of all the states which this crown holds and possesses in Eastern India and adjacent parts, and consequently [of all those] in the Western Indias; and as it is positively known that there is no other way of assuring this end except by the commerce conceded to the islands with Nueva España—which is in such a condition that by only reducing it, or by deranging it as regards its amount, or the manner in which it is carried on, it will be necessary that it cease; and that if the inhabitants lose what supports them, all the islands will be lost: some persons, and especially Captain Francisco de Vitoria Baraona, with less attention and knowledge than is requisite in treating a matter so remote, serious, and politic—which demands so much more than ordinary foundation for its proper understanding [on account of not understanding it—MS.]—proposed to your Majesty certain expedients or counsels; but, although these should be directed to the increase of the forces which the arms of España maintain in the seas of the Orient, in order to oppose them to the numerous enemies who are trying to overthrow our power in those seas, and have the desire to end it, one would believe that they were directed with especial purpose to weaken and obscure that power, and thereby to extinguish the best and most creditable [finest—MS.] military post that this great monarchy possesses outside of Europa. And inasmuch as the matter pertains not only to the conservation of those vassals, but also to the general subject of your Majesty's service, your vassals, attending more to this consideration than to even that result—although the one does not suffer without the other, since some orders originating from the expedients proposed by the said Captain Francisco de Vitoria, have begun to be put in force in Nueva España— and recognizing from their beginnings how much the issues are in danger and how important it is to heed in time the dangers that threaten, and successfully to prevent them, on account of the impossibility that they can be checked later (for it is easy, at the beginning, to overcome what, when it is once introduced, is usually impossible to conquer), are attempting to represent those dangers in this informatory memorial, which they lay at your Majesty's royal feet. In it, taking occasion from that which is most important and weighty, all the affairs of the Filipinas Islands will be touched upon, and those of their conservation, government, and commerce—and all with the truth, thoroughness, accuracy and knowledge that ought to be used, not only in general, but in each one specifically; so that once explained, in a complete report of the disadvantages and advantages existing in each point, the decision most advantageous to the service of God and of your Majesty, and to the welfare of those islands, may be made in them all. The claims made in behalf of the islands are reduced to the petitions which are presented in a separate memorial, through which the inhabitants hope to receive the favors that their necessities and condition demand.

Number 2. Condition of the commerce of the islands, and dangers from any changes therein

To begin with the fact that furnished a reason for so purposely discussing these matters: it is presupposed that the commerce of the Filipinas to Nueva España was carried on with some degree of prosperity, although with all the restriction that could be endured—albeit the royal orders were in certain cases less closely observed than seemed desirable, and it was an obligation to attend only to what demanded correction, and to what was sufficient to adjust the commerce, and reduce it to its best method. But another method was proposed which would have completely checked or suppressed it, by advising measures that would so alter the former one that, even if there were any irregularities in the old method which are avoided in this, that is accomplished by impeding and ruining the commerce; so that it will become necessary, in order not to permit one slight loss, to cause many, so irreparable that either the ruin of the islands will follow from them, or the total expense of their conservation will fall back on your Majesty's royal treasury. And although it is always right (and today more than ever) to take care that since your revenue is not increased, it be not diminished, it is not a successful expedient to represent the saving of expense and the increase of income, if from what is gained on the one side, results on the other, either the loss of what it is advisable to defend, or the addition of heavier expenses for its defense. For there are matters which have attained so even and regular an equilibrium and balance, that, from whichever of its parts one subtracts or adds, the other side inclining is unsettled, and the structure that they compose is destroyed. One can easily understand that if your Majesty were to dispense with the payment of avería2 on the royal treasure that comes from the Indias in the war and trading fleets of their line, there would be a clear gain annually of more than half a million, in both silver and gold; but from that gain would result the failure of means to maintain the principal. And if the freighters, and those who are interested in the rest [of the trade] can with just cause excuse themselves from attending to the avería; and it is necessary that this treasure, as well as that of private persons which is brought with it, be accompanied by an armed force sufficient to resist those who have so great desire to pillage it: the alternative is either that it come without that force, and thus liable to lose more in one year than the expense for its defense in ten, or that all the cost be loaded on to your Majesty's treasury, by which doing away with the avería would be a greater expense than would paying it. Who can deny that if the customs duties in the ports of España were to go up to fifty or one hundred per cent, they would not be worth ten times more than they are worth at present? But who would say that such an expedient would ensure the duration of commerce, and the ability of your vassals and the foreigners to maintain it? If the immediate result of increasing the duties must be the loss of the principal from which they are collected, the ruin of trade, the desertion of the ports, the impoverishment of your vassals, the depopulation of the cities, and the ruin of everything, one can easily understand that this scheme would, under pretext of increasing the royal treasury, ruin it and destroy the kingdom. These examples are no different from what is observed in the commerce of Filipinas. It is represented that, by the measures which are ordered to be put in force, the duties in the port of Acapulco alone will be increased one million seven hundred thousand pesos; and although this calculation, as will be seen, has no foundation, supposing that it did have, that increase would result in such a decline of trade there that everything would go to ruin. [In the margin: "In numbers 83, 85, and 91."]3 And if the wealth on which that trade depends should fail, either your Majesty will alone sustain the Filipinas, or you will have to abandon them. The first is almost impossible without spending twice as much as is now spent. The second has the disadvantage that will be explained. [In the margin: "In numbers 6–44."] Therefore the execution of the methods proposed at once carries with it irreparable injuries, which, after they have happened, will be so difficult of remedy, that the return of things to their present condition may not be possible. As this [present] condition has become established during the course of many years, it is preserved both by the wealth that those who sustain it have acquired during those years, and by merely allowing it to continue. But, if those two requisites fail, first will be experienced the loss of courage in the ruin [that will ensue], as the return [of courage] can be seen in the restoration [of the present condition].

Number 3. Commissions given to Licentiate Quiroga, and their execution

Your Majesty was pleased to order Licentiate Don Pedro de Quiroga y Moya, who went to Nueva España the past year of 635, on this and other affairs, by instructions in regard to the commerce of Filipinas, to establish a new system in the port of Acapulco, which is the point where their ships arrive. And although it is understood that the mandate was general, in order to correct and prevent the illegalities which are committed at that port in the trade of the islands by taking greater quantities of silver away from Nueva España, and bringing in more cloth from China, than is allowed by the [royal] permission; and although he was ordered to attend to this with the greatest care—not only to investigate the past but to provide for the future—and that he should issue ordinances for everything, give instructions, and advise your Majesty in the royal Council of the Indias, with full commission limited to certain times among both the officials and those who are not, with appeals to the tribunal whence it emanated: orders were also given him to go to Acapulco to visit the ships from the islands, and ascertain whether they transgressed the law by carrying either more than was allowed, or without register what they were allowed to carry in the ship, in order to escape the royal duties. This is what is known of his commissions in general terms; and in detail some memorials were given to him and information of the damages, and of the remedies that could be applied; so that from these he could accept what was practicable, and might either execute or give advice of what he deemed most advisable, both in the increase of the duties, and in making the appraisals of the merchandise, in which consists the most serious and the most dangerous aspect of the matter.

Number 4. Uneasiness caused in Nueva España, and what can be feared in the islands

The innovation and disquiet caused by these commissions in Nueva España (where it is known that they have arrived) has been very great, and as notable is the uneasiness and embarrassment among the citizens and exporters of Filipinas, who—without recognizing in themselves any guilt which accuses them, any crime which burdens them, or any proof which condemns them—have, for the sole purpose of not becoming liable to denunciations,4 whether false or true (for all denunciations are troublesome), and to what ignorant witnesses, the evil-intentioned, or their enemies may depose, tried to serve your Majesty beyond what their wealth allows and their abilities permit. On that account, so great has been the assessment on the inhabitants of Filipinas, that it will be impossible to pay it without their total ruin, and they are not those who are guilty of the violations of law which some are attempting to prove. Consequently, the inhabitants have petitioned that this assessment be not made. Nothing is said at present of the other things that will result from it to [the harm of] the islands. [In the margin: "In numbers 45 and 87." —Ex. his.] This memorial will hint at some things, and time will continue to show them, if not by the causes that are now operating, then by the effects, which will reveal themselves. And even if these are less than those that may be expected, they will require very considerable attention and cause very sensible injury—as is usual with any innovation of the magnitude of this; for that which only changes and embarrasses the course of affairs, causes more damage than gain in what it reforms.

[V. Purpose to which this memorial is directed. — Ex. his.]

In order to avert the dangers that threaten, it is the intention to present some measures and the reasons on which they are based; so that, without departing from what must be considered in the first place (namely, the service of your Majesty), and then the conservation of those islands and of their citizens and residents, the evils may be corrected, the violations of law prevented, and the welfare of that so remote and afflicted community attended to—which, although so far away, attends so conscientiously to its obligations, ever preferring those duties to the possessions and lives of those who form and sustain that colony, risking and even losing them for the defense of that (although remote) very important part of this Catholic monarchy.

[VI. Proposition to abandon the islands, and its foundations. — Ex. his.]

The Filipinas Islands, which dominate the archipelago of Sant Lazaro, merit, for many claims, causes, and reasons, the esteem in which they have always been held. Contrary to all these, it was represented already, in the times of the sovereigns your Majesty's grandfather and father, that it seemed advisable to abandon the islands, and leave them to whomever cared to occupy them. It was remarked in the Council of State, where the matter was ventilated, and where a consultation was held, the question being presented with the motives for this resolution, that those islands not only did not increase the royal revenues, but even decreased and diminished them, and were a continual cause of great and fruitless expense, as they are so many, so remote, and so difficult of conservation. The instigators of this proposition availed themselves, as says the author of the History of the Malucas,5 of the example of the kings of China—who being the sovereigns of the islands, and so near that they could reënforce them in a short time, as being so adjacent and near their great continent, abandoned them, in order not to be under obligation for the expenses and cares that were necessary to maintain them. They said that España's method of governing them was very burdensome and prejudicial to the monarchy, and was without any hope of being improved, because of the great amount of silver that was sent to the islands from the Indias on that account, both for the ordinary expenses of war, and for the conservation of commerce—all of that silver passing to Assia, whence it never issued. They said that the states, so scattered and so weakened by so many wide expanses of water and remote climes, could scarcely be reduced to union; nor was human foresight sufficient to introduce union in that which nature itself, and the way in which the world was put together, separated by so distinct bounds. That was proved not only by reason but also by experience, which had discovered and proved how difficult and even impossible was the conservation of those islands, unless the cost were very greatly in excess of the profit—although, in this matter, one should first decide whether [questions of] honor and polity counted for anything.

Number 7. More attention should be paid to the conservation of states than to the increase of the royal revenues.

These reasons, and others which were advanced, were originated and accepted by some who paid more heed to the increase of the royal revenues than to the advantage with which those revenues ought to be, and generally are, spent; for, although kings are obliged to regard that increase as the blood of the mystical body of their states, it must be without injury to the reputation of the states. For since, as is a fact, they must try to acquire riches in order to preserve their reputation and to increase their treasure by avoiding superfluous and little-needed expenses, it will not be a well-founded argument that, in order to avoid spending their revenues, they should allow what they already possess and enjoy legitimately to be lost. Such a course would be to prefer the less to the greater, and the means to the ends; since we see not few millions spent on the conservation of a fortified post to which belongs, at times, nothing but the reputation of arms. If its defense is justifiable for that reason, it would be more justifiable if on such a place depends not only the reputation of the crown, but the preservation of many other reputations, which would be risked by losing that post, and which will be assured by maintaining it. Such is the peculiar importance of the Filipinas Islands, as will be proved in this memorial. [In the margin: "In numbers 41, 42, and 43."]

Number 8. As, and for the reasons that, Flandes is preserved, the islands should be preserved

What state does your Majesty possess that costs as much as Flandes, although it is almost the least one of this monarchy? Because in Flandes all the reasons may be verified that are alleged in regard to the islands—namely, that they are costly, difficult to preserve, a drain of so much money, and separated from the other states—would it be prudent to influence [the crown] by those reasons to abandon that state? There can be no doubt that even the first proposition of such a nature would be condemned as imprudent, and lacking the basis of policy that such measures ought to have; and that from its execution would result, leaving aside other damages, the loss of many states of this crown, and their allies, which are now maintained by only maintaining Flandes, although at the price of so costly a war. Therefore, if the Filipinas possess that same importance, and if the conservation of the two Yndias results from their conservation—or at least from their being less exposed to notorious risks, which, were that Flandes of the new world lacking, would threaten them—what more notable reason of state can there be for not deserting them, and for characterizing as justifiable and necessary all that is spent in them, as is above mentioned?

Number 9. Resolution of preserving the islands well founded

Giving more heed to this than to all the propositions [made to him], King Felipo [Phelipe—MS.] Second, not lending ear to so pernicious an opinion, resolved that the Filipinas should be preserved as they had been thus far, by adding strength to the judiciary and military—one of which maintains and the other defends kingdoms—devoting and applying them both to the propagation of the holy gospel among those remote nations, although not only Nueva España, but also old España were to contribute for that purpose from their incomes. And thus did that most prudent monarch declare, in order that it might not be understood that preaching was denied to them, and that he excused himself from sending them ministers for it, because of the lack of gold and silver, even though it should cost him other provinces. He put into effect that Christian axiom, that kings possess some states because they need them, and others because those states have need of them.6 Well are these two propositions proved in the Filipinas; for they were ordered to be maintained because their natives and neighbors need [to be under] the seigniory of this monarchy in order not to lose the faith which they have received, and to make it easier for others to receive it. Also, as has been said, and as will be proved, [In the margin: "In numbers 19, 34, 35, 36, 41, 42, and 43."] this crown needs those islands now more than then, in order to preserve other posts not less important, since in losing them much more would be lost than what is spent on them. Consequently, both then and afterward, that talk of deserting the Filipinas was and has been regarded as worth little consideration, and was ill received and considered unworthy the greatness, Christian zeal, and obligation of the kings of España; and accordingly it has sunk into eternal silence.

Number 10. The conservation of the islands is more necessary today

If these reasons could so powerfully influence the devout minds of the so Catholic princes in that epoch, much more should they influence that of your Majesty in this, wherein they have not only the same but greater force, because of the many unexpected difficulties that have been encountered through the entrance of the rebels of Olanda into so many parts of the two Indias. Consequently, if the Filipinas be now deserted, not indeed for the sake of authority and reputation, but only for political convenience, the advantage that might result would be very doubtful, and the loss very evident. And although the effort is not at present made directly to have the islands abandoned, expedients are being or have been proposed from which one fears, not indeed the abandonment of them willingly, but what is worse, the loss of them unwillingly. Before proving that the measures which are beginning to be executed may conduce to that end, the reasons on which their conservation, importance, and necessity are today founded will be discussed; so that, what is advisable being understood with all clearness and certainty—since it is not expedient to add to their forces, as that is now impossible, nor to deprive them of what force they possess—the reader may draw as a conclusion that, if the weakening of the islands follow from the orders issued, and their loss be risked, those orders may either be corrected or suspended, or the most prudent decision in all respects may be adopted.

Number 11. First reason of the importance of the islands: their discovery

The first reason for which the Filipinas should be valued is that of their discovery, which was made by Hernando de Magallanes in the year of 1519, after so many hardships, by the new navigation through the strait until then undiscovered, to which he gave his name. That expedition was not for the discovery of lands or wealth, as were others, but to obey the order and satisfy the desire of the emperor Carlos V, of glorious memory—who, years before, had made known this desire and endeavored to carry it into effect; and at that time he succeeded in doing so, by making the agreement for that heroic voyage, which astonished and encompassed the world. It is to be noted that that discovery was directed toward the islands of Maluco, so that the crown of Castilla, which was then separate from that of Portugal, might enjoy for itself alone the trade in the spices that grow there. That was obtained, and the vassals of both crowns having fought together for the conservation of those islands, their weapons were reduced to pens, and to various councils and disputes as to the situation and demarcation of the islands. Although it was recognized that they belonged to Castilla, according to the division of the world made by the apostolic see—as it then had no other lands or islands near those of Maluco, from which to succor them, except Nueva España which is so distant—yet, as it was judged difficult to maintain them, in a region so remote, against the invasions of Moros7 and pagans, and against the obstinacy of the Portuguese (who could never be persuaded that those islands were not theirs); and seeing that the action of abandoning them was unworthy of him who had spent so great a sum in their discovery, and in planting therein the gospel: it was accepted as a more creditable and expedient resolution to dispose of them in pledge8 to the crown of Portugal. That country held and maintained them alone, until the year 1564, when the Castilians, under the command of Adelantado Miguel Lopez de Legazpi, continuing what Magallanes had commenced, went to settle the Filipinas Islands, by the proximity and protection of which they recovered the islands of Maluco; and more, when these two crowns had been united, was the mutual aiding of their vassals facilitated. In order to assure their defense, by the agreement of both countries (the circumstances of the transfer having become almost obscured) the Malucos were detached from the crown of Portugal and joined to that of Castilla; and they became subject, as today, to the Filipinas. Consequently, the argument with which the author of the History of the Malucas affirms that if God had permitted the king of that time to exclude the Filipinas from his monarchy, leaving them exposed to the power who should first occupy them, Maluco would have so bettered the condition of its affairs that it would have been impregnable, is not very clear. That statement must be understood with reference to the Moro kings, who would have been more powerful had not the proximity of the Filipinas subjected them; since it is evident that, if when the emperor disposed of the one [group of islands], the others had been settled, he would not have made that bargain, but would have defended them and kept them all. That is verified, because when Felipe II, having succeeded to the crown of Portugal, wrote to the governor of Filipinas to reënforce the Malucas and other places in India whenever he had an opportunity, that was a matter of so great fear to their kings that the king of Terrenate, Sultan Babu, feeling himself oppressed by a greater and nearer force, sought defense in peace, and to secure it sent, as ambassador to these kingdoms, Cachil Nayque. From the above it is inferred that, if the first intent was to discover the Malucos because of the wealth of their trade—which is now united with that of the Filipinas, as will be seen; [In the margin: "In number 29."] and if the maintenance of the one group consisted in that of the others, even when they belonged to different crowns: now that they all belong to Castilla, more necessary is the conservation of the Filipinas, in order that the islands of the Malucos may not decrease from what they were then.

Number 12. Second reason for the importance of the islands: their size and number

The second reason is that of their size and number. Cosmographers recognize five archipelagos in that sea that is included between China, the Javas, and Nueva Guinea9—namely, that of Moro or Batochina, that of the Celebes, that of the Papuas, that of Maluco, and that of San Lazaro, which is that of the Filipinas or Luzones. [The last name is given] because the principal island is that of Luzón, whose form is that of a tenterhook, one hundred and thirty leguas along its longest side and seventy along the shortest. The islands renowned after that island are Mindoro, Luban, Borney, Marinduque, the island of Cabras, the island of Tablas, Masbate, Zebu [Zubu—MS.], Capul, Ybabao, Leyte, Bohol, island of Fuegos, island of Negros, Ymares, Panay, Cayahan, Cuyo, Calamianes, Parauan, Tendaya [Tandaya—MS.], Camar, Catenduanes, Mindanao, and Burias, besides other smaller islands. They number in all forty, without counting the small and desert islands, which are many. Among those named are some larger than España, some as large, and some smaller. One of these it Zebu, which is10 fifty leguas in circumference. Near to it are the islands of Maluco, which are properly five in number, namely, Terrenate, Tirode [i.e., Tidore], Motiel, Maquien, and Bachian—although the last named is not one island, but a group formed of many small islands, which are divided by various arms, straits, and channels of the sea; but which are reckoned as one island, as they all belong to one king. That of Tirode belongs to another king, and that of Terrenate with the two remaining ones to another, as well as so many islands adjacent to these that they number in all seventy-two. Those two archipelagos of Maluco and Filipinas occupy more than twenty-six degrees of latitude, running from two or three degrees south of the equator to twenty-four north of it; and extend more than four hundred and fifty leguas, while they are one thousand four hundred in circuit.

Number 13. Grandeur and characteristics of the distinguished and very loyal city of Manila

The center of all that distant region is the famous city of Manila, which on account of its remarkable characteristics deserves equal rank with the greatest and most celebrated cities of the world. It is located on the island of Luzón, in the angle made by its two aides or points, with a capacious, deep, and strong harbor. It was anciently the settlement of the Luzón islanders; it was occupied by the Spaniards, and the government established there, in the year 1572. On account of its location, renown, and prominence, it was given by a royal decree of June 21, 1574, the honored title of distinguished and ever loyal,11 together with that of capital and chief city among all the cities in those islands. By a decree of November 19, 1595, it was decreed that it could enjoy all the privileges enjoyed by all the cities that are capitals of kingdoms; and by another decree of March 20, 1596, it was granted a special coat-of-arms, which it uses;12 while another decree of May 8, of the same year, allows it jurisdiction for five leguas around. However, it has greater jurisdiction in regard to government and superiority than any other of this monarchy, since the district of the royal Audiencia resident therein, according to the declaration by provinces, of the fifth of May, 1583, and the twenty-sixth of May, 1596, consists of the island of Luzón, with all the Filipinas of the archipelago of China (including the five already mentioned [i.e., the Malucos]), and the mainland of China, discovered or to be discovered hereafter, which is an immense distance. Its inhabited part— although it has suffered great disasters, which will be mentioned later [In the margin: "In number 93."] and in spite of which it endures—is today very sightly in its buildings and plan, as they are mostly of stone, and as it is surrounded by a wall in the modern manner, with sufficient fortification. But what most ennobles it is the valor and loyalty of its inhabitants, who, notwithstanding their small numbers in proportion to those of the enemies, sustain the city with so much reputation and renown, that it is one of the best military posts in all the Orient, and one in which the royal standards of your Majesty preserve the valor and fame of Spaniards—who are feared and respected by all the kings who rule in those islands and regions—and of all the fleets that plough their seas. All the above makes that city, and the region that it governs in the most remote places of the world meritorious; this crown, therefore, should preserve that city for its dignity, and maintain it as the daughter of its power.

Number 14. Third reason of the importance of the islands: their native and acquired character

The third reason is the character, both native and acquired, of the Filipinas Islands. That of Luzón produces a quantity of gold, of which a quantity has always been found and obtained in its rivers. Rich mines have been discovered, now more considerable than ever. By a decree of August 12, 1578, the [reduction of the] royal fifth to the tenth was conceded to the inhabitants.13 That had some extensions later, from which it is inferred that metals were obtained. There are persistent rumors regarding the Pangasinan hills, which are forty leguas away from Manila, namely, that they are all full of gold-bearing ore. In the year 620,14 Alférez Don Diego de Espina [España—MS.]15 discovered the rich mine of Paraculi in Camarines. It extends for nine leguas, and it is hoped that it will have a considerable output. That has occasioned the command that the privileges of miners in those islands be observed, by a decree of September 22, 1636. They also abound in copper, which is brought from China with so much facility that the best artillery imaginable is cast in Manila, with which they supply their forts, the city of Macan and other cities of India, and it is taken to Nueva España; for the viceroy, the Marqués de Cerralvo, sent the governor, Don Juan Niño de Tabora, twenty-four thousand pesos, in return for which the latter sent him eighteen large pieces to fortify Acapulco. Of not less importance is the quicksilver of the Filipinas, whither the Chinese carry it in great quantities. It can be shipped—as is permitted and ordered by different royal decrees of August 15, 1609, and May 15,16 1631—to supply the deficiency of that metal for working the mines of Nueva España.

Number 15. Commerce of the islands, domestic and foreign; and in what the domestic consists

The greatest treasure of those islands, and that in which their wealth consists, is commerce, which demands a more extended treatment. It is divided into domestic and foreign. Of the latter, which is the rich commerce, we shall treat later. [In the margin: "In the year—sc.: number—20 to 37."] The domestic, which is slight, consists in the fruits and commodities produced in their lands, which are cultivated by their inhabitants: rice in the husk, and cleaned; cotton, palm wine, salt, wax, palm oil, and fowls; lampotes, tablecloths, Ilocan blankets, and medriñaques. These are the products in which the Indians pay their tributes, and in nothing else—except some who pay them in taes of gold, of eighteen carats, which is that obtained in those islands, and which is worth eight reals. Nutmeg, as good as that of Borneo, is found in them, as is mentioned in a royal decree of October 9, 623, in which it was ordered to bring some to these kingdoms.17 There is abundance of swine and cattle, deer, and carabaos or buffaloes. The coast waters are full of fish, the fields of fruits, the gardens of produce and vegetables. The most useful plant is the palm, from which an infinite number of articles are obtained. There are groves of them, as there are vineyards in España, although they require less labor and care. From the rice they make the ordinary bread, which they call morisqueta. What most shows the wealth of the country is the gold that its natives wear; for scarcely is there an Indian of moderate means, who is not adorned with a chain of this rich metal, of which the women use most.

Number 16. Number and diversity of Indians in the islands

What most assures the provinces of the new world is the greater or less number of the natives. In that the Filipinas are eminent, for there are the indigenous Indians, who are tributarios; but these are not many, as not all of them are pacified. Of those who have been pacified some, the larger encomiendas, have been assigned to the royal crown. There are other foreign Indians whose number is great in Manila and its environs, and where there are Spaniards, to whose service the Indians engage themselves for their day's wages. These include an infinite number of nations: Chinese, Japanese, Champanes, Malucans, Borneans, Joas [i.e., Javanese], Malays, and even Persians and Arabs. But those who are tributary to the royal crown are:

Number 17. Indians tributary to the royal crown in the Indias

In the provinces of Oton and Panay, twelve chief villages, which have 6,035 tributes.

In the island of Zebu, three which have 2,529 tributes.

In that of Camarines, there are 87 tributes of vagrant Indians and Sangleys (who are Chinese Christians).

In Mindoro and Luban, 1,612 tributes.

In the province of Tayavas, in five villages 1,343 tributes.

In that of Bay, in nine villages, 2,232 tributes.

On the coast of Manila, in twenty-eight villages, 4,250 tributes.

The vagrant Indians of Manila and its environs amount to 781 tributes.

The Japanese foreigners, 218 tributes.

The Christian Sangleys of the village of Baybay, outside the walls of Manila, 580 tributes.

In the province of Pampanga, in six villages, 3,650 tributes.

In the province of Pangasinan, in four villages, 899 tributes.

In the province of Ilocos, in five villages, 2,988 tributes.

In the province of Cagayan, in eight villages, 2,192 tributes.

Consequently, the royal crown has 44,763 tributes, as appears from an official statement made in the year 630. At ten reals per tribute, the amount reaches 53,715 pesos.

Among private persons there are distributed and assigned as encomiendas 48,000 other tributes, which for the 230 citizens of Manila— without reckoning those of the cities of [Santísimo] Nombre de Jesus, [Nueva] Caceres, and [Nueva] Segovia, and the town of Arebalo, who number about 300 more—does not amount to 160 tributes per man. They amount to a like number of pesos of eight reals, for the two additional reals are for the royal crown. And even on the eight reals so many charges are made that there is left but six or a trifle more. This is the wealth, and natural and proper commerce of the Filipinas.

Number 18. Fourth reason for the importance of the islands: their location, as18 is explained

The fourth reason which persuades one to value and conserve them is the one drawn from their notable location, almost opposite this hemisphere of España. Consequently, some think that Manila is the antipodes of Sevilla. Although according to the latitude of the world that is not exact—as it is in a different latitude from that required to be opposite by a straight line which passes through the center of the earth—according to the longitude the idea is not so far wrong; for although both cities are not on one great circle, their meridians lack only a difference of two or three hours to be diametrically opposite. From this it follows that, as the world has two poles upon which its frame moves and rotates, so does this monarchy also have two, one of them being España, and the other the Filipinas, which is the most remote part of España's possessions. And although in respect to the Indias, which led to the discovery of Filipinas, they are called the Western Islands, yet if sought by the voyage by way of India, they are the most eastern, and the finest that have been discovered in that ocean—whose dominion belongs to them even by nature and by their relative position among all the islands of that hemisphere. Therein they are surrounded by an infinite number of rich islands, which were formerly frequented; these promised great increase in the promulgation of the gospel, and no small hope based on the wealth of their commerce, before the rebels of Flandes entered those seas and embarrassed their navigation and trade. The islands are also at equal or proportionate distances with the kingdoms which extend from the straits of Sincapura19 and of Sunda (or Sabaon), to China and Japon.

Number 19. Importance of the islands because they offer opposition to the Dutch

From this so unusual location results the best proof of the importance of those islands—an importance well understood by the Dutch, who are striving, by means of immense military expenses, fleets, and numerous presidios, which they sustain in their seas and environs, as will be seen [In the margin: "In number 32."] to blockade, restrict, infest, and attack the islands, with no other end in view than their seizure. For they believe (and not without reason) that if they should attain this end, and remove that obstacle (which is the one that restricts the course of their fortunes in those regions), they would be absolute masters of all that extends on from the straits; and that they would cause from there so great anxiety and danger to India, that they would oblige its citizens to spend on its defense a greater sum than is now spent on the conservation of the Filipinas. And now, when the Dutch have been unable to gain a foothold in any of the islands because the arms of your Majesty sustain that country with the same reputation as in Flandes, the enemy maintain themselves by aggressive measures against the Spaniards—usually keeping for that purpose in the seas of those islands forty or fifty armed vessels, which are used to pillage whatever they can find, and to guard the presidios which they have established, and the commerce which they have introduced of the most precious drugs and commodities valued by Europa, whither they take them. However, that is done at a greater cost than they are willing to pay, because of the opposition made against them by the Filipinas. In order for the Dutch to overcome the Filipinas, it has not been sufficient for them to unite and ally themselves with the Moro and pagan kings of other islands and lands of Asia, persuading them that they should take arms against the vassals of España, whose defense lies in the Filipinas alone. And if the banners of your Majesty were driven from the islands, the power and arrogance of Olanda, which would dominate all the wealth of the kingdoms of the Orient, would greatly increase with the freedom and ease of commerce; while they would gain other and greater riches in Europa, and would so further their own advancement that more would be spent in this part of the world in restraining them than is spent in driving them away in those regions [i.e., the Orient]. Consequently, those islands are the bit that restrains the enemy, the obstacle that embarrasses them, the force that checks them, and the only care that causes them anxiety, so that they cannot attain their desires—an evident proof of the importance of those islands, and a fundamental reason for their conservation.

Number 20. The foreign and general commerce of the islands makes them more valuable

The above is not the sole motive of the Dutch for desiring to gain control of the Filipinas, but they recognize that they are, by their location, the most suitable of all the islands in the Orient for carrying on the general commerce of these kingdoms and nations. Already we have discussed the domestic and private commerce that is now conducted, which is scanty and limited; and we have stated that what most enriches the islands, and makes them most valuable, is the foreign trade. For it is rich and of great volume, and furnishes so great profits to the European merchants that, for the sake of these, in spite of the expenses, risks, and dangers of so long a voyage, the Portuguese go to seek it by way of India, the Castilians by Nueva España; the Turks by way of Persia, the Venetians by way of Egipto; and the Dutch, now by the Eastern route, entering India, or by the Western, crossing the immense open stretch of the South Sea, or even by way of the north and Nueva Zembla.

Number 21. Estimation of the commerce of the Orient, and its condition

That commerce, then, consists, according to what the Filipinas can enjoy of it, in different products and trades because of the difference of the kingdoms or islands with which they do or can communicate. And inasmuch as the explanation of this commerce is the chief part of the matter; and so that one may see in what estimation it has always been held, and what it deserves, and that there is no other medium by which to maintain this crown except by the conservation of India and the Filipinas: we will here describe, as briefly as possible, the times through which that trade has run, and its varying conditions up to the present. Now it all belongs to the two royal crowns of Castilla and Portugal, but it is usurped in part from both by the Dutch, whose only aim is to secure possession of it; and this they will attain on that day when either of the two extremes presented [for which these—MS.] which are maintained shall fail.20

Number 22. Oriental commerce; why it is valued

For many centuries has the oriental commerce been known as the foremost, and most valuable and rich in the world, as appears from Divine and human writings.21 The kingdoms of Europa, Asia Minor, and part of Africa produce, for their mutual intercourse, certain fruits almost the same, and commodities for merchandise, which differ rather in quality or quantity than in essence. But in Asia and the regions of the Orient, God created some things so precious in the estimation of men, and so peculiar to those provinces, that, as they are only found or manufactured therein, they are desired and sought by the rest of the world. Accordingly, different voyages and routes have been taken, which have been varied by the change of monarchies, on which such accidents depend.

Number 23. Beginnings of the Oriental commerce by way of Persia

The islands of Maluco, to begin with what is most suitable for my purpose, were peopled by Chinese [sic] and Jaos, who, with the practice of navigation, commenced to traffic in cloves, a precious and peculiar drug of the forests there, with India, there meeting the traders in pepper, cinnamon, and other articles; thus going from port to port and from nation to nation, all these spices reached the Persian Gulf. There came together various peoples, with still greater diversity of drugs, perfumes, and precious stones, which were brought into Persia; and, being disseminated throughout Asia, these commodities were imparted, although at a great price, to the eastern lands of Africa, and to the south of Europa. That commerce having become known for the precious and wonderful character of its wares, was at once esteemed so highly that it was one of the causes which induced Alexander the Great to direct his conquests toward India, in order to make himself master of the kingdoms which he imagined (and without error) to be the richest of the world, as from them originated the most precious thing that was known in it.

Number 24. Commerce of the Orient through the Arabian Gulf and other parts

Later, the monarchy of the Persians having become extinct and ruined, a part of that commerce passed, on account of the division of the states and the increase of trade among the peoples, by way of the Red Sea to the Arabian Gulf. Then, entering by way of the two Arabias, the nations of Asia Minor snared the spices and drugs; and through Africa they went down by the river Nilo to Egipto, stopping now in Cayro by land, now in Alexandria by water. As the latter was a frequented port in the Mediterranean, the communication of that commerce was easy, almost without knowing from what beginnings it sprang. By that voyage, the commerce increased so greatly that the king Ptolomeo Auleta22 collected there as many as one thousand five hundred talents in duties: if these were Attic talents, they amounted to nine and one-half million Castilian escudos. The Romans came into the monarchy, and, having made Egipto a province of the empire, they enjoyed that commerce by way of the Arabian Gulf — by which the spice-trade penetrated at that time (even to the city of Arsinoe, or that of Berenice), and by the Nile, or went overland to Alexandria, which came to be one of the richest cities in the world because of this trade. Later, as the sultans of Babilonia went on gathering power, until they gained possession of the best part of Asia, the spice again came to have an exit more by way of Persia and Trapisonda [i.e., Trebizond] to the Caspian Sea, whence it was taken down to the ports of the Mediterranean, and in one or another place, was received by the merchants of Italia, who imparted it, in the utmost abundance, to Europa. In Asia Minor, the Ottoman house succeeded, and the Turks got control of that commerce, which they divided — directing it, through the cities of Juda and Meca, to the interior of their lands; and, by the gulf and port of Suez, to Alexandria.

Number 25. Commerce of India confined to Portugal

The Turks did not enjoy the commerce for many years, for after the year 149723 the Lusitanian banners in India conquered their coasts, and the Portuguese, masters of the navigation of the Orient, blockaded the ports of the two gulfs — the Persian and the Arabic — with their fleets, preventing the entrance of that commerce there; and, conducting it by the Atlantic Ocean, they made the great city of Lisboa universal ruler over all that India produces. Thither [i.e., to Lisboa] resorted immediately not only the European nations, but also those from Africa and Asia, by which they despoiled the Turks of the source of their greatest incomes, forcing them to beg from these kingdoms what all had formerly bought from theirs. The wealth of Portugal increased so greatly by the commerce of India that, in the time of the king Don Manuel, payments of money in copper were more esteemed than those in gold. That trade furnished the profits with which to maintain wars, squadrons, and great presidios in the Orient, with which the Portuguese defended their coasts and seas, not only from the native kings, but also from the fleets that the Turks sent up through the Red Sea in order to recover what they so resented losing. Those fleets always returned either conquered or without the result for which they had sailed, until, having lost hopes of the restoration of that commerce through their lands, they desisted from the attempt—contenting themselves with some ships which, with the danger of encountering the Portuguese ships, they take to certain ports and lade with such spice as the fear of robbers allows them to take.

Number 26. Entrance of the Dutch into India, and their · · commerce

The commerce of the Orient lasted in Lisboa, without any other nation but the Portuguese sharing it, for almost one hundred years, which appears to have been the fatal century of their career. But as always they set upon that trade the value which has been made known in the wars of Flandes and the prohibition of trading with Olanda, their rebels determined to try to secure it; and in the year 1595 their first armed fleet entered India, to carry a portion of the spice to their islands, imparting it through them to all the northern nations, and even to those of the Levant by way of the strait of Gibraltar. Returning merchandise of great richness, they introduced a new trade, so remunerative as may be understood from the peril that they undergo, and from the expenses that they incur, in order to maintain it. Whatever they have acquired by that voyage (and it is not little) they have pillaged from this crown. The Dutch spreading through the Orient, recognizing the wealth of those regions, established their business, took part in barter there, erected factories, built presidios, fortified ports, and (what can well cause more anxiety) collected sea forces, by which they have succeeded even in driving out the Spaniards from their houses, in disquieting them, and, at times, in blockading them. They began to go out to the ocean with this trade, becoming the general pirates of the two Indias—where there are those who affirm that they have pillaged more than one hundred and thirty millions in less than forty years. They established the chief seat of this commerce in Bantan,24 the principal port of Java Major, whither people go from all the islands—Banda, Maluco, Gilolo, Sumatra, Amboino—and from the mainland of Coroman [Goroman—MS.], Siam, Pegu, Canboxa [Ganboxa—

MS.], Patan, Champa, and China. Turks, Arabs, Persians, Gusarates, Malays, Jaos, Egyptians, and Japanese go there. Consequently, with the presence of so many nations and so various sects (all of which are evil) Bantan may better be called "the Oriental Ginebra [i.e., Geneva]." There are two markets or fairs held there daily, at which more than thirty thousand persons come together to buy and sell.

Number 27. Commerce of the Orient, which the Dutch carry on from Ba[n]tan

The commerce acquired by the Dutch from that place is notable and large; for it consists of all the drugs, perfumes, and products found in those seas. The money carried by the Dutch is Castilian silver, as that is the kind that is most valued throughout the Orient. The money that circulates in the country is that of the leaden caxies [i.e., cash], of which one thousand five hundred are given for one real of silver. Two hundred caxies make one satac, and five sàtaques one sapacou. Rice is carried from the islands of Macaser, Sanbaya, and others. Rice forms the chief food bought by the Dutch, not only for the supply of their forts and fleets, but as a means of gain in that same port. Cocoanuts are taken [thither] from Balamban; this is another product that is consumed widely, and is of great use. They go to the confines of the island for salt, which is very profitable in Ba[n]tan [Bamtan—MS.]; and which is of greater profit, taking it, as they do, to Sumatra [Samatra—MS.], where they exchange it for wax from Pegú, white pepper, and various articles made from tortoise-shell. Twelve leguas away lies Jacatra, whence, and from Cranaon, Timor, and Dolimban, they get honey; and from Japara, sugar; from Querimara [Quarimara—MS.], east of Bornio, iron;25 from Pera and Gustean, tin and lead; from China come linens, silks, and porcelains. Their most abundant article of trade is pepper, for huge quantities of it are gathered in Java and Sumatra. And inasmuch as even those islands do not suffice to fill all their ships, they buy the pepper in other parts where they go: as on the coast of Malabar, as far as the cape of Comori—a land that produces whatever is taken to Portugal, and that which the Moors carry to the Red Sea; at Balagate, that which goes to Persia and Arabia; at Malaca, that which goes to Pegu, Sian, and China. The large variety comes from Bengala and Java, while the Canarin, which is the least valuable, is gathered from Goa and Malabar. The best is bought at Bantan, for forty thousand caxies (which amount to 27 reals in silver), per sack of 45 cates,26 or 56 Castilian libras, and it sells at one-half real [per libra?]. The ships which are unable to lade there—either because many ships go there, or because they are looking for wares that are not carried to their markets, or because they try to get them cheaper at their home market—go to other factories and places of trade. They go even to Meca in the Arabian Gulf, and cast anchor in Juda, twelve leguas away. For that voyage they carry drugs, food, and Chinese merchandise, which they sell for silver money — of which there is a quantity stamped with the arms of your Majesty in this kingdom, while the rest of the money consists of Turkish ducados. With that they go to other ports, and buy very precious commodities, as money is more precious [in those ports] than anything else. They get the aromatic mace from the island of Banda, which belongs to the Filipinas, and where Jacobo Cornelio left the first factors in the year 600; and in that of 608, Pedro Guillelmo Verrufio erected a fortress, although at the cost of his life. There, then, they barter the mace and the nutmeg, which is grown in no other part of the world, and obtain it there in so great quantity that they can lade annually one thousand toneladas of it. They take it dry, in order to carry it to Europa; and to Meca, Ormuz, and all the Orient in a conserve; for it is highly esteemed, as it is a very delicate relish. With mace, pepper, nutmeg, and other drugs they go to Pegu and Sian, where they trade rubies and wax in their factories. They barter those substances in Sumatra for pepper, which they also carry to Ormuz. There and at certain ports of Cambaya, they buy indigo (a royal product, and of which there is a monopoly in India), manna (a medicinal drug of Arabia and Persia), and rhubarb. What they are most eager to buy at Ormuz are the pearls that are fished from the Persian Gulf as far as Besorà. They also get them between Ceylan and Comori, between Borneo and Anion, and in Cochinchina. At Ormuz they trade most for precious stones27 — fine bezoars, turquoises, chrysolites, amethysts, jacinths, garnets, topazes from Cahanor, Calecut, and Cambaya, copper wire, and not very good agates. They have a factory in Patan, since — although they do not desire the trade of those people, as it consists only of silver money — a great quantity of Chinese merchandise is found there; and, as the Dutch cannot enter that country, they barter there [i.e., at Patan] for silk in the skein and woven, porcelain ware, and other things, and for calambuco wood, which is found in Sian, Malaca, Sumatra, and Cambaya. They get ginger from Malabar, not to take to Olanda — where they have too much with what they plunder in the Windward [Barlovento] Islands — but to take to Ormuz, which with that from Malaca, Dabul, and Bacain is traded in Persia [Percia — MS.] and Arabia. They trade cardamomum in Malabar, Calecut, and Cananor, [that plant] being used throughout the Orient to sweeten the breath. From the coasts of Sofala, Melinde, and Mozambique, they get gold, ivory, amber, and ebony, which they also get from Champá, whose mountains apparently raise no other [varieties of] woods. From Bengala they get civet, and mother-of-pearl. The best benzoin is that of Ceylan and Malaca; but as the Dutch have but little trade in those parts, they get along with that of the Javas, which is not so good, and with some of fine quality that they obtain in fairs and ports. The same is true of cinnamon which they are unable to obtain at Ceylan, except through third persons; accordingly, they secure but little, and content themselves with the wild cinnamon of Malabar, although it is very poor. Sandalwood was formerly the most profitable product in India, and was traded by the Portuguese. It was obtained in the island of Timor, where they had a fortress; but, as it is near Bantan, the Dutch have gained possession of it and its trade. This is the white sandalwood, for the red comes from Coromandel and Pegu. They buy snakewood [palo serpentino],28 brought from Ceylan [Seilan—MS.], in the fairs of Sumatra; eaglewood from Coromandel; camphor in Sunda and Chincheo, but better in Borneo; myrobalans29 in Cambaya, Balagate, and Malabar; incense from Arabia; myrrh from Abasia [Abaçia—MS.]; aloes-wood from Socotora; all of which they obtain at Ormuz. They trade but few diamonds, for the fine ones come from Bisnaga and Decan, and are taken to the fair of Lispor, between Goa and Cambaya; and since the Dutch do not go thither, they have no share in them, but they get some at the fair in Sumatra.

Number 28. Commerce in cloves, and how the Dutch entered it, and took possession of Maluco

The most noble product, and that which is must earnestly desired, as it is of the greatest profit and gain, is the clove. Cloves are produced in the celebrated islands of Maluco and that of Amboyno; and a little in the islands of Ires, Meytarana, Pulo, Cavali, Gilolo, Sabugo, Veranula,30 and other islands adjacent to the Malucas—which are the chief producers of cloves, and produce the best quality. As now, it was formerly the most valued product of the Orient; and now it forms one of the royal commodities of its commerce. In the islands where it is grown, one bare costs 460 Castilian reals. [The bare] has 640 libras, so that it does not amount to 2531 maravedis [per libra]; while it is sold for at least one ducado in Europa, so that each libra gains fourteen, which is an excessive profit. From the time when those islands were sold to the crown of Portugal, for the above-mentioned reason, for the sum of three hundred thousand ducados, that crown possessed them and the clove trade until the year 1598, when Jacobo Cornelio Nec went to India with eight ships. Dispersing those ships through its kingdoms, two of them went to Terrenate, where they left six factors, the first that Olanda had in that archipelago [In the margin: "In the year 11"]. In the year 601, of twelve other ships which entered the Orient, seven went to Amboyno, and by an arduous attempt gained the fort held there by the Portuguese; and although it was immediately recovered by Andres de Mendoca Furtado, commander of the fleet of India, and he, victorious, overran the islands of Maluco, subduing those of Tidore and Maguso [Magusié—MS.], he was unable to enter that of Terrenate [Teranete — MS.], where the Dutch had taken refuge and made its king rebel — the reënforcement of two hundred soldiers sent (in one ship and four fragatas, in charge of Captain Juan Galinato) by Don Pedro de Acuña, governor of Filipinas, being of no use. Thereupon everything was in a ruinous condition. In the year 605 [sic] Estevan Drage, who went to India with twelve galleons, attacked Amboyno and recaptured the fortress; and, going to Tidore and the rest of the Malucas, gained possession of them all.

Number 29. Recovery of Maluco by the governor of Filipinas, and its annexation thereto

That loss was felt keenly in España. The difficulty of relief from India having been recognized — as that country was so distant, and its forces were so broken; while those of the Filipinas, because they were greater and nearer, were more suitable — letters were sent to the governor of those islands, with orders that, aided by the Portuguese, they should endeavor to recover Maluco and restore it to this crown. Don Pedro de Acuña, having determined to make that expedition, and being already in possession of the aid that India could furnish, assembled a fine fleet in Iloylo, consisting of five large ships, six galleys, three Portuguese galliots, another open galliot, four junks, three champans, two English lanchas, and fourteen fragatas; and with them thirty-eight small boats, one thousand four hundred and twenty-three Spaniards, one thousand six hundred natives, seventy-five pieces of artillery, and everything else needed. With that he gained Terrenate, reduced Tidore, and subdued Siao, Sula, and Tacome, Gilolo, Sabugo, Gamocanora; and left those islands obedient. He moved the fortress of Terrenate to a better site, and garrisoned it with six hundred Spaniards, as it was the capital of all the other islands. Thus he placed on the enemy a curb, which some disasters have [since] removed. Inasmuch as the Malucos had been recovered by the Filipinas, and obtain from the latter the most certain succor, it was deemed inexpedient to return them to the crown of Portugal, or to its viceroy of India, which is so far distant from them, by the consent of both crowns; and a royal decree of October 29, 607, ordered that all the Malucas should remain, as at present, in charge of the governor of Filipinas.

Number 30. The clove trade, which is carried on by way of India

In regard to the clove trade, it was proposed that it be introduced by way of Nueva España, carrying to barter for it the products of the island of Panay and the merchandise of China at the account of the royal treasury; and that with the 100,000 ducados that would be invested in that, one might trade for all the cloves that were gathered in those islands. In the five chief islands alone that amounts to 4,400 bares of cloves of prime quality (which is the selected spice). At 640 libras, that amounts to 2,816,000 libras, in which two millions are concerned annually, for the maintenance of those islands, and the gaining of large increases for the royal treasury. In regard to it a decree of instruction had been given February 16, 602; but it was not then considered advisable to disturb that trade of India, either because of the injury that the Portuguese would receive, or in order not to cause a greater withdrawal of silver from Nueva España. However, that argument had little force; for, in exchange for the 100,000 ducados, two millions would be returned. Accordingly, although Maluco remained under the crown of Castilla, it was ordered that the clove trade be carried on by way of India, by a decree of November 17, 607; and the Portuguese go from India to buy the cloves at Manila, and take them to Malaca. Only what is needed there it shipped to Nueva España, and the rest is conveyed to various parts and kingdoms of the Orient which are convenient to Manila and the Malucas. The Dutch have again attempted to usurp that trade, as will be told later.

Number 31. The Dutch return to Maluco; and the deeds of the governor of Filipinas

Don Juan de Silva, who succeeded Don Pedro de Acuña in the government, tried to preserve during his term what his predecessor had gained. Immediately upon his arrival, learning that four ships from Olanda were near Manila, he prepared five ships and three galleys, and went to give them battle with one thousand Spaniards. Of the three ships that he found, one was destroyed by fire, and the other two surrendered; and their booty amounted to more than two hundred thousand ducados. That victory was not sufficient to make the enemy lose their liking for that commerce, and they returned in greater force to seek it. Don Juan de Silva made an expedition against them, and went to find them in the strait of Maluco; but that expedition did not have the desired success. Having written to the viceroy of India, by a secret letter of arrangements, dated December32 13, 615, asking the latter to join with him to endeavor to drive the Dutch from those seas once for all, he resolved to put forth his utmost efforts in order to accomplish it; and had he had the good fortune to carry out that plan as he desired, it would have been an exploit worthy of his great courage and valor. He built seven galleons of one thousand or one thousand five hundred toneladas, in addition to three others that he had; and cast one hundred and fifty large pieces of artillery—although, for lack of master-workmen, they did not turn out well. He sent to request ten other galleons and six galleys from the viceroy of India, and sent sixteen thousand pesos for the purchase of certain articles. That was taken by Don Christoval de Azqueta and forty Spaniards, who were never seen again, the disaster of that expedition thus commencing. The governor repeated the embassy by means of Father Juan de Ribera of the Society of Jesus. The latter obtained a reënforcement of four galleons and four galliots, and a few poorly-disciplined men; and (what was worse) they left so far ahead of time, that they had to await Don Juan de Silva at Malaca before the season to arrive, and at the worst time possible; for scarcely had they entered port when the king of Achen attacked them with four hundred boats. He fought with the four galleons of Goa, and burned one of them, whereupon he desisted from the blockade. As soon as the Jaos had gone, six galleons from Olanda entered, and after fighting with the three galleons of Portugal, burned them. Learning that Don Juan de Silva was coming, the Dutch retired to their forts, in fear of the force that he was carrying. Then the governor left Manila with ten galleons, the best that have ever been on that sea, and four galleys, in the year 616. He learned of the loss of the Portuguese, and although he ought to have attacked Bantan, where the enemy were fearing him, he entered Malaca without doing anything; and, while hesitating there as to what he could accomplish, he was seized by the illness from which he died. His fleet, being left without a leader, returned to Manila, destroyed and conquered by itself. The disaster of that voyage was recognized not only in what has been said, but also in that if he had gone to Maluco, as he had been advised, he would have accomplished an important feat of arms. If he had been a fortnight later in leaving Manila, he would have prevented the depredations committed by the Dutchman Jorje Spilberg. The latter—having entered the South Sea, and fought the battle of Cañete, near Lima, which was of but little consolation for the Peruvians—arrived at the bar of that city [i.e., Manila], and then went to Maluco, thinking that the governor had gone to their islands. Hearing that he was in Malaca, he took ten galleons from them, and went to look for him. Not finding him, and hearing of his death, he caused the rebellion of all those who were peaceful. The Mindanaos went out with sixty caracoas, and attacked the province of Camarines, where they caused considerable depredation. Having disagreed, the Mindanaos divided into two companies—one going toward Manila to join the Dutch, the other to the island of Panay. There Captain Lazaro de Torres destroyed them with only seven caracoas; and, capturing four of the Mindanao caracoas, made the rest of them take to the open sea, until they were all lost. The Dutch, with their ten galleons, sighted the same island of Panay, and Captain Don Diego de Quiñones with seventy soldiers fought with seven companies of them that landed, and made them return to their boats with great loss, and but little reputation, so much can a good captain do. The enemy went in sight of Manila again, where the fleet taken out by Don Juan de Silva had already entered; however, it was in so bad condition that it did not have sufficient strength to attack the Dutch. Finally six galleons could be prepared, to oppose the other six which were infesting the coasts. The battle was fought, and the flagship of Olanda was sunk, and two galleons burned, while the almiranta, with two others, took to flight. But that victory had its diminution, for the galleon "San Marcos," having become separated [from the others], met two Dutch galleons which had not taken part in the battle. In order to avoid a new battle with them, and the captain losing courage, the "San Marcos" was run ashore and burned. Thus the Spanish side was victorious, but weakened. The enemy, although conquered and having lost three galleons, went to Maluco with the seven remaining ones, and were able to keep what they had acquired. It is recognized that Maluco is of the importance that has been stated, because they have maintained it at the cost of so many losses, fleets, and men.

Number 32. Dutch forts and presidios in the Filipinas district

The above is confirmed by mentioning the forts which they have established with presidios, and which they have now in the district of the Filipinas Islands, both for the defense by their arms and for the continuance of the clove trade.33

In Terrenate they possess the fort of Malayo, which they call Granoya. There lives the Dutch governor, who has the rest of Maluco in his charge. It is a regular city in which there was usually a garrison of 850 soldiers, but which now has only 150 [140 — MS.]. At a quarter of a legua is Toloco, a strong site, in which there are, for garrison, one alférez with twenty soldiers. Tacubo is also near Malayo, whence they garrison it as is necessary. Malaca is one-half legua to the north of Malayo. Tacome, which they call Vuillemistat,34 three leguas from Toloco, is a principal fort, and has a garrison of one company.

They had no fort in Tidore formerly, from the time of the expedition of Don Pedro de Acuña until the year 612, when they gained a small rampart where the governor of Maluco, Don Geronimo de Silva, kept an alférez with 14 [15 — MS.] soldiers. There the Dutch built the fort called Marieco the great, where there is a captain with sixty soldiers. However, they do not get any profit from that island.

Motri [Morri — MS.], which lies between Tidore and Maquien, became depopulated through the fear of the natives for the men of Tidore. Persuaded by the Terrenatans, the Dutch founded a fort there in its northern part, taking a colony from Gilolo; the natives were thereupon assured of safety, and settled there. It has a captain with fifty soldiers.

There are three forts in Maquin or Muchian, one legua from Motir [Morir—MS.]: Nofagia, at the north, with one alférez and forty married soldiers; Tafazen, at the west, with one lieutenant of the governor, and one hundred married35 soldiers; at Tabelole, in the east, a small fort of but slight importance, with one sergeant and twelve soldiers.

In Bachian is the fort of Bernevelt, with one captain and sixty soldiers.

In Gilolo or Batochina,36 three leguas from the fort maintained there by the Spaniards, the Dutch maintain that of Tabori, with one alférez and fifty soldiers; and three leguas farther on is another fort, with one lieutenant and twelve soldiers.

In Amborino [i.e., Amboina],37 eighty leguas from Terrenate, is a large fort, with a watered moat capable of floating a galley without its oars. Its garrison consists of a commandant with one hundred soldiers.

In Siao, thirty leguas from Terrenate, the Dutch own Sagu Maruco [Marico—MS.]. A Spanish alférez was there with five soldiers in the year 614 for a certain purpose. The Dutch came, and after driving out the Spaniards, fortified themselves in that place, as they always crave what España possesses. A sergeant was stationed there with sixteen soldiers, although it is not a post of importance.

They have two forts in Banda: Moçovia and Belgio, each one with one hundred and twenty soldiers. Although the natives are hostile, those presidios are kept up with the hope of reducing them, and because of the nutmeg which is gotten there, which is but little.

In Java Major there are three factories, namely, in Baatan, Jacava, and Japara. Bantan is the chief stronghold that the Dutch have in India. The governor or prefect lives there, in whose charge are all the forts of the Orient. There is kept account of all that is laden and of the ships, so that it is the accountancy and register of their trade. There are two galleys and more than thirty barks, armed and garrisoned, in which they cross to Jacatra, which is the arsenal and dockyard where their ships are repaired, as it is the first and last station that they make on leaving and on entering by the straits of Sincapura and Sonda. It is one day's journey from Bantan. However, the English, in confederacy with the Jaos, a few years ago seized certain of those ports. In the year 629, the king of Matalan [i.e., Mataram] besieged Jacatra, where he remained for five months. They destroyed the city, and killed three hundred of the Dutch, and the latter only retained their fortress.

In Borneo, which is the most westerly of the Filipinas, and the largest, being five hundred leguas in circumference, the Dutch do not possess fort or factory, but they are allowed to trade there.

In the island of Hermosa, between the Filipinas and China, they have established a presidio and seized a port. España has another fort there, each on its own point, as the island is long. That has caused anxiety, as the island lies on the way to China. Accordingly, the governor [of Filipinas] has been ordered to endeavor to drive the Dutch away.

In the island of Sumatra, at the city of Jambo in the strait of Sincapura, they have a factory for the pepper trade, which is of great importance to them.

In the kingdom of Patan, they have another factory, which ranks with that of Jambo; another in that of Sian; another in Camboxa; and another in Cochinchina. They have no entrance into China; on the contrary, they are the declared and common enemy [of that country] because of the great piracies that they have committed against those natives. They have a factory in Japon, from which they get food and ammunition, which is worth not a little to them.

They have other ports, which they have abandoned as it was convenient for them to do so — as that of Gemalanor, in Gilolo; the forts of Bouson, Solor, and Timor; the factories of Gresco in Java, and that of Asqueo, because of a war which they had with their king. They abandoned another in Macasar, in the island of the Celebes, where they got a quantity of sago [*segu*], which is the bread of the country, and a quantity of rice. Accordingly, they tried to return there, but were unable.

In all those forts and presidios Jorje Spilberg found, in the year 616, three thousand regular soldiers; one hundred and ninety-three bronze pieces, and three hundred and ten of cast iron, with three hundred swivel-guns; and thirty war galleons, besides those galleons in which they made the journey to and from Olanda.

Number 33. Arguments based on the forts of the Dutch

From this account which has been given of the Dutch forts in the seas of the Filipinas, are deduced certain arguments that belong to the purpose of this memorial and the matters of which it treats.

Number 34. First argument: for the condition and danger of the commerce

The first argument is the quality and importance of the commerce of the Orient, its condition, and the risk to which it is exposed.

Number 35. Second argument: participation in the clove trade of Maluco

The second is the special point of the trade in the cloves which are obtained in Maluco, in which it is to be noted that the Dutch share by means of the forts that they maintain. Accordingly, they obtain 600 bares [misprinted *baus*] from the cloves of Terrenate annually, or 384,000 libras; from Motir, 700 bares, or 468,000 libras; from Maquien, 1,400 bares, or 896,000 libras; from Bachian, 400 bares, or 256,000 libras; from Amboyno, 1,800 bares, or 1,152,000 libras. The total of the cloves obtained from Maluco, exclusive of Amboyno, is 1,098,000 libras. Since the total yield from all those islands is, as has been stated, 2,816,000 libras, there is left for the Spaniards, Portuguese, Castilians, and other nations who get some of it, 1,718,000 libras. Even that is because of the protection and proximity of the Filipinas; and if that protection were lacking, not only would all the clove trade belong to the Dutch, but, not needing the presidios that they maintain for it, they would enjoy all the trade at a much less cost and with greater gains, as can be understood from what is here stated.

Number 36. Third argument: the profits of that commerce, and the effect [on it] of the Filipinas

The third, the great profits of that commerce; since for its maintenance alone the enemy employ and support so many fleets and presidios. And although the states of Olanda are so poor and of so little importance, when compared with the grandeur of the monarchy of España, they obtain [from that trade] with only good management and the freedom with which they conduct it, so large profits that with that gain they maintain so great a force on the sea; and their profits would be much greater, if the Dutch were not opposed by the force which your Majesty has in the Filipinas Islands. For it is affirmed that when two ships and one patache were coming laden from India to their country, and the ships were wrecked, and the patache saved, from that vessel alone they made up the loss, and had a considerable gain. That shows how advisable it is that the enemy do not increase and that the [colony in the] islands be permanent, and be protected, and its citizens succored.

Number 37. [Fourth argument:] Commerce of China sustains the Filipinas, and how it is carried on.

Returning to the commerce that the islands have and what they can have—namely, all the above and that of Japon and other kingdoms of those regions—the first and chief thing in which consists the preservation of the Filipinas is the Chinese trade. Although the commerce is shared by Portugal, it is with great peril and danger, as the Portuguese have to go through the strait of Sincapura, which is always occupied by the Dutch. It has this difference, that the Portuguese go to China itself to get the goods, where they have a settlement in the city of Macan; while the Castilians enjoy the trade in Manila, to whose port many ships come annually from China, laden with all the products, natural and artificial, that that great kingdom yields. Governor Don Francisco Tello granted permission to Don Juan Zamudio, in the year 1599, to go to China, and to establish the trade as the Portuguese have it. He went with a ship to the city of Canton, and although he experienced not a little opposition from them, he opened a port for the inhabitants of Filipinas. That of El Pinal was assigned them, and a house in Canton, together with chapas and passports, so that they might go to form a settlement there whenever they liked. Don Luis Perez Das Mariñas being wrecked afterward on the coast of China, the Chinese welcomed him, and the Spaniards entered that port. Although, as that was in violation of the royal decree of 593, a censure was sent to the Audiencia, yet the governor was charged by a secret letter of October 15, 603, to call a council to consider the advisability of continuing that enterprise. From that conference it appears that the royal decree of July 25, 609, resulted, by which that trade of China and Japon was permitted to the citizens of Manila. However, it is a fact that they do not avail themselves of it directly, but that they are content to await the Chinese who bring their merchandise to them, as the citizens have not the forces or the capital to go to their country for it. The Chinese are allowed to sell the goods at wholesale, in accordance with the order that was introduced by Governor Gomez Perez Das Mariñas. The goods are appraised in a lump by persons deputed for that purpose; and then the goods are divided and distributed among the inhabitants, so that all may have a share in the commerce. That method was approved by a letter of instructions of January 17, 593, and is the method called "pancada;" to the governor was left only permission to send one ship annually to Macan, in order to buy military supplies and no other thing, by a decree of February 4, 608. For some little time past the Portuguese of that city have begun going to Manila, or sending thither merchandise from China. That is a great damage to the citizens, for the Portuguese sell the goods dearer than do the Chinese. Formerly those Chinese goods were taken freely to Nueva España, Guatimala, and Panamá, and passed on to Perú; but on account of their cheapness and the extent to which they were consumed, and the profit made on their cost, they were a menace to those kingdoms, and the damage caused by them to the commerce of Sevilla was regretted. Accordingly, the exportation of those goods to Guatimala and Panamá was forbidden, and afterward their transportation to Perú; and the permission was left only for Nueva España, as will be related, as that is the principal point under discussion. [In the margin: "From number 62 on."]

Number 38. Fifth argument for the importance of the islands: their superiority in those seas

Concluding with the arguments that make the Filipinas important, the fifth is the superiority that they have in the Orient over not a few crowned kings. Your Majesty does not provide any post in all the kingdoms of this monarchy, that are equal in that region to that of governor of the islands, unless it be the viceroyalty of India. As such governor, the king of Borneo, confessing himself, although a Mahometan, a vassal of the crown of Castilla, rendered homage to Doctor Francisco de Sande. During the term of Gomez Perez Das Mariñas, the king of another island, Siao, went to Manila and rendered homage. Don Pedro de Acuña took their king prisoner in the expedition to Terrenate, and kept him in that city [i.e., Manila]. When Don Juan Niño de Tavora went [as governor], he bore an order, by a decree of November 10, 626, to give that king his freedom if he considered it advisable; but he was not freed, and died a prisoner in 629, as did also his son shortly before. He was succeeded by a cachil who had been a prisoner with the king, and who remained hostile. The king of Tidore is an ally, and recognizes the governor as his superior; and the arms of España as his protection. A treaty of peace was made in the year 618 with the king of Macasar, as that was important for the maintenance of Terrenate. The watchfulness maintained with the king of Mindanao is constant; and although he has been subdued several times—especially in the year 597, through the valor of Don Juan Ronquillo, who had many encounters in that island with the natives—he has once more revolted. Although he has been severely punished, never is there assurance of him except when he knows that there is a force in the Filipinas. Consequently, such a force is necessary, in order that he may not dare to commit greater depredations, for the Mindanaos who shall be taken in war are declared to be by that very fact slaves, by a royal decree of May 29, 620. By a decree of July 4, 1609, it is ordered that peace be maintained with the emperor of Japon; and harmonious relations were long maintained with him, by sending him a present annually and receiving his, and by admitting ships and commerce between the two countries. [This was done] until the year 634, when the Dutch so angered him against the Catholics that they roused up a new persecution against them in his kingdoms, and put an end to his friendship with Filipinas. That is no small injury, not only on account of the cessation of intercourse with them, but because that barbarian is powerful, and the Japanese are general pirates. Peace with Great China and its king has been better managed, and is maintained by means of commerce and some presents which are sent. Doctor Sande wrote that he would dare to conquer that kingdom, which was a very confident promise; he was answered on April 9, 586, that he was not to consider such a thing, but to preserve friendship with the Chinese. Accordingly, that has been done, and so many Chinese are in Manila that they have two villages: one that of Vindonoc [i.e., Binondo], which is near the city, and composed of married Christians; and the other the Parián—which is, as it were, an enclosed suburb—in which live those who bring merchandise, and all these are called Sangleys. The kingdoms of Champa, Camboxa, and Sian, which occupy the mainland, are frontiers of war. The conquest of Champa is regarded as lawful, by agreement of the theologians, as its natives are notorious pirates on those who pass their coasts, and they have many Christian captives; and because they consent to and defend the law of Mahomet, and are nearly all Moors, as is mentioned in a royal decree of October 13, 600. The king of Camboxa is not so pernicious, and allows woods, which abound in his kingdom, to be taken [thence] for shipbuilding in Filipinas, besides other products and valuable drugs. There is a history of the ambassadors whom the king, Apran Langara, sent to Manila, whence went to him the reënforcement taken to him by Captain Gallinato, and the success that he had; consequently, that kingdom has always been well affected toward the Spaniards. The king of Sian is like him of Champa; he holds more than fourteen thousand Christians captive, from various nations. In the year 629, that king captured two ships from Manila in his ports, and detained them. Therefore the governor, Don Juan Niño, sent two galleons, which inflicted a sufficient punishment along their coast; and then an embassy to demand satisfaction for the two ships, saying that, if it were not given, they would continue to collect it. The king was dead, and his son agreed to do what was demanded from him. Thereby your Majesty's arms kept the reputation that they have always preserved in those seas among so many Moorish and pagan kings, and in presence of the forces of Olanda and Inglaterra.

Number 39. Sixth argument for the importance of the islands: the effects of their preservation

The sixth and last argument which shows and proves the importance of the islands, and how advisable is their conservation and maintenance, consists in the excellent and considerable effects that result from it, which, although they are numerous, can be reduced to five chief points.

Number 40. First effect of the conservation of the islands: the promulgation of the faith

The first effect is the conservation of the Catholic faith, and the continuance of its promulgation, which has entered the rich and extensive regions of the Orient through the agency of both crowns of Castilla and

Portugal. In that are seen so38 miraculous advances that it would be for the kings of España to disregard the obligation that they so much value, in [not] giving them the protection possible—so that while the faith does not advance, it may not decrease, nor lose what has been planted in the vineyard of God our Lord. This will be attained (humanly speaking), as long as the two extremes on which this mean depends do not fail, those two extremes being the states maintained by the two crowns in the Orient: that of Portugal, in India; and that of Castilla, in Filipinas. As India is the gateway for all the kingdoms that belong to this part of the straits, so also are the islands for these kingdoms about them, such as Great China, Japon, the Javas, Nueva Guinea, and the islands of Salomon—for whose discovery three voyages had been made from Lima at great cost, but with little result, although they could be reached with greater ease by sailing from Manila.

Number 41. Second effect of the conservation of the islands: the security of India

The second effect will be to assure the safety of those states, of which as they are found today, one may understand that, if one be lost, the other will become endangered. India has declined in its commerce and wealth, and consequently, in its power, because of the relationship that there is between these two things; for when a kingdom loses its wealth, it loses its strength. Both have been usurped by the Dutch, as is proved; for they, commencing with the commerce, have appropriated it to themselves, as well as the strength that is annexed to commerce. Therefore India needs to avail itself of the Filipinas, and that not only for such special aid as was requested by the viceroy, Conde de Linares, in the year 631 (who was governing India with the care, prudence, and success that is known by the excellent results that he obtained, and by the great talent and valor of his person, experienced in that and in other charges), to whom Governor Don Juan Niño sent two galleons; but also so that the enemy, being diverted, may have less power. Thus was he [i.e., the governor of Filipinas] charged to do by decrees of April 4, 1581, and December 5, 1584. The same must also be understood of the islands, which although they do not now have less strength than for the last forty years, have more enemies and more to which to attend. If India should fail them, they would be maintained with greater difficulty. The Portuguese aided in the expedition made by Don Pedro de Acuña, and also in that of Don Juan de Silva, but not with equal success in both; and it is ordered that the two forces unite for the recovery of the island of Hermosa. The city of Macan, in China, is so far from India that it would be in danger should the islands fail it. The governor of the islands had an order to aid that city, by a decree of December twenty, six hundred and twenty-three. He did so by sending it six pieces of artillery, with ammunition and other supplies, which were of so great importance that the Portuguese averted their danger. That action is recommended by the good treatment and welcome that the men of Filipinas receive in India—especially in Cochin, where they go to buy ships and other things—as was written, in acknowledgment therefor, to Don Felipe Mascareñas [Mascarenhas—MS.] in the year 630.

Number 42. Third effect of the conservation of the islands: to deprive Olanda of commerce

The third effect is to deprive the Dutch of a great part of their commerce, not only by España maintaining it in the Filipinas, which otherwise would all belong to the Dutch, as has been said, [In the margin: "In number 36."] but also by forcing them to keep the presidios and fleets that have been mentioned, [In the margin: "In number 32."] in order to preserve what they have usurped; and thus, the expenses being heavier, consequently the profits would be less. It was already proposed, with arguments that gained no little approbation (thus they secured its execution), how advisable it was for a royal fleet to cruise among the Windward Islands. Among the effects that were assured was one (and the most important), that of compelling the enemy who should go to infest those islands and commit piracies along their coasts, to erect a fort, and form settlements in some [of the islands], as they have done; and to do it with presidios and garrisons, because of their fear of being attacked and punished—and not as they usually do, when with two little ships carrying each six pieces and twenty men, they pillage what they wish; and with a hundred [common] laborers, and one captain to command them, without arms or defense, they settle on this or that island, confident that there is no one on the sea who can oppose them, or attack them ashore. For if they were in fear, and were obliged to carry an armed force, they would, as that requires cost and preparation, be unable to make so many settlements; nor would their profits be so great that they would not some time or other be ruined and take warning from experience. The Filipinas are doing this in the Orient, and are resisting the enemy in such manner that they not only compel them to maintain forts in their seas, but also to suffer so great losses in them that at times the losses, as is known, exceed the profits. On that account, it is understood that the East [India] Company of Olanda is less rich than formerly; and that, leaving it, they have established the West [India Company]. As the latter does not consume [demand—MS.] so much expense, although the profits are less, it is more appreciated. This is an argument that ought to be heeded in order to establish a fort in the Windward Islands, as there is in the Filipinas, so that the same result might be experienced in the former as in the latter.

Number 43. Fourth effect of the conservation of the islands: the relief of the Indias

The fourth effect is the relief of the Western Indias; for with the diversion and expense that the enemy encounters in the Eastern Indias and the posts of Maluco, he is forced to pay less attention to the Western Indias, and to infest them with weaker forces — which would be greater if he could dispense with employing them in the Orient to counteract the forces of Filipinas; and the profits of commerce there increasing, he would, freed from the expense [of those armaments], be at liberty to occupy himself in the West. If the Dutch should enter there with all their forces, they would cause much more anxiety [than now], and more costly means of defense than those which are made in Filipinas.

Number 44. Fifth effect of the conservation of the islands: the reputation of this crown

The fifth and last effect is that this crown will sustain its reputation and renown, a consideration which so urgently persuades it to preserve a post so honored, avoiding the scandal that would result from losing it, or from abandoning as difficult and costly the most noble exploit that has been offered to any prince. That would [will—MS.] persuade the enemy that it was for lack of forces, or that the gospel ministers whom España sends only go where riches and advantage await them, and not where these are not found. That was one of the motives, if not the greatest, of the kings your Majesty's father and grandfather; and your greatness has not only to preserve what you inherited by so many legitimate titles, but also to increase it as much as possible.

Number 45. Means existing for the conservation of the islands

Granted, then, and declared by so many and so evident arguments, the importance of the Filipinas, in regard to both its causes and its effects, it is to be noted that there are to be found but two means for the attainment of their conservation. One is for your Majesty to supply from the royal treasury all the expense that should be necessary, without heeding what income they furnish. The other method is to concede to them the commerce with Nueva España, in such quantity and manner that, with what should proceed from it, there should be enough to defend the islands. Each of these means is insufficient by itself, nor is it possible; for your Majesty cannot spend all that is necessary for the maintenance of Filipinas, and it is not advisable to permit their commerce to the extent that the duties derived from it may equal the

expenses incurred for the islands. Consequently, the least damaging and the most certain expedient seems to be to combine these measures so that your Majesty may aid in part, and may protect that commerce in such manner that the islands having the means therefor, may attend to their own wants; since the greater the sum derived from the commerce, without increasing it too much, the less the expense from the royal treasury.

Number 46. Points to which the execution of the means proposed can be reduced

In order to adjust these two means, as they are the only ones for this end, it is necessary to make known what the Filipinas are costing today. This will be the first of five points to which this matter is reduced. The second, what they contribute. The third, what commerce they exercise with Nueva España. The fourth, the present condition of this commerce. The fifth and last, what illegal acts are committed in this commerce, and how these can be avoided or corrected without ruining or destroying it. These points having been declared, the decision that can be rendered in regard to the petitions that are made in behalf of the islands will be clear.

Number 47. First point: of the expenses of the islands; and the first division of it, the administration of justice.

In regard to the first point, namely, the cost and expense of the islands, it consists in what results from eight branches or main divisions to which it is reduced. The first is that of the justice which your Majesty, as natural seignior, ought to furnish and administer to those vassals. The head of it is the royal Chancillería which resides in the city of Manila. It was first established (for everything is done with a foundation), by a royal decree of March 5, 582, with a president (who was to be governor), three auditors, and one fiscal.39 The governor and president, who was then Licentiate Santiago de Vera, was assigned a salary of four thousand pesos ensayados;40 and the auditors and fiscal, two thousand. For the payment of those salaries, by a royal decree of May 10, 1583, twelve thousand [pesos] ensayados in tributes of the Indians were ordered to be assigned (and they were assigned) to the crown. Later, it having been understood through some less authentic reports that the Audiencia was unnecessary in Manila, it was suppressed by a decree of August 9, 1589; and Gomez Perez Das Mariñas, of the Habit of Santiago, was appointed governor and captain-general, with a salary of 8,000 pesos ensayados, and with authority to have a guard of halberdiers to uphold the dignity of the post (as is done by his successors to this day). It consists of one captain with 240 pesos pay (although this post is always held by an infantry captain who receives no more than the ordinary pay, which will

be mentioned), twelve soldiers at 96 pesos, and one corporal at 108 pesos, making a total of 1,260 pesos of eight reals (all this account and summary being reckoned in pesos of that denomination). He was given a lieutenant-general as counselor, with a salary of 2,000 pesos ensayados. But scarcely was the Audiencia suppressed, than results showed the unreliability of the reports which had led to that step. Don Francisco Tello having succeeded to the government, the Audiencia was again established, and he was given the title of president, on December 21, 595. There were four auditors and one fiscal, who was to be protector of the Indians; and all were given the salary that they had before, except the president, who was left the 8,000 pesos ensayados that had been assigned him as governor. Thus the Audiencia is still maintained, with an expense of 18,000 pesos ensayados, or 29,000 pesos, 2 reals of common gold. To the court scrivener was assigned 300 [pesos]; to one reporter, 600 one fiscal solicitor, 300; to the captain, 350; to one herald, 48: a total of 1,898, to be paid from fines of the exchequer. The sum paid to corregidors is as follows: to two, for the island of Mindoro and the province of Catanduanes, at the rate of 100 pesos, to two, for the islands of Mariveles and Negros, at the rate of 150 pesos; to those of the islands of Leyte, Samare, Ybabao, and to him of Ibalon (who is also a sentinel), at the rate of 200. To twelve alcaldes-mayor of Tondo, Pampanga, Bulacan, Pangasinar, Ilocos, Cagayan, Calamianes, Zebu, Camarines, Laguna de Bay, Balayan, and Atilaya, at the rate of 300 pesos; and to him of Oton, who serves in the post of purveyor for Terrenate, 700 pesos. Therefore the total in this department is 37,077 pesos.

Number 48. Second division: the conversion, preaching, divine worship, and the hospitals

The second is that which pertains to the conversion, and to preaching, divine worship, and the hospitals. The first bishop appointed for the church of Manila was Fray Domingo de Salazar. He was succeeded by Fray Ignacio de Santivañez, with the pall as archbishop—the church being erected into a metropolitan, and the three of [Nueva] Caceres, Zebu, and [Nueva] Segovia into suffragans, in the year 596, although the latter have no prebends. The archbishop was assigned a competence of 3,000 ducados, and the three bishops each 500,000 maravedis, all from the royal treasury; the tithes enter into the treasury, as their amount is small. Thus the four prelates receive annually, 9,637 and one-half pesos. To the dignitaries of the metropolitan church are paid: to the dean, 600 pesos; to the archdeacon, precentor, treasurer, and schoolmaster, each 500; to four canons, each 400; to two racioneros, each 300; to two medio-racioneros, 200; to two curas, each 50,000 maravedis; to two sacristans, each 25,000 maravedis. To the chaplain of the seminary of Santa Potenciana, which belongs to the royal patronage, 300 pesos. For four regular priests of St. Dominic, four of St. Augustine, and four of the Society of Jesus, who administer instruction in Manila, to each convent are given, 1,072 pesos; and for four others, Augustinian Recollects, 697 pesos to their convent. To two secular assistants of the bishop of Zebu, each 576 pesos, by a decree of March 14, 633; and a like sum to two of [Nueva] Segovia, by a decree of April 11, 635; and the same to him of [Nueva] Caceres. To twelve curas, and twelve sacristans, in the three cathedrals, and in nine other churches of those islands, each 50,000 maravedis, and 25,000 [respectively]. To two religious who administer the sacraments in the island of Hermosa, each 536 pesos. To the convents of St. Dominic and St. Augustine, each 400; to that of the Society of Jesus, 200; to that of St. Francis, 300; to the nuns of St. Clare, 200. To two infirmaries, maintained by the Dominican religious in Cagayan and Pangasinan, each 400. To the Spanish hospital in Manila, 3,000 pesos; to the physician, 300; to the surgeon, 400; to the barber, 312; to the apothecary, 200; to the steward, 182 and one-half, and one tonelada in the trading ships. To the hospital of Cavite, 700; to that of San Lazaro of the natives, outside the walls, 3,442; to that of Los Baños of Nueva España, of holy41 waters, 1,472, and 100 more for medicines; to that of the Sangleys of San Gabriel [Graviel — MS.], 425; to that of Terrenate, 1,000; to that of Cagayan, 300; to that of Oton, 250; to that of Caraga, 50; to that of Zebu, 250; to that of the artillerymen, 500; to that of the trading ships, 1,000. To some churches which have alms of oil are distributed annually 3,940 gantas, which are worth 760 pesos. [The expenses for] this department amount to 37,297 pesos.

Number 49. Third division: the presents sent by the governor

The third is but little, and consists of [the expenses caused by] the custom in those islands of the governor sending some gifts, donations, and presents to the kings of Japon, Camboxa, Tidore, and others. These are necessary to maintain their friendship, and to keep them well-disposed for what is asked from them; for not one of them receives an embassy favorably, unless it is accompanied by some present. In the year 580 a present was sent from España to Great China, consisting of twelve falcons; twelve horses, with their trappings and saddle-cloths embroidered with the royal arms; and six mules,42 with their wrought coverings, which carried twelve boxes, filled with various curious articles. For securing this amicable relation, there are spent annually one thousand five hundred pesos.

Number 50. Fourth division: the management of the royal treasury

The fourth division is that of the management of the royal treasury. To the three officials — treasurer, accountant, and factor — are paid salaries of 5,625 pesos. To eight greater and lesser officials, 2,300 pesos; to one computer-in-ordinary of accounts, 1,000; to his chief clerk, who is a royal notary, 450; to three other clerks of accounts, 900; to the assayer and weigher, 550; and to its officer of justice, 300. The full total is 11,550 pesos.

Number 51. Fifth division: land warfare

The fifth division is that of land warfare. There is one master-of-camp in the camp of Manila, with 1,654 and one-half pesos pay; one sargento-mayor, with 990; two adjutants, with 360; one chaplain of the regiment, with 360; one field captain, with 180; one chief constable, with 96; one head drummer, with 126; ten substitutes stationed near the person of the governor and appointed by your Majesty at different rates of pay, which amounted in the year 635 (the year when all this report was drawn up) to 6,675 pesos; one military notary, with 200 [20 — MS.]; and one procurator for the infantry, with 126. Of the presidios of Manila, the castellan of the fort of Santiago receives 800 pesos, and his one lieutenant, 420; three wardens for the presidios of Zebu, Oton, and Cagayan, each 300; their three lieutenants, each 96; one chaplain for Oton, 180; one lieutenant of the captain-general of Pintados, 800; one lieutenant of the governor and captain-general, for the presidio of the island of Hermosa, 1,200; one sargento-mayor of that presidio, who is also a captain of infantry, has captain's pay; three adjutants of the sargento-mayor of Oton [Octon — MS.], Cebu, and Cagayan, each 180; another in the island of Hermosa, 250. The infantry of the camp of Manila, which includes that of the island of Hermosa, consists of eighteen companies — sixteen of them with a like number of captains, and the two which are commanded by the master-of-camp of the army and the castellan of Santiago. All amount generally to 1,576 infantrymen, 88 men to each company. As to pay, the captains receive each 600 pesos; the alférezes, each 240; the sergeants, each 120; the corporals (there being four in each company), each 12 pesos over the common soldier's pay; the 56 infantrymen, including page, fifer, two drummers, and one standard-bearer, each 96 pesos; the [remaining] infantrymen, who are musketeers, each 126 pesos. To each company is given 30 escudos per month over the regular pay. The total expense in pay to each company amounts to 9,555 and one-half pesos. And inasmuch as they are never without crippled soldiers, who receive 72 pesos without serving, there is a fund of 1,000 pesos for them. There are 140 other soldiers of the Pampango tribe, who are stationed in the presidios of Manila, Oton,

Zebu, Cagayan, and Caraga, who receive each 86 pesos per year. Their captain receives 288, one alférez, 192, one sergeant, 96. Consequently, this company causes an expense of 7,296 pesos. For the artillery, there is one captain who receives 800; four constables, in Manila, the fort of Santiago, the fort of Cavite, and the island of Hermosa, each 300; one hundred and ten artillerymen in the camp and presidios, each 200; the total amounting to 32,596. The total for this department is 229,696 pesos.

Number 52. Sixth division: of the defense of Maluco

The sixth is for the war and defense of Maluco. The castellan and governor of the forts of Terrenate receives 2,750 pesos; two adjutants of the sargento-mayor, each 825. There are seven companies of infantry with 570 soldiers. The captains receive each 600 pesos; each alférez, 240; each sergeant, 120; each corporal, 30 pesos in addition to the regular soldier's pay; and the others as in Manila. Each company gets 30 escudos in addition to the regular pay. They were ordered to spend [the money for] four substitutes that they had, each of 440 pesos, and that pay was also given as additional pay. Thus each of these companies causes an expense of 9,809 pesos. In addition there are two Pampango infantry companies, with 200 soldiers. Each captain gets 288 pesos; each alférez, 192; each sergeant, 144; and each infantryman, 72. The two companies cost 13,312 pesos. There is one surgeon who receives 664 pesos; one artillery captain, 480; one constable, 300; one field captain, 330; one war notary, 200; one accountant and factor, 1,150; one chief clerk, 400; another minor clerk, 150; one notary of the royal treasury, 250; one [book] keeper and paymaster, 523; twenty sailors, 150 [pesos] and one ganta of rice apiece; one cura, 50,000 maravedis; one sacristan, 25,000 maravedis; and seven religious, four of St. Francis and three of the Society, to whom are given 1,330 pesos. Consequently, [the expense of] this department amounts to a total of 97,128 pesos, three reals.

Number 53. Seventh division: the navy and marine works

The seventh is that of the navy and what pertains to marine works. There are six galleys, used as a guard for the islands. They have one commander-in-chief, who receives 800 pesos; one lieutenant, 600; six captains, two of whom live in Manila, two in the island of Hermosa, each 422 pesos, and two in Terrenate, each 699 and one-half pesos; one accountant, 400; one chaplain [captain—MS.], 200. Each galley has one leader, who receives 170 pesos; one master, 300; one boatswain,43 250; one boatswain's mate, 217 and one-half; one alguaçil, 230; one oarmaker, 230; three sailors, each 133. In all [six galleys] there are 1,080 convicts who receive 27 pesos and two reals, and three pesos in clothing. These six galleys cost 45,026 pesos annually.

There are twelve pilots in the ports of Cavite, the island of Hermosa, and Terrenate, each of whom receives 200 pesos when he is not afloat (for when afloat they receive more); ten boatswains [contramaestres] of as many boats, who are paid each 325 pesos; ten boatswain's mates, each 225. There are 520 sailors, each of whom receives 175 pesos, among whom are included those who sail to Nueva España, Terrenate, and the island of Hermosa, and other parts. There are 200 common seamen, each of whom receives 60 and one-half pesos; seven coopers, each 325; four Indian coopers, each 72 and one-half; one diver, 350; one hundred and sixty Sangleys (24 of whom are pilots), who serve as sailors in the champans and bring the food and war supplies, all of whom together get 7,504 pesos; twenty Indians, who serve in the boat that acts as a scout-boat in the island of Marivelez, who receive five hundred and forty pesos; one hundred and thirty Lascars, natives of India, who are sailors and common seamen, 9,754 pesos; one master of ropemaking, one hundred and seventy-five pesos; two Indian ropemakers, each 78 pesos; fifty Indians who work at the rigging, each 24 and one-half pesos; six Spanish carpenters, each 325; five hundred and fifty Indians, carpenters along the Cavite coast (six of them, who are bosses, each 97 pesos; 120 workmen and laborers, each 61; and the rest, each 49); 50 other Sangley carpenters and sawyers, who are paid 4,220 pesos; seven Spanish calkers, each 325; four slave calkers, each 47 and one-half; fourteen Sangley calkers, who get 1,165 pesos; one master of the smithy of Cavite, 425; another of the Manila foundry, 375; another of the smithy of the army, 350; one hundred Indian smiths, for the three smithies, get 5,377 pesos; thirty Sangley smiths, ten of them bosses of forges, are paid 2,280 pesos. Therefore this part amounts to 180,731 pesos.

The ships that sail annually to Nueva España carry one commander-in-chief, or head, who, in addition to four rations that are given him, receives a salary of 4,325 pesos; one admiral, 2,900. Although it is ordered in the royal decree for the grant of the last of December, 604, that these ships have an overseer and accountant, with pay of 2,000 ducados apiece, in order that they may keep account in their books of what is carried and taken, as in the last reports of expenses and salaries, those offices are not found. It is doubtful whether they are provided, and accordingly they are omitted. There are two masters, each of whom receives 400 pesos; four pilots, each 700; two boatswains, each 325; two boatswain's mates, each 225; two notaries, each 225; two keepers of the arms and stores, each 225; two calkers, each 325; two water guards, each 225; two surgeons, each 225; two constables, each 325; twenty artillerymen, each 225 (who ought to serve a like number of pieces, according to the seventh section of the royal decree of 604); six Cahayanes [i.e., Cagayans (Indians)?], each 60; two coopers, each 325. These wages amount to 20,535 pesos, for sailors and common seamen belong to those whose posts are continuous. On the return trip [to Filipinas], when the usual reënforcements are carried, there is a sargento-mayor, who gets 600 pesos; one adjutant, 412; one royal alférez, 865. It is ordered by a royal decree of December 14, 630, that the latter officers be aided with only four months' pay at Acapulco, and that they be paid for the time of their service. Furthermore, there is a shoremaster at the port of Cavite, who receives 600 [650 — MS.] pesos; and although it was ordered by a royal decree of April 22, 608, that he should not receive this salary, that office must have appeared indispensable. There is one builder for ships and another for galleys, each of whom receives 690 pesos; one gunner to sight the guns, and an overseer of the royal works of Cavite, 800; one manager for the artillery foundry, 500; one founder, 450; one powder manager, 500; another of the rigging, 272. One galley is built every year, on an average, which costs 20,000 pesos finished and ready for sailing, exclusive of the men who work at it. The purchase and equipment of 18 champans cost 2,300 pesos. Therefore, according to the items above mentioned, the expense of this department amounts to 283,184 pesos.

Number 54. Eighth division: the food, munitions,44 and other expenses

The eighth and last is that of the food and munitions. As much as 50,000 pesos are given annually to the factor of the royal treasury, for expenses and the purchases of food, and the pay for the careening and repair of ten galleons and six galleys. For flour biscuit for the voyage, besides the rations, are spent 5,000 pesos; for iron, 1,250; for wax, cotton, and other things, 1,300; for balls and fuses, 1,000; for saltpetre, and the making of powder, 4,000. A quantity of money is sent to the alcaldes-mayor and the persons who bring in the supplies for the provision of the royal magazines, the amount being estimated at 86,000 pesos. On extraordinary watchmen are spent 2,000 pesos. To the keeper of the magazines of Manila is given 750 pesos; to his clerk, 222; to the keeper of those of Cavite, 395; to his clerk, 212; to the keeper of that of Jambolo in Pangasinan, 173; to the keeper of the magazines in the island of Hermosa, 300; to his accountant, 500; to his clerk, 200. The expense of this last department amounts to 153,202 [15,302 — MS.] pesos.

Number 55. Summary of the expenses of the islands, and the persons employed

The above is what is spent annually on the average, more or less according to the times, for all purposes in the Filipinas Islands, a summary of which (both of persons and money) is as follows.

The first department, that of justice, supports 32 Spaniards, and costs	37,077 pesos
The second—the conversion [of heathen], worship, and hospitality in most of the convents, and the hospitals and churches—supports 73 Spaniards, and costs	37,297 pesos.
The third, the maintenance of friendly relations with the kings, costs	1,500 pesos.
The fourth, the management of the royal treasury, in which 19 Spaniards are employed, costs	11,550 pesos.
	[21,550—MS.]
The fifth, the land warfare of Manila and its islands, in which 1,762 [1,702—MS.] Spaniards and 140 Indians are employed, costs	229,696 pesos.
The sixth, the war in Maluco and its islands, in which there are 612 Spaniards and 200 Indians employed, costs	97,128 pesos.
The seventh, the navy and marine works, in which 832 Spaniards and 2,200 Indians are employed, costs	283,184 pesos.
The eighth, the commissariat, in which 8 Spaniards are employed, costs	153,302 pesos.
	[53,302—MS.]
	850,734

Consequently, exclusive of the four convents and fourteen hospitals which are cared for, and the alms which are given for wine and oil to certain churches, your Majesty pays in the Filipinas Islands and Maluco, and in their navigations and trade-line, salary, pay, and special wages to 5,878 persons, 3,338 of whom are Spaniards, and 2,540 are Indians or men of various nations. The cost of all included in the eight departments here presented, as it appears, is 850,734 pesos of eight reals.

Number 56. Second point: of that which the Filipinas produce

Having seen what it costs to maintain the Filipinas Islands, the second point is to ascertain how far they aid in this cost, and with what they supply your Majesty's royal treasury, in which notice is to be taken that there are eleven departments of revenue.

1. The tributes of the encomiendas which are assigned to the crown, paid by not only the natives of the islands but the Chinese and Japanese, are annually valued—in reals, and in products which proceed from 44,763 tributarios—at ten reals apiece   53,715 pesos.

2. In the encomiendas of private persons, who, as has been said, possess 84,439 tributes, there is a [royal] situado of two reals for each tribute—only eight being reserved for the encomenderos, which are valued annually at 21,107 and one-half pesos .... 21,107 pesos.

3. The licenses which are given annually to the Sangleys, in order that they may remain for some time in the islands, amount to about 14,000, which at eight pesos that are paid for them as fees, amount to 112,1000 pesos .... 112,000 pesos.

4. The tribute of these 14,000 Sangleys at five reals apiece— four for the tribute, and one for the situado—are worth 8,250 pesos .... 8,250 pesos.

5. The fifth and tenth of the gold that is collected from what is declared by the natives, is 750 pesos .... 750 pesos.

6. The ecclesiastical tithes—which are collected for the royal treasury, because all the clergy are paid from it, as has been seen—amount to 2,750 pesos. .... 2,750 pesos.

7. The fares for passengers, who leave the islands for other parts in royal ships, 350 pesos. .... 350 pesos.

8. The fines of the exchequer are worth 1,000 pesos annually. ... 1,000 pesos.

9. The customs duties on the merchandise of China, India,45 and other parts, which are imported and exported, 38,000 pesos. .... 38,000 pesos.

10. The imposts and freight charges, customs duties, and other charges that are collected in Nueva España on the merchandise exported annually from the islands, are worth 300,000 [309,000—MS.] pesos which is reckoned as income of the Filipinas, for those islands cause it. Accordingly, it is ordered by a royal decree of February 19, 606, that the proceeds from this department be remitted to Manila, and that so much less a sum be sent from Mexico; besides which they ought to make good to it 30,000 more, because of what in Nueva España proceeds from the traffic and commerce of this merchandise for the excise duty and other imposts. .... 300,000 pesos.

[309,000—MS.]

11. It cannot be ascertained what the mesada taxes in the ecclesiastical estate, and the half-annats in the secular, are worth; nor that concerning sales and resignations of office, and other petty transactions, for all of which a figure of 6,000 pesos annually is set down...... 6,000 pesos.

These eleven departments of royal revenue amount to 573,922 pesos; and the Filipinas produce that sum in revenue for your Majesty.46 [In the margin of Extracto-historial reprint: "Note—This sum seems to be inaccurate, because it should amount only to 543,922 pesos."]

Number 57. The excess of expenditures for the islands over the receipts

It is ordered by a royal decree that the amount reported from the islands to be lacking for the total amount of situado be sent annually from Nueva España; and as the situado, according to the calculation set forth, is 850,734 pesos, there is an annual deficit of 276,512 pesos or thereabouts; [In the margin of Extracto-historial reprint: "The deficit should be 306,812 pesos."] for this account is made for only one year, and is not fixed, although it it usual every year. In this matter it is to be noted that this [itemized statement] answers the current report that every year six hundred thousand pesos and more are taken from Nueva España for their expense. That report gives rise to the belief and understanding that they spend that amount in addition to their receipts. That is an error; for if from the tenth division the sum of 330,000 pesos is made good, which is collected in Acapulco and Mexico, and other parts of Nueva España (and this is recognized to belong to the islands by the above-cited royal decree of 606 and is therefore ordered to be returned to them), when 600,000 or more pesos are sent, not one-half that amount is supply of deficiency, and expense, since more than one-half is returns. And even this is counterbalanced somewhat by what is derived from the bulls of the crusade, the proceeds of which are ordered by a royal decree of December 21, 634, not to be taken to Mexico, but to be kept at Manila, and that to the treasurers in Mexico a like amount be furnished. Although this order is opposed by the crusade, as it is advisable it ought to be executed, and a second decree issued ordering its observance; thus two dangers might be avoided to this sum, one in going and the other in being returned—as is done with the possessions of deceased persons, by a royal decree of December 13, [of the year] 16, which are kept in the Manila treasury, and paid into that of Mexico.

Number 58. The islands contribute more than they spend

From the expenses and contributions of the islands, and the excess of the debits over the credits, some, through lack of acquaintance with the matter, are wont to derive the main argument against them, imagining that the islands are of little use but of great expense. Although the first of these propositions is quite confuted and answered by what is thus far alleged, the second also lacks foundation in the meaning in which it is put forward, which attributes to the islands more expense than profit; for the Filipinas alone contribute more than what they cost. Until the year 607, the islands of Maluco belonged to the crown of Portugal, which spent a great sum of money on them — as was necessary on account of the great distance from Goa, upon which their government was dependent. Although, nevertheless, those islands were maintained, that appeared impossible after the Dutch entered the Orient; for with their advent the expenses of Maluco were so increased that the islands were lost, inasmuch as there was no money with which to maintain them. It was ordered that the Filipinas recover them, and they did so. In order to assure the safety of the Malucos and to economize expenses for the convenience of both crowns, they were joined and united to them [i.e., Filipinas], imposing on the crown of Castilla, and in its name on the Filipinas, the obligation to attend to their wants, thus adding to Filipinas at least 290,000 pesos of expense — the amount of what pertains to Maluco from the second, third, and fourth departments, all the sixth, half the seventh, and a third of the eighth. If your Majesty is petitioned for 276,000 pesos annually for both groups of islands, as is attested, and those of Maluco alone cost 290,000, the deduction is evident that the Filipinas per se cost less than what they contribute — and more, if it is considered that the crown of Portugal saves 400,000 pesos which the Malucas must have cost it when they were under its charge. Since the Filipinas did not ask for that union, and were not a party in causing it to be made, they ought not to be charged with increase in expenses which those islands cause them.

Number 59. How and in what the inhabitants aid in the support of the islands

But it is proper to remark at this point, what is the kernel of the matter under discussion, that the Filipinas and Malucas are not supported with the 850,000 [890,000 — MS.] pesos, which are the amount of their expenses. Neither that sum nor a much greater one would be sufficient, if the inhabitants of Manila did not serve, aid, and help with their possessions and lives on the occasions that arise, both extraordinary and ordinary. Now [they serve] as soldiers in the wars when the enlisted and paid troops are outside, or are not sufficient to resist the enemy, standing guard and assisting in military duties with the [same] punctuality and discipline as if they drew pay; and although they are few, as has been said, they count for many in the valor, willingness, and generosity with which they serve. Again, they give their slaves to labor on the public works and shipbuilding, and ordinarily for the levies for the galleys, as happens daily; and in the term of Don Alonso Faxardo, had not the inhabitants furnished the crews, the galleys could not have sallied out, as they did, against the enemy. Then they lend, when the aid from Nueva España is delayed or insufficient, very great quantities [of money] for any sudden expense—as was that above mentioned in the case of Don Alonso Faxardo, to whom they lent at that time two hundred and fifty thousand pesos. So they do every year, and always without interest, the payments sometimes being delayed two or three years. In regard to that, there is a royal decree of February 29, six hundred and thirty-six, in which it is ordered that those who make such loans shall be promptly repaid, in order that the royal treasury may be accredited when it needs help. They help, too, with very large and continuous gifts of money, and food and products (which are generally more important than money), which the governor assigns for the aid of Terrenate, the island of Hermosa, and other posts. They also accept expeditions and embassies, by which they go at their own expense to the kings of those archipelagos. So have gone General Juan Xuarez Gallinato, to the king of Camboxa; Gregorio de Vargas, to him of Tunquin [Tumquin—MS.]; Juan Tello de Aguirre and Juan Ruiz de Ycoaga, to him of Siam; to whom also went Admiral Andres Lopez de Asaldegui; Don Luis Navarrete Faxardo; and afterward Don Antonio de Arco, to the emperor of Japon, at the cost of life; Don Juan Zamudio to China; and others to other kings—each one spending ten or twelve thousand pesos to serve your Majesty. In short, the occasions that the inhabitants of Manila have for helping, and to which they respond as loyal vassals, are as many as will be seen in the future, and as one can imagine would be found in a post and frontier so infested by so many and so strong enemies—Dutch, Chinese, Japanese, Mindanaos, Terrenates, Zambales, and those of other nations, which keeps the inhabitants in arms continually. Scarcely is there a year when the inhabitants do not engage in hostilities, and it necessarily costs them heavily. If it were all at the expense of the royal treasury, the cost of the islands would increase so that it would almost exceed their possessions.

Number 60. To what degree the inhabitants of the islands ought to be favored

By all this is represented to your Majesty what those vassals merit who are always and continually serving, not in posts and duties that increase their wealth and advance their households, but in land and naval warfare, in which they lose their lives and possessions—fighting now with the Dutch, who harass them more sharply than in Flandes, and make daily attacks; now with the numerous nations who surround them. Consequently, they deserve that their services be considered, not only in consulting as to rewards, but in giving them; and that they be gratified with honors and rewards—if not equal to their services, as those are so great, at least equivalent to what good government permits, and to what the same land which they defend can support. That is in accordance with the royal decree of February 29, 636, in which the governor is ordered to observe the rules ordering that military offices and encomiendas be given only to those who shall have served under your Majesty's banners, and always preferring those who shall have rendered most service. It will be proper and very consoling for the deserving citizens and residents of those islands, that the royal Council of the Indias — which, as it were a crucible for the new world, estimates services, approves merits, and deliberates as to rewards, with so much acumen, equality, and justice — allow the claims of Filipinas before those of others who, by serving in Flandes, Italia, and Alemania, try to get hold of the best posts, not alone of the Indias, but even of the islands themselves which they never entered. For, if the latter do not exceed the former in the hardships, perils, and services that the citizens of the islands suffer and perform, for your Majesty and for that colony, and those citizens should be preferred justly in the rewards of their own land, then they have sufficient ground for asking that they be not despoiled of this favor and privilege, which they try to merit by so many and so repeated acts of valor and loyalty; but that in the dispensing of that favor they may recognize that they may expect sure rewards for their children, by leaving them as an inheritance the blood shed and the property spent in defense of their king and the preservation of their fatherland. And since their services differ so widely in quality from those of others, who have no services, it will be just that their papers and claims be examined with a different kind of attention.

Number 61. It is not advisable that the magistracies of the islands be sold

In this matter also it is to be noted that the magistracies of the city were formerly conferred by the governor on the most deserving and venerable persons who were to be found. They, because of their experience and zeal, accepted those offices, and attended to the duties of those charges as was demanded. In order that those offices might be held by them for life, it was sufficient for them to come to ask for confirmation of them from your Majesty, in accordance with the royal decree of March 17, 1608, and February 8, 1610. And although, since they were ordered to be sold, persons of equal ability and position have bought them, and fill them and attend as they ought to the government of the community (which in this, above all else, has always been fortunate); and although the governor is ordered by a decree of June [July — MS.] 12, 636, to employ the regidors of Manila in charges and posts according to their rank and the competency with which they can serve your Majesty, and that he honor, favor, and aid them in whatever else arises: the deserving men of that city cannot be prevented from expressing their resentment that, while there are so few rewards to which they can aspire, so many the occasions in which to serve, and so remote the qualification of their merits, that small part should be taken away from them, and that, in order to enjoy those offices, they should have to be bought. Moreover, the command, by decree of June 3, 620, that the magistracies of the Filipinas be sold only to conquistadors and settlers, or to their descendants (which was only recognizing that it was fitting to do so, but not assuring the reward), is no favor; for those to whom it is ordered to sell them, since it is so just that those who conquered and seeded should govern, are generally the poorest of all. And although they desire to enjoy the offices which belong to them, some of them do not possess the money with which to buy these; while others do not care to spend the little wealth that they have acquired for what is not of any use or profit to them, but rather a burden and inconvenience—since, by defending that community, they have had many contentions with the former governors. Consequently, it is very advisable that the magistracies be given to men of years, and old residents in the colony, who have held military posts, and who can oppose the governors when the latter try to exceed the provisions of your Majesty's decrees. For this and other reasons, it has been experienced that eight vacancies have existed in the magistracy of Manila for many years, because there were no buyers for them, as appears from the royal decree of February 29, 636, in which it is mentioned. And since the greatest value of those offices is one thousand one hundred pesos, and, if one consider the twelve magistracies, they do not produce an income of five hundred pesos per year, that is so small a sum, and there are so many damages and disadvantages that may result from it, that it would be a gain for the royal treasury and a great service to your Majesty to have the sale of the said offices stopped, and to have them given as formerly by the governors to the oldest residents, and to men of greatest experience and worth and as favors to individuals—that, while they do not give any profit, they may give honor to the citizens of Manila. Since there is not a city in all the Indias of its rank, nor one in which the inhabitants render so much service and with less advantage, this measure will not be a conclusion of which others may avail themselves to demand the same.

Number 62. Third point: of the commerce of the islands with Nueva España

From the service rendered by the inhabitants of Filipinas, one may deduce how necessary it is to maintain the rich, or to give them capital sufficient for them to attend to their business. For that the only method (and the third point of the five arguments proposed), is the commerce of the islands with Nueva España, for in the proportion in which that shall increase, their possessions will increase, and with that the defense and security of the islands. For there is no more powerful argument than that which establishes the conservation of a province in the strength, that is, the wealth of its inhabitants, and depends on the abundance of that for its conservation. Commerce is a natural law of nations, by which they make common to all provinces what each one produces, grows, or manufactures—now by selling, now by exchanging. Although commerce ought to be free, and was in the beginning, when kingdoms and seigniories were less powerful (for as they had narrower territories, so they had fewer matters to which to attend), as the monarchies increased and extended it became necessary to limit the commerce in parts, prohibiting it with some, in order to oblige or cause it to be maintained or increased with others. If that of Filipinas with the Indias were free and absolute, as it was immediately after their discovery, it is evident that they would enjoy the greatest prosperity; while Nueva España would have greater abundance of what was necessary to it, and Peru of what it lacked. But the commerce of España, which would perish and be ruined, was opposed to that; for since the goods sent thence to the Indias were dearer than those of Filipinas, if merchandise entered from both parts without restriction it would be to the advantage of the consumers to seek that from Filipinas rather than that from España; and the former commerce would continue to increase, and the latter to decline. Accordingly, it was right and proper to restrain the one so that the other might endure, and that, heeding the principal thing, namely, the conservation of these kingdoms (the heads of the monarchy), trade to them might be free, and to the others restricted—maintaining such a proportion in this that in securing the prosperity of España the ruin of the Filipinas might not result; for natural laws influence us to concede what is to the advantage of another, when it involves no injury to one's self. And thus it is no considerable damage that the kingdoms do not increase as much as is possible, if they maintain what they have; for the former is a matter of gaining, and the latter of not losing, until each one is left what is sufficient, if from conceding more results the lack to others of what is necessary. Accordingly, to Perù47 is conceded one ship annually for Nueva España; to Nueva España two for Filipinas; and to España the number that its commerce demands and is entitled to, in consideration of its amount—so that thus neither may the islands be lost nor Nueva España and Perú be deprived of all the freedom of their trade, nor España feel so much weakness in the trade of the Indias that it should lose that; and that all may remain in suitable relations [to each other], since they are members of the mystical body of this monarchy.

Number 63. Why the islands need the commerce of Nueva España

This matter being thus explained, it is also supposed that the Filipinas retain the trade above described with various kingdoms of the Orient; and that all that trade is free and open without any restriction, except that of China, and that of the Western Indias, which they maintain and observe in a certain manner. For since all those different traffics require the return of suitable kinds of merchandise in order to sustain the exchange in which they consist, and the islands need them—for the rice, cotton, wines, blankets, textiles, and other products, are not desired by China, Japon, Sian, or any other pagan nation, because they abound in the same products, or have better ones—those different branches of commerce must necessarily cease, if there were not another foreign and different commerce, which, desiring the products of those regions, can extend and carry on another trade, which their nations desire and crave. This is that of the Indias, from which is conveyed and bartered silver (a most noble commodity), in return for which are carried the drugs and merchandise that are produced in China and other Oriental kingdoms and provinces, and traded in Filipinas, by which all come to be sustained, united, and joined.

Number 64. Commerce of the islands: why it is injurious to España

This commerce of the Indias with the Filipinas is to the prejudice of España for two causes or reasons, from which result great disadvantages. The first, because the silver is withdrawn and conveyed to the islands, whence it passes into the possession of the enemies of religion and of this crown, Moors and pagans; and finally remains in China—which, according to what we understand, is the general center for the silver of Europe and Asia. For as it always is current, gaining and increasing in value until it reaches that great kingdom, whence it must issue with a loss, it does not issue, and remains perpetually among those inhabitants. From that cause result many damaging effects: such as enriching our enemies, giving them the most noble product of all the commerce of the globe; making easy for them the possession of that which private persons among them maintain, and increasing their number; preventing that silver from going to España so that the royal duties might increase thereby, the avería and the commerce be sustained; and, in short, making this crown lose and its enemies gain. The second cause is that, in addition to the aforesaid losses (which are obvious) from the withdrawal of silver, no less are the damages that are experienced on what is sent in return for it to Nueva España, and passes to Perú— namely, a great quantity of the merchandise of China in textiles of gold, silk, and cotton, and other articles. [These are sold] at so low prices that, when the merchandise of these kingdoms arrives (which is worth more, as it is of better quality), it is not sold and has no outlet, as the country is full of the others [from China]; so that those who ship it lose. Consequently, losses are multiplied; and from all results so extreme weakening of the commerce of España with the Indias, that it is almost extinct and will be diminished just as that of Filipinas increases.

Number 65. Reply to the damages of the commerce of Filipinas; and to the first, regarding the withdrawal of the silver.

These two reasons are [alleged as] those which hinder the advancement of the islands, and restrict its commerce. However, a reply is not lacking, which, if it does not destroy, weakens them. For to the first, regarding the withdrawal of the silver and its retention in China, answer is made, that on the silver which goes [from Nueva España] nine per cent [duties] are paid at Manila, and at Acapulco fourteen per cent, a total of twenty-three per cent. Consequently, the duties on its transportation to España are not lost, for they are paid there in larger measure. The effects are not those which are represented; for, although it is true that the silver goes from Manila, it is for China, and for the very reason that it does not issue from that country, it does no harm. But the retention of what comes to these kingdoms is a greater injury, as it all goes to Olanda, Genova, and Venecia [Venencia — MS.], and thence to Turquia, while some portion goes to India by way of Portugal, and those same Dutch, and the Persians, Arabs, and Mogores share the silver; and, although at last it goes to remain in China, it is after it has enriched the greatest enemies of this crown. That is not the case with what goes by way of Manila; for, if it goes thence, it is through the hands of your Majesty's vassals, and it does not reach the hands of the enemies. But even this reply is superfluous, for it is not necessary to the islands nor to their inhabitants that more silver be sent to Manila than is permitted; rather is it important to them that the [amount for which] permission be observed and executed with rigor, as will be said. [In the margin: "In numbers 98 and 99."] Therefore, of the damages caused to the commerce of España by that of Filipinas, only that to the merchandise should be made good; for the silver either is within the limits of the permission, and does not conflict [with this statement] (for neither does it cause any loss, nor can it be dispensed with), or it is in the illegal amount that is stated, and the citizens request that this be corrected and prevented. For if there is any damage to España, it is not any advantage to them; but, on the contrary, destroys and ruins them, as will be seen.

Number 66. Reply to the statement touching the merchandise exported from the islands

As for the second reason—that of the merchandise, and the trade of the islands therein—it is not denied that it would have the effects that have been stated, if it were free, open, and without restriction; but these cease, because experience and good government have chosen a method such that neither the commerce of España should be destroyed, nor that of the islands be annihilated, by permitting the commerce to one in such quantity that it should not prove damaging to the other. And although España petitioned that the commerce from Filipinas be totally suppressed, by which they thought that they would assure their own increase, it was also considered that the islands would surely be lost in that case; and that they would be settled by the Dutch, who would make themselves masters of all the Orient. Consequently, that would not only expose India to evident danger, as has been proved, but would also, by increasing the forces of the Dutch, render them more powerful in the trade of the Indias, and in all the regions where they navigate and traffic. Therefore, if the trade of [the merchants in] España should increase for the one reason, their risks and expenses would be greater for another; and nearly all the trade of Portugal would be ruined. Thus from an imagined benefit would result damages so certain and considerable that, were they weighed as they ought to be, the present losses would be considered as more tolerable. Such is the mutual relationship of states which are many and extended that, if attention to all of them be difficult, it is advisable that decisions be adjusted to the least harmful course. Accordingly, it is proper that the islands should not continue to increase, but that they be allowed the commerce that is sufficient to maintain them; and that that of España should not be increased in that region, but that the trade of the islands be restricted in such manner that it shall be as little obstructed as possible. For, by each kingdom losing a part of its right, all will be maintained and conserved.

Number 67. Commerce of España with the Indias: why it is decreasing

This will be more apparent with the conditions and the changes which the commerce of Filipinas and that of España in the Indias have sustained and suffered. That of España has decreased so much from its usual status that it appears to be less than the half of its former amount. Although the fault is attributed to the Filipinas, that is because the matter is not probed below the surface, and causes are not sought at their sources. The physician who understands only the effect of a dangerous illness, namely, the death of the patient, generally attributes the sickness to uncertain causes and sometimes so remote that they have no connection with the case in question; and, since he prescribes his remedies for such causes, the true, proximate, and essential causes which are working out of sight without any check, end, if not by killing the patient, by placing him in evident risk. All see and recognize that the commerce of the Indias is in a feeble condition, that the merchants are losing, that the exporters do not obtain their capital [from what they ship], and that the ships which go are smaller, and return with poorer cargoes. Although this loss is so well known, there are some who ascribe the cause of so great an effect to the Filipinas, and not to the misapprehension of España—which is persuaded that the wealth of the Indias must be inexhaustible, and that the merchants can still gain on their investments the same amounts as fifty years ago, while the causal means of it all have been lacking, which have been noticed by few, and ignored by many.

Number 68. First reason for the decline of the commerce of the Indias

First, the abundance of gold and silver. So great was the abundance of these metals in the Indias, that one could say the same as of Jerusalem in the time of Solomon, that they were regarded as the stones of the street. Accordingly, articles were paid for at so exorbitant prices, as is apparent from the histories of their conquests. That region has failed, for the ores that yielded three hundred pesos per quintal by smelting, now yield eight or six by quicksilver, which costs more than smelting; and [such ores] are worked as good ones. Potosi, which is the heart of the Indias, is threatening to give out; for it alone yielded for forty years an amount that it cannot now yield, although aided by the opening of many mines which sustain its reputation. The mines of Nueva Reino [i.e., New Granada] and of Nueva España have lost a part of what they had. The cost of mining is greater, the mines are poorer, and, consequently, the gains less, and less the amount obtained. Therefore, since this was the first cause of the greatness of the Indias, it is not remarkable that with its deficiency their commerce has declined.

Number 69. Second cause for the decline of the commerce of the Indias .

The second cause is the decrease of the Indians and the increase of the Spaniards. The latter number thirty times more than formerly; where there were five hundred, there are now three or four thousand. Without exaggeration, there has been a decrease of the Indians of more than six millions. Although not all of them used Spanish commodities, they consumed many, and to so great an excess that it became advisable to prohibit this to them and order them to dress as did their ancestors. What is most to be regretted is the cessation of the service for the mines, the cultivation of the fields, the gross sum of the tributes, and the local commerce of many provinces. With fewer people and less wealth, there must be less consumption and smaller profits; and, if everything diminish, it is impossible that trade should not do the same.

Number 70. Third cause for the decline of the commerce of the Indias

The third cause has proceeded from the above two; for with the increase of the Spaniards, not only has the consumption not increased, but it has been and is much less. For, besides the fact that so many stuffs and figured goods are no longer worn out in the Indias as formerly, and he who clad himself in silk now contents himself with cloth, all bulky goods that are exported from Sevilla are manufactured there [in the Indias] — where with the number of people their necessity has increased, and with their necessity their skill. The consumers are fewer, and the officials more; there is little money, and those who seek it are many; and they seek it more eagerly as their courage is small, since their funds are already scant. The springs are drained dry, for there is less water, so that scarcely can they dampen what they formerly soaked. What few formerly shipped and many bought is now quite the contrary, and many send it and there are few who use it — as is evident by the wine which was and now is consumed by Nueva España. On that account it has been necessary that the former profits cease, and that the exportation and consumption of merchandise be restricted — not only on account of the goods which are manufactured there, but because of lack of consumers and lack of wealth, all of which are causal circumstances of the decline of the commerce.

Number 71. Fourth cause for the decline of the commerce of the Indias

The fourth and last cause is the little favor extended to the Indian trade, both in the Indias, and in these kingdoms — either because of the straitness of the times, or because of other accidents — together with the burdens that have fallen upon everything, the imposts and duties increasing, although greater relief was needed as the amount of wealth was less. The avería, which increased from two and three per cent to six and seven, and was then judged to be so exorbitant that it seemed impossible for the commerce not to be ruined with that excessive tax, has increased so greatly that one year it rose to forty, and with the other expenses is never lower than twenty. What were formerly risks at sea are now great and evident losses, which, aided by the necessities of this crown—which force loans and considerable gifts, and the exchange for juros48 of what was formerly the capital for commerce—have so weakened commerce, that one is more astonished that it has not been entirely ruined, than that it has declined to its present condition. And all the more justifiable have been the reasons why this crown has profited from the exporters among the merchants of the Indias, and from what has come from the Indias, the greater the loss has been, as it was known to be unavoidable on account of what occurs on land, and more hazardous because of what is risked on the sea—by which some have been ruined, others have retired from trade, and others have changed their business; and all who take part in it are aware that this commerce is ruined, and with it whatever depends on it. It is certain, and has been observed in Manila, that since the loss of the trading fleet of the year 629, and their unfortunate experiences with [storms in] the Northern Sea, the winterings, the disasters, the averías, the embargoes, the delays, and the burdens [imposed] at Sevilla, the merchants in Mexico have decided to export more to Filipinas than to España. And although these things are found by experience to be thoroughly damaging and irreparable, and [it is evident] that they demanded new exemptions and safeguards, by which the losses might be recuperated, and those who suffer them be encouraged, there has not been lacking a person to propose as an expedient that the duties and customs should be raised still higher in the Indias, affirming that they are the most free, and that they pay less— although they really are quite the opposite, as is known.

Number 72. The Filipinas do not damage the commerce of España

The above and many other causes which might be mentioned are those which have weakened and are ruining the commerce of the Indias; and although it would be more advisable to counteract some of them, or to seek reparation for those which are most hurtful, the Filipinas Islands come to be the ones that suffer the penalty, without being implicated in the guilt. And although their commerce is in the lowest condition that it has ever experienced or suffered, yet even in this condition they are not allowed or permitted [to improve] it, and there are some who propose its destruction as a remedy, so that it may share in the universal destruction of all trade; and this is in so far as it touches the commerce of España.

Number 73. Beginning of the commerce of the islands

The commerce of these islands began with their second discovery and the first settlement, which was in the year 565.49 However, it was at the first scanty and of little weight, until during the government of Guido de

Labazarris, in the year 576, the trade of China was introduced, and with it considerable profits, which extended it freely to Nueva España, Guatimala, Tierrafirme, and Perú, by a royal decree of April 14, 579. As it continued to increase, it was believed necessary to restrict it; and accordingly, by a decree of November 11, 587, it was ordered that Chinese cloth brought from Filipinas should not pass from Nueva España to Perú or to Tierrafirme. That decree was later confirmed by others of February 13, and June 13, 599. And in order that what was prohibited in one way might not be obtained in another, decrees were despatched on February 6 and December 18, 591, ordering the total cessation of commerce between the islands and Perú. That was later extended to Tierrafirme and Guatimala, by decrees of January 12, 593, and July 5, 595, forbidding the trade of China and its merchandise to all the Indias, except to Nueva España, which was left open to the Filipinas.

Number 74. Permission for the commerce of the Indias, and its final form

The commerce of Sevilla was not satisfied with even these orders and restrictions. That commerce continued to decrease, although the cause was unknown. They regretted the damage, and tried to apply the remedy, but in vain. As the trade of Filipinas was already the stone of offense, they immediately descended on that. Not only was the prohibition of commodities from the islands strengthened, but their quantity was limited, reducing it to a fixed amount that was permitted, and a certain form. It was ordered that only four ships should ply in that trade-route—two which should sail to Nueva España, and two to the islands, and all at the account of the royal treasury. In these could be carried two hundred and fifty thousand pesos' worth of such merchandise as they should have in Manila; and in return they could take five hundred thousand in silver, including in this sum the principal and the profits. And inasmuch as this permission, from its beginning, was never in favor of Nueva España, but of the islands, it was declared that only the citizens of the islands could navigate and trade, as was already ruled by a royal decree of January 11, 593. In accordance with this, the commander [of the fleet] was despatched on the last of December, 604, with various instructions and declarations, which gave form to this commerce. And since his permission was for only the citizens of the islands, and those who were not residents of the islands but of Nueva España had begun to take part in it, it was ordered that the toneladas of the two ships which sailed should be distributed in Manila by the governor, the archbishop (or the senior auditor), the fiscal, and two regidors. That order was confirmed by decrees of May 4, 619, and May 29, 620, and by others, which regulate this matter, and declare that the respective shares of the silver which must be sent back as returns for the merchandise must be allotted in Nueva España.

Number 75. Administration of the permission for the islands for its citizens alone

Notwithstanding this last order, the citizens of Mexico, who had before taken possession of part of this commerce, continued in it, availing themselves of certain underhand work and management—by which the citizens of Manila perceived the damage that they were receiving, in that others were enjoying what had been conceded to them. Accordingly, as soon as they received the decree of 593, which was the first decree that granted to them exclusively the permission and trade, they decided, in order that they might manage their cargoes, to appoint four or six men to go to Nueva España in the name of all, and there attend to the sale of the merchandise in the ships, and to the returns for it. That determination had no effect then, nor in the year 597, when Governor Don Francisco Tello ordered it executed by an act of January 24. It was again proposed in the year 623, when open cabildo-sessions were held in Manila for that purpose, and persons appointed for it; but neither were they sent, because of certain obstacles in the way. But since the necessity became more urgent, because of the injuries experienced, the matter was undertaken more effectively in the year 629, and six commissaries, citizens of Manila, were actually appointed and went to Nueva España, where they are today administering the commerce permitted to the islands. That has been examined in the royal Council of the Indias, together with all the acts which have been made upon it; and it was approved by a decree of March 25, 635, and extended for four years more than the six (for the one of 593 was for six years), by another decree of February 16, 635. The chief motives that induced the inhabitants of Manila to carry out this resolution, were three. The first was, to prevent the consignments of silver which the merchants of Perú and Nueva España made through their agents and correspondents, the result of which—to say nothing of the violations of the royal orders in sending silver in excess of the amount allowed—was so prejudicial to the citizens of the islands that it deprived them of the benefit of the permission, while those who were expressly excluded from it enjoyed it. The second was, that with the great amount of silver that entered Manila the price of the Chinese merchandise advanced so greatly that the inhabitants could not buy it. The third was, that prices fell in Nueva España for the same reason, so that the principal could scarcely be realized, as will be told. [In the margin: "In number 98."] [Those were] damages that were repaired by the decisive action above mentioned. And lest that should not be sufficient, it will be advisable that, in the distribution of the licensed toneladas that is made in Manila, measures be taken that no one have a share except the citizens [of the islands] in accordance with the third petition. [In the margin: "In number 103."]

Number 76. Declaration of what is or is not included in the five hundred thousand pesos allowed.

Inasmuch as there were certain doubts in regard to the sum of the five hundred thousand pesos of the returns, it was declared by royal decree of August 19, 606, that it should include the legacies, bequests, moneys for charities, payments for service, wrought silver, and whatever else might be shipped, except by those who bound themselves to reside for eight years in the Filipinas. Such might carry their possessions in money, in addition to the general permission, as was declared by a decree of November 20, 608; and the seamen of that trade-route might take their wages in silver, registered, also in addition to the amount permitted.

Number 77. Smuggled Chinese goods shall not be sold in Perú

Peru was excluded from the above-mentioned concession, and the former prohibitions forbidding the importation of Chinese stuffs into Perú remained in force, while the penalties were rendered more severe. Inasmuch as from their enforcement it resulted that merchandise of this character, which was seized as forfeited and confiscated, was sold as smuggled goods, and thus the goods remained in the country, they were (although remaining with that warrant and reason) the cause of as much loss and damage as if they had been brought in either secretly or by permission; for the country was filled with these wares, at more moderate prices than those of España. Accordingly, it was ordered by decrees of April 18, 617, and July 30, 627, that Chinese cloth which should be smuggled, and as such condemned as forfeited in Perú, should not be sold in the provinces; but that, in the same form in which it had been seized, it should be carried to these kingdoms and sold here.

Number 78. Permission to trade between Perú and Nueva España, and its condition

Perú and Nueva España appealed from the mode imposed on the commerce of the islands, and from the above-mentioned prohibitions, representing certain disadvantages that resulted from barring them from the commerce that those two most opulent states had maintained between themselves, almost by nature, the chief one being that they were deprived, in this manner, of all the mutual relationship and dependence that they ought to enjoy. Therefore another permission was conceded, for two ships: one to leave annually the port of Callao de Lima, and to carry silver to the amount of two hundred thousand ducados to the port of Acapulco, in order to invest it in the products peculiar to Nueva España — of agriculture, stock, and manufactures — and in no others, even though they be products of these kingdoms; and the other, to sail from Acapulco to Callao with these returns. The prohibition of Chinese cloth was left in force, and it was declared that no Chinese cloth could be sent in the returns for the two hundred thousand ducados, nor beyond that sum. Severe penalties were imposed for its enforcement, by decrees of the last of December, 604, June 20, 609, and March 28, 620, which gave final form to this permission. This last is now suspended and ordered to cease by a decree of November 23, 1634, without the reason that has inspired it being known, other than the expedients that have been proposed for the destruction of the islands. And this order, forbidding ships to go to Acapulco from Perú, is so menacing to the Filipinas, that it alone may prove sufficient to ruin them. For if no ships go from Perú to Acapulco the islands are exposed to the failure of their succor, in any year when their ships should not arrive — whether because of having been wrecked, or having put back in distress, or having arrived late — since, in such cases, it is usual to supply their lack with the ships of Perú, sending in them the ordinary aid of men and money. If the latter do not go and the former do not arrive, there will be no vessels for the above-mentioned purpose; and the islands might remain for several years without the succor that sustains them, and with evident danger of being lost.

Number 79. Fourth, point: of the condition of the commerce between the islands and Nueva España

In regard to the fourth point, which is to declare the present condition of the commerce of the islands, it is supposed that although all the orders above mentioned were to their evident injury — restricting their prosperity, if not prognosticating their ruin — that which was permitted to them was sufficient, when enjoyed by their citizens, to preserve the islands, as it has preserved them, although with some decrease. Moreover, the enemy having increased the expenses and obligations of the islands, they needed, when the succor sent from India, and at times that from Nueva España, failed them, new favors and less strict trading permissions, in order not to be ruined as they fear — being exposed to a more continual and dangerous war than any stronghold of this monarchy endures, with resistance equal to the strongest of them, and with danger greater than that of those most harassed, as they have no other aid than what they themselves can supply. Nevertheless, although it seems as if it were advisable, on account of the importance of their conservation, not only to [let them] go beyond the amount permitted, but also to increase still farther that favor, they find it is greatly restricted, and that their commerce is reduced to such condition and mode that it will be almost impossible for them to enjoy or to continue it. That which should be considered is, that this innovation does not originate as at other times, from Sevilla — which now, undeceived as to the causes that weaken them, knows better — but from the counsels given for action in the matter by Captain Francisco de Vitoria [Victoria — MS.]. He, with no knowledge of the past or heed of the future, judged only by a hasty conclusion that for the present a sum of money might be obtained where there is none — although from it may result the damage that can be understood, not only to your vassals, but to the whole monarchy, as if there could be distinctions and peril between the vassals and the monarchy that would not be common.

Number 80. Allegations of transgressions of the permissions given for the islands and Perú

As an argument for that course, it is alleged that notable transgressions are committed in regard to the two permissions for Filipinas and Perú. Although this memorial only defends that of the islands, the one is most completely verified by treating likewise of the other; and the illegal acts in both consist rather in the exaggeration with50 which they are mentioned than in the arguments by which they are proved. Who has ever said, or what possibility can there be, that the two ships which come every year from the islands to Acapulco, whose permitted cargo is of 250,000 pesos (not of 500,000, as is affirmed), carry four millions in merchandise? That, even in pearls and diamonds, seems impossible to be contained in two small vessels; and how much more so in the goods of so great bulk as those that are carried in them! The schemer tries [to say] that those four millions are worth eight in Nueva España, or even ten for the returns [on investments]; and that that sum goes back to the islands with the 500,000 pesos allowed by the permission, with another 600,000 which is sent as the ordinary aid, granting the net profits at one hundred and fifty per cent, or at the least at one hundred per cent. Were that so, those islands would be most wealthy in one year, for their citizens, as has been said, numbering 230 (counting married and single men), if ten millions entered their possession annually, which would be more than 43,000 pesos for each one, neither Venecia [Venençia — MS.], Genova, Sevilla, nor Lisboa, nor these four empires together, would equal their wealth. With the same extravagance does the captain talk of the ship that sails annually to [from — MS.] Perú, [saying that] its permission, which is for 200,000 ducados, extends to three millions of silver that goes unregistered.

Number 81. The violations of law in all commerce, and why they are not remedied

One cannot deny, Sire, that there are illegalities and abuses in all the navigations and commerces in the world, without excepting one; and that, under pretext of the permission and register that goes, which is not permitted and registered. This is known, and is not remedied for two principal reasons. The first is that it is impossible to remedy it, unless a greater damage results from the remedy; for if the bales and boxes were opened in Sevilla, or in other ports of heavy trade, and the articles that enter and leave were measured, weighed, and counted in detail, the employees there would not suffice, nor six times as many; nor would there be time to despatch one-tenth of the trade. Thus the salaries increasing, because of the greater number of administrators, and the trade being embarrassed by this method, it is evident that the damage caused would be greater than the gain acquired. The other reason is that in imposing the duties of import and export, the customs, the excise, the avería, and other similar duties, care is taken that it is not done with the strictness that is due; and thus they amount to more than it would be convenient [to obtain] if it were paid by measuring, weighing, and counting them all. It is a general decision of all who carry on commerce that, if something be not dispensed with in that direction, the trade and traffic cannot be maintained at all. Accordingly, collection is made on the bales by the packings of the cargoes, by the memoranda of the ships, and by the registers, without making any other moral efforts to ascertain whether more is being carried than is declared — punishing what is discovered, but not discovering the fourth of what is hidden.

Number 82. Tacit permission for what is secreted in the commerce

Many examples might be mentioned which prove this truth. Let the first be the one that was disputed in Sevilla by the exporters of the Indias, namely, that they had not furnished sworn invoices of their cargoes. And although the administrators of the customs insisted upon that, the exporters secured [permission] to furnish, as they are doing, mere lists [of the goods]. Nevertheless, they do not open the bales or boxes; and, although at times these contain cloths, silks, and fine Holland linen, and other rich stuffs, they pass as coarse linen,51 in great part,52 and at most as Rouen linen; and they pay as duties the fourth part of what they would have paid had the bales been opened. Let the second be the existing ordinance that no bale be opened, until it is apparent by information that it carries more or different articles than are stated on the enclosures. That ordinance is observed in all ports of Europa. The third, the custom that has been introduced into Sevilla of imposing on every bale exported to the Indias a certain duty above the amount of the invoice and measure of it that is presented. That can only be justified by the presumption from evidence that the bale carries different goods from what are declared. In the Indias, in the appraisals that are made at Cartagena for the collection of the customs, although it is apparent to the royal officials that the merchants are selling the entire invoices at a profit of ten or twelve per cent over the cost in España, they add to them forty-four per cent of the cost that they [nominally] bear, and then collect ten per cent on the bulk of all. That would be an excessive burden and grievance, if it were not understood as certain that this is charged upon what is shipped registered and what is concealed by substituting some goods for others. Let the fourth be the notable denunciation made in the year 624 by Don Christoval de Balvas, while factor of Tierrafirme, in which he gave information against seventy exporters and merchants concerned with the one fleet that went that year under command of Don Gaspar de Azevedo Bonal. He ascertained that they had carried and shipped to Perú by the house of Cruzes, located between Puerto Velo and Panamá, besides 1,446,346 pesos which were registered, another 7,597,559 pesos, by which the royal duties were defrauded of 1,370,656 pesos. And when it was feared that for so flagrant a violation of the law there would be an equal punishment, the affair was all settled for 200,000 pesos, besides 6,000 which were given to the informant, whereupon the whole case and matter was relegated to silence; and there was no change in the despatch [of the ships], nor in the registers, nor in anything else of the previous practices. For if the burdens of your vassals are not eased in this manner, so that they can make up their losses, risks, injuries, expenses, and other damages that they suffer in so long voyages and so distressing navigations, everything will be ruined. If that has been experienced in Sevilla, and in the trade of the Indias, the magnitude of which is what is known, and where rigor would be more important than in Acapulco (which can not at all be compared to the other), why, if the greater transgression is overlooked (although there is the same and stronger argument), should not the less be excused, and why should not the islands be treated like all the ports of the world?

Number 83. The illegalities in the two commerces of the islands and Perú cannot be such as are alleged, in the withdrawal of silver.

It follows that it is not to be denied that in the two traffics permitted to Filipinas and Perú the same illegal acts might be found as in the other parts where there is trade; but it is not conceded that these excesses are so enormous as are represented. Nor are they greater than those in other regions, where, in the shadow of 200,000 ducados of silver, 50,000 go concealed, while in that of 250,000 in merchandise will come another 60,000; and perhaps both one and the other will be so much less that they merit no attention, and never [is the concealed merchandise] so much more that it exceeds the principal. Some arguments can be advanced on this point. The first is that there is no place whence so much silver can be obtained that three millions of it should be sent from Perú to Nueva España, and ten from Nueva España to the Filipinas. For if six millions and upwards come every year from Perú to these kingdoms, one remains in their land, and three go to Acapulco, then their mines yield from ten to eleven millions. Those of Potosi never amount to six,53 while all the others together do not yield two. Consequently, the supposition that eleven millions are mined is false. That will be better proved by what has come [thence] and what shall come in the future; for since it is ordered that the ship that was permitted shall not sail from Perú, it will be necessary for three millions more than usual to come from its provinces, since those who trafficked by way of the South Sea cannot let their money remain idle, and must employ it on the Northern Sea. The same consideration ought to hold for Nueva España. Three millions are sent [here] annually from that country, and one-half or one [no — MS.] million remains there in the country. Let us suppose that ten millions are sent to Filipinas. It is proved that the three millions cannot be sent from Perú; but admitting for the sake of the argument that they can be sent, it follows that it [i.e., Nueva España] alone yields another eleven millions from its mines — which is impossible, as is gathered from the royal fifths, and from the facts that in some years ships do not go to Filipinas, and that more silver is not for that reason sent to these kingdoms, as would be necessary.

Number 84. The concealment of silver in the galleons argues for the two permissions

All people say openly and believe that much silver is sent unregistered in the galleons of the royal armada for the trade-route of the Indias, and as its vessels number eight, and sometimes twelve, and it acts as convoy to twenty or thirty other and smaller vessels, the highest figure named by those who exaggerate this excess is one million; but never, by dint of diligent efforts and the experience of so many years, has there been known, found, or discovered one-half million. Therefore, if it can scarcely be supposed with probable foundation that thirty or forty ships, with a registered cargo of nine or ten millions, carry one million hidden, how can one believe that three millions can go unregistered in only one vessel (and that a small one), and that ten millions can go in two? The fact is, that he who is looking for transgressions does not think that he is accomplishing his purpose unless he increases them. Besides, if three millions are sent from Perú, it is in order to have them returned in investments in the merchandise of Nueva España (all of which are bulky), for those who send their money [there] will not do so for the purpose of having it remain there. And three millions of investments (which will amount to four millions in Perú), in one ship of three hundred toneladas—[why,] there is no one who will even express an opinion that such a ship can be found that can hold so much. Hence, it is inferred that the above sums are imaginary, fantastic, and fabulous, and consequently, [so is] whatever is based on them.

Number 85. Excess in the merchandise, over the amount permitted to the islands, cannot be what is stated.

In regard to the merchandise, the extravagance of the report is also recognized, namely, that what is carried in each of the two ships is worth four millions; for there is not another like sum in all the Filipinas, even though the cities be sold, with whatever possessions are owned by their citizens and inhabitants. And that such an excess is impossible is apparent for many reasons. First, because the opinion [proposed] regulates the merchandise by the silver that it assumes as the returns. Accordingly, on four millions, with a profit of one hundred and fifty per cent, it gives ten millions of silver; and if there is no foundation in this sum, as is proved, neither is there any in the other. Second, that there is not enough merchandise with which to increase the permitted cargo of the ships, some years, and fewer toneladas are sent than those that are allowed to be distributed. It is improbable that there should be a deficit in the [amount sent by] permission, and yet that outside of it there should be sent four millions, or one, or a half-million unregistered. In regard to that, the islands make now the ninth petition, which will be seen [later]. [In the margin: "In number 109."] The third is the controversy in regard to the distribution of the toneladas—of which the citizens complain that some have been taken away from them, and given to those who are not residents. Thus it is ordered, by the general decree of 604, that no toneladas be assigned to the officers, captains, soldiers, sailors, and artillerymen, and that such cannot receive or buy them. A decree of May 29, 620, orders that there be moderation in the toneladas given for their clothing and ship's stores to the commanders and chief officers. It cannot be believed that those who carry goods would go to law about two or four additional toneladas of allotment, if they were given as many as they wanted. The fourth is very much to the point. In the year 587, while the Englishman Tomas Candi[sh] was sailing through the South Sea to India and the Malucas, he pillaged the ship "Santa Ana" on the coast of Nueva España, which was one of the most rich and valuable ships that has left the islands for Acapulco [Capuico—MS.] The very report of the Englishman himself says that nothing was concealed, and that the valuable merchandise that it carried was worth 122,000 pesos54 of four English sueldos [sc.: shillings] apiece, besides some bales of so little value that they were left to burn with the ship. And since that commerce was then free and unrestricted, they could carry more than now, when the commerce is reduced to a certain amount permitted. The fifth is almost evident, because this merchandise comes in two ships of 300 toneladas. Suppose that they are of 500 toneladas, and that they do not carry any products of the islands, nor any ship's stores, or spices, or anything else but silk, of which every six boxes make one tonelada; accordingly, the thousand toneladas of the two ships would mean 6,000 boxes. Each box is worth 1,500 pesos, and therefore all would be worth 900,000 pesos. Now if from this amount supposed be deducted the toneladas occupied by the men, artillery, ammunition, and food, those toneladas that the ships have below 500, and those toneladas which are of other kinds and not of silk (for those containing cotton cloths are estimated to have a value of 100 pesos and less, and usually exceed [in all] 2,000 and at times 4,000), it easily follows how impossible it is to carry four millions in merchandise in these two vessels—if indeed the three and one-half millions do not come in gold, pearls, and diamonds (products of which 20,000 pesos' value are not brought).

Number 86. Permission for the merchandise of the islands: how it is understood there

The sixth reason is founded on the truth regarding the commerce of the islands, namely, that in regard to the value of the two hundred and fifty thousand pesos allotted by the permission, the governors have granted favors in two ways. One is by admitting registers of more merchandise than is included in the permission, for certain reasons and motives that they have had, guiding themselves more by the burden of the ships and their toneladas, and by the volume of the goods, than by their intrinsic and real value. That has not been any fault or transgression in the citizens, nor in the government employees—of the former, because they are masters of what is allotted to them, but not of its restriction or its increase; of the latter, because it is clear that they must have had an order or sufficient reason for it—and even if such order or reason were lacking at the beginning, those who have succeeded and have found them in this practice and procedure, have not greatly transgressed in following it. The other method is by allowing the citizens to export more than the amount ordinarily allowed, in the products of their own land, which they get from their harvests or their encomiendas. Such are white and yellow wax, and civet; talingas, manteles, lampotes (which are cotton fabrics); and certain kinds of blankets [mantas] from Ilocos, Moro, and Bemben. Of these products, eight hundred piezas (which make one hundred toneladas) are generally sent; and they are declared and appraised at Acapulco, as will be told of the rest. [In the margin: "In numbers 96 and 97."] That practice seems to have been introduced on the ground that it was considered probable that the permission was for the Chinese cloth and other foreign stuffs, and not for those peculiar to and native to the islands; these latter were always admitted, and never needed any permission to carry them to Nueva España—both because of their little value, and because, as will be said, they do no harm to the commerce of España. This is where the excess [over the permission] lies, and not where it is imagined by him who is not conversant with the facts. It is even to be noted that not eight hundred boxes of those products and commodities are always shipped, nor all of them outside the permission—but at times much less than is contained in the per mission, and sometimes very few, are sent; and these are registered and pay the royal duties, as do the others.

Number 87. Imposition of the two per cent, and the reason why it should be repealed

The seventh and last reason is that which is deduced from the imposition of the two per cent which an effort has been made to introduce, on the merchandise of those islands which is exported to Nueva España, and on the silver which is taken to them, by way of avería. It was ordered that this be collected, by the general decree for the permission of 604, and by another of April 22, 608. Governor Don Rodrigo de Bivero tried to execute the first, and Don Juan de Silva the second, and both found so many disadvantages that they suspended it. In the year 625, the royal officials again insisted upon its observance, during the governorship of Don Fernando de Silva, and later during that of Don Juan Niño de Tabora—who, recognizing that the motives that influenced their predecessors were more cogent than before, because of the greater decline in which they found that commerce, the poverty of the inhabitants, and the loss in their business, conformed to the earlier decisions. Licentiate Don Francisco de Roxas put forth more diligent efforts for the actual collection of the said two per cent, but he learned by positive evidence that that collection would mean the destruction of the trade of the islands. For their citizens were resolved not to export their goods, or to take advantage of the permission, as it was apparent to them that, if they paid this additional two per cent besides the three per cent that they pay and the other three per cent on the Chinese merchandise, with the freights and expenses of the ships, the duties in entering Acapulco, and afterward on the silver when they depart [thence]; and that, if without that two per cent, they are continually losing, with it they will be completely ruined, and will be able neither to advance, nor even to preserve their wealth for their support: therefore, the inhabitants have represented several arguments of not a little force to your Majesty. First, that although it was a fact that the profits made formerly on the Chinese trade were large, they were indeed quite small after the entrance of the Dutch into those seas; for by their plundering the Chinese merchandise its cost has so increased that the profit made on it is indeed very little, and there are so many risks in it that there are some years when the merchants lose everything. Second, Governor Don Juan de Silva, seeing that it was difficult to enforce this imposition, supplied its place by the three per cent duty that he ordered to be collected on the Chinese merchandise, whereupon its price again rose. Third, because the duties paid and the expenses incurred by the commerce of the islands are very large. For each thousand pesos the citizens there and in Nueva España pay 270 pesos; and on freight, expenses and costs, 280 more—a total of 550 to the thousand. Fourth, since the costs are so heavy, the profits cannot be large, while the perils are enormous; so that it is impossible for the inhabitants to maintain that commerce; and consequently, they will have to abandon it, and the result will be its total loss. Fifth, the visitor, Don Francisco de Roxas, understood this, and contented himself with getting four thousand ducados for that time, as a gift for suspending the execution [of the two per cent]. Sixth, if from the collection of the two per cent would result the sure and certain cessation of the commerce, or its so great decline that it will bring in less with the greater duties than now with the less, it is better to leave it as at present. Seventh, because of the decline into which the commerce has fallen since the Dutch began to frequent the Orient. Eighth, the services performed, past and present, by the inhabitants of those islands, for which they deserve this and greater rewards. These arguments, although more at length, were presented to your Majesty; and you regarded them as so cogent and sufficient that you were pleased to order that the execution of the decrees for the two per cent should be suspended, by another decree of June 13, 636—by which the inhabitants, on account of their shortness of means, should aid the crown with a gift, in accordance with the condition of the country and their funds.

Number 88. Scanty profits of the commerce of the islands

Two things are inferred from the above. One is the scanty profits of the commerce of the islands, which are so greatly exaggerated by him who is proposing measures for destroying that commerce; for, were its profits half of what is alleged, it cannot be believed that vassals so loyal and so liberal in your Majesty's service would hesitate so much about paying two per cent, and gaining less, when there is so great experience of the love and good-will with which they offer you their possessions and lives. This was not the only time in which this imposition was considered, since Governor Gomez Perez Das Mariñas imposed an additional two per cent besides what was stipulated in Nueva España,55 in the year 591, for the building of the walls of Manila; and although it was confirmed by a letter of instructions of January 17, 593, orders were given, on account of the opposition manifested to it by the inhabitants, that that duty cease when the work was finished, by decree of March 12, 597, which was put in force. For it is certain that considering the expenses, the risks, the hardships, the shipwrecks, and the losses of that voyage from China to Manila, and from Manila to Acapulco — so remote, so long, so troublesome, and so full of dangers, in which many ships have been wrecked, and the enemy have pillaged others, and not a few have put back in distress, and have suffered other disasters, as will be related [In the margin: "In number 93."] — the profits become very small and the gains so limited. This is recognized in the amount of wealth possessed by the citizens of those islands at the end of sixty years, which is the best and most evident proof; since if it were not indeed ten million annually, as has been imagined, but only that which is permitted, without any illegal gain, and the profits one hundred per cent net, the islands would be found in a very different condition from what they are in at present.

Number 89. The new resolution incompatible with that for the two per cent

The second thing that is inferred from the proposed resolution for the two per cent is, that it seems to be incompatible with what it is claimed to introduce. For if there were so many difficulties in adding two per cent on the duties of the commerce, and its execution was suspended after forty-five years of dispute and attempt, and the arguments proposed were considered as sufficient for that step, and your Majesty, yielding to those reasons, approved and confirmed them, how can an increase of duties be suffered now, which will cause so great an innovation in the manner and despatch of the commerce, which will result in so increasing the duties that what is being attempted is exceeded by this way, and did not seem advisable by the other? And [how is it] that the reasons and arguments which were sufficient in order not to impose the lesser burden are not sufficient to prevent the imposition of the greater?

Number 90. Argument for the two per cent that was proposed in Nueva España

That disadvantage was indeed set forth in Nueva España, although in a different manner, making an argument from this imposition of the two per cent to that which results from the present attempt to disturb the commerce. On account of the attempt of Licentiate Don Francisco de Rojas to enforce that collection, the citizens of Filipinas resolved not to export [any goods] in the ships, nor even to avail themselves of the permission; as they believed that they were going to lose instead of gain, notwithstanding the fancied shipments in excess, as will be [if it is not—MS.] apparent to your Majesty by the reports of the visitor. The latter recognized therein that, if the duties went farther, all those now derived from that navigation would be lost, which, as has been seen, amount to more than three hundred and sixty thousand pesos [In the margin: "In number 56"]; and it would be necessary to supply them from the royal treasury, or leave the islands exposed to ruin. And they would have been ruined if the commissions borne by Licentiate Don Pedro de Quiroga had been fulfilled, as these were beyond comparison more rigorous and prejudicial to commerce; and the same effect would result to the inhabitants—as it appears, inevitably. For, not being able to suffer the lesser burden, they could ill endure the greater; and the damage would exceed the benefit by many odds, since in the two or three years that it would take to obtain the decision, even though it were as favorable as that regarding the two per cent, either it would have cost your Majesty the loss of the Filipinas, or you would have spent in their conservation almost two millions, without any recompense. And what is worse is, that those vassals would have become so impoverished that, even though the commerce were to be restored afterward to its first condition, the inhabitants could not enjoy or continue that condition, or get from the commerce in many years what it now produces and contributes; for, the substance and power in which it consists having been consumed, late or never could that be again accumulated. That is an argument worthy of considerable thought and reflection, which those who propose the measures in question do not answer, although they note and consider it, and they only justify those measures—although your Majesty has a right to impose what duty you please, which is the only thing in which there is no doubt. But they do not avert, for they cannot, the damages which must result.

Number 91. The commerce of the islands pays more duties than any other

By these statements it may be seen how groundless is the supposition that the commerce of the islands pays small duties (and it is seen that in this it not only equals but exceeds that of Sevilla, according to the information concerning that); while in all the Indias it is noted as an incontestable fact that in Filipinas the boxes of the permitted lading are not appraised by the cheapest and worst goods, as is done in other ports, but by the best and those of highest quality and value. [In the margin: "In number 82."] For since there are among them those goods which will be hereafter mentioned, and since the most noble and esteemed is silk—as if all the other boxes contained nothing else, each one of them, whatever it may be, passes and pays [duties] for one pico of silk, the equivalent of five arrobas; and conformably to its cost at embarcation, according to the investigation that the royal officials make for its appraisal, the duties are paid and collected. On arriving at Nueva España, they increase its weight by the fourth or third part, and the pico is held to be about six and one-half arrobas of silk. Then another report is made, of the kinds of silk that are received that year; and, distributing it proportionally through them all, the appraisal is made, and the customs duties are collected, higher than in any other port. For the whole cargo is considered to be silk, although there are in it many other articles, inferior in value and quality. Licentiate Don Pedro de Quiroga, as he had reported, had a box of those which pass for six and one-half arrobas weighed, and found that it contained ten—from which three were deducted and discounted for the wood, nails, tarpaulins, ropes, rattans, papers, and other things which have to be placed around the package to strengthen and secure it for so long a voyage. It was found that one arroba or thereabout was exempted, which, compared to the allowance made on what is sent from España, is very little; and even that is compensated by making the valuation by the [standard of the] most valuable commodity, as above stated, although not all the boxes contain silk. Each box, if of silk, is usually worth one thousand five hundred pesos. It pays as first duties and excise two hundred and thirty pesos, while it is a fact that no bale is sent from Sevilla which pays so much as that, even though it be worth four or six thousand pesos. Therefore the proposition that the commerce of the islands pays more duties than that of Sevilla or any other port seems well proved.

Number 92. The profits [navigations—MS.] of the citizens of Manila do not equal their losses

But if these duties were less, and the profits greater, or even greater than what they are said to be, the city of Manila would not be compensated for the damages and losses suffered there and in its trade, past and present— partly through serving your Majesty, partly by being bound to danger and difficulty by their navigation (which is a circumstance that should be considered, since the same profit on what is sent from Sevilla to the Indias, or on that which goes from Madrid to Toledo, is not sufficient for Filipinas), and partly because of the special disasters that have happened to it from its foundation. These damages and losses have been so excessive that if they were noted in detail with the attention that they merit it would seem not only inevitable that that city, as noble [notable—MS.] as unfortunate, would be poor and ruined, but impossible that it should not be finished, destroyed, and deserted; and impossible that, struggling against so many disasters as it has suffered, it should still survive with some luster and wealth. Inasmuch as it is the purpose to avoid in this memorial generalities that do not influence or persuade, the mention of the misfortunes that have happened to Manila has two special and necessary ends. One is the presentation of the services, valor, and merits of its citizens; the other is the notable and lamentable recompense for the profits of its commerce and navigation, since it was necessary that the profits be much greater, to offset thereby the losses and expenses. Their evil will be mentioned by years. Many which are yet unknown, or which are minor, will not be mentioned; and it will be seen whether that city deserves to be protected, its inhabitants rewarded, its commerce aided, and its petitions decided in the most favorable manner that the matters and cases proposed will permit.

Number 93. Misfortunes, losses, and damages that have been suffered by the city of Manila and its inhabitants.

The Spanish government was established in the distinguished and very loyal city of Manila, as capital of all the islands of those seas, in the year 1572.

In the year 575, the pirate Limahon, a Chinese, attacked it with a fleet of seventy large warships. Finding it in so incipient condition, and poorly fortified, he entered and sacked it. The Spaniards defended it rather by valor than by number, in a small fort that they had built.

In the year 578, while Guido de Labacarris was governor, the ship "San Juanillo" sailed for Nueva España, in command of Captain de Ribera, in which it was thought to recover the loss inflicted by the pirate; but the loss became greater, for that ship was lost, and it was never known how or where.

In the year 580, Captain Don Juan Ronquillo del Castillo sailed for Nueva España, in a ship that carried no small cargo. After having sailed for many days, and having found himself in the neighborhood of Nueva Guinea, he put back in distress in a very bad condition. In this it is to be noted that among the losses which Manila feels keenly, is that the ships of their commerce have to put back in distress; for in that year besides failing to obtain the profits of what they invest, and the investment of what is sent in return, they lose most of the principal, which they export—not only in averias, but in the costs and expenses.

In the year 581, Governor Don Juan Ronquillo de Peñalosa imposed a duty of two per cent on the merchandise exported to Nueva España, and three per cent on that carried by the Chinese to Manila. Although he was censured for having imposed those duties without having any order for it, they remained.

That year a fleet sailed from Manila, in command of Don Juan Ronquillo, to succor Maluco and protect the Portuguese who were then in possession of those islands; but after the cost, expense, and expedition, in which many of the inhabitants took part, it had no effect.

In the year 583, on February 27, while the funeral honors of the governor were in progress, fire caught in the church of St. Augustine; and as the edifices of that time were of wood, all of the city was burned and made desolate, and not a thing was saved—not even the fort, in which almost all the possessions of the citizens were lost—while some people met death. That was one of the greatest losses that that city has suffered.

That year, building was recommenced; and, in order to avoid a similar damage, it was determined that all the houses should be built of stone. That caused the inhabitants the expense that one may understand, and the city became one of the most beautiful that can be seen.

In the year 584, Captain Pedro Sarmiento went to Maluco with reënforcements, with another fleet, which had the same expense and effect as the first.

In the year 585, another fleet sailed in command of Captain Juan de Moron, from which, as from the others, Manila derived nothing else than having incurred the expense.

That year, an insurrection that the natives of the country were attempting was discovered. It was quieted with some damage, although less than it might have been.

In the year 587, the Englishman, Tomas Candi[sh] besieged Nueva España, and pillaged and burned the ship "Santa Ana," which was en route to Acapulco very richly laden.

In the year 588, the same pirate tried to burn a ship in the shipyard of the islands of Pintados. He was resisted by Manuel Lorenzo de Lemos, who was in charge of its building. Some men were killed in this affair, and all the men of the islands were placed under arms.

In the year 590 the royal Audiencia of Manila was suppressed. It had been established in the year 584, [sic] and its suppression must also be reckoned among the hardships of that city, because of those which it suffered until the year 597, when the Audiencia was reëstablished.

In the year 591, the commerce of Japon—which was of great advantage, because of the provision of food which was taken thence to Manila—began to be disturbed. That was occasioned by the barbarian emperor Taycocama trying to make the governor of Filipinas pay him vassalage and tribute. That peril lasted as long as the life of the emperor. The islands suffered from it, not only because of the lack of those friendly relations, but because it was necessary to place themselves in a state of defense against the tyrant, who was threatening them with his fleets.

In the year 593, the two ships "San Felipe" and "San Francisco" sailed for Acapulco. They put back in distress, one at Manila, and the other at the island of Zebre [Zienbre—MS.], very much crippled and wrecked.

That year was even more unfortunate. For Governor Gomez Perez Das Mariñas sailing for the conquest of Terrenate with nine hundred Spaniards and more than two hundred boats (reckoning galliots, galleys, fragatas, virreys, and other craft), and arriving at the island of Caça, the Chinese who were taken as rowers in the flagship galley mutinied, and killed the governor and forty Spaniards who were with him. Thereupon, the expedition ceased, and the expenses incurred by the citizens for it, as most of them had embarked in it, were lost.

In the year 596, the galleon "San Felipe," one of the trading ships, under command of Don Matias de Landecho, made port in distress at Japon, where it was wrecked. Those pagans seized the goods aboard the ship, and martyred some of the Spaniards, together with the religious and natives. The Church has placed the latter in the list of the holy martyrs.

In the year 598, Don Luis Das Mariñas left for the expedition to Camboxa with two ships and one galliot, and two hundred Spaniards. After many misfortunes he put in at China, where his vessels were wrecked and beached, some of the men being saved.

In the year 600, two ships under command of Juan Martinez de Guillestigui sailed for Acapulco. Both put back and were lost—the ship "Santa Margarita" at the islands of the Ladrones. The natives entered it in the island of Zarpana, as it was almost destitute of men, and pillaged all its cargo; and the men who were saved remained there some years. The ship "San Geronimo" put in at the island of Catanduanes, where it was wrecked although the men escaped.

That year the Englishman [sic] Oliverio de Noort came in sight of Manila with war vessels, in order to await those ships which were expected from Nueva España. Therefore it was judged advisable to drive him away. Doctor Antonio de Morga, auditor and lieutenant-general of Governor

Don Francisco Tello, sailed to attack him. He took one moderate-sized ship, another of less size, one patache, and one galliot, with one hundred Spaniards in each boat. He attacked the pirate, and the flagship, having been conquered, was set afire. Thereupon that of España cast off its grappling-irons, but was so hardly used that it immediately sank. Some of the men escaped in the small boat, and Doctor Morga reached an island by swimming; while the ship was lost, with the rest of the soldiers. The other ship conquered the English almiranta, and took it to Manila. It was an important capture, but very costly.

In the year 601, the galleon "Santo Tomas" en route from Nueva España, under command of Licentiate Don Antonio de Ribera Maldonado (who had been appointed to the post of auditor), having been blown by a storm to the Embocadero of Capul and the bay of Catamban, was driven ashore and was wrecked. However, the men and most of the cargo were saved. The latter was taken to Manila overland and by sea, a distance of eighty leguas.

In the year 602, Captain Juan Xuarez Gallinato went out in a fleet to attack the Mindanaos, who were infesting the coast of Manila. Although he inflicted some punishment upon them, the cost was greater than the remedy.

That year the ship "Espiritu Santo," en route to Acapulco, after it had cast out all its cargo because of the gales that it encountered, put in at Japon, where it was in danger of receiving the same treatment as had been given to the ship "San Felipe." It was saved from that by the watchfulness of Don Lope de Ulloa y Lemos, its commander. The ship "Jesus Maria," with a like loss, put in at the islands of the Ladrones; and, at the end of five months of navigation, both ships returned to Manila, almost without crew and without cargo.

In the year 603, on the eve of St. Philip and St. James, some houses caught fire; and although many of the edifices were now of stone, the fire leaped to others which were built of wood, and so many were burned that the loss was estimated at more than one million.

That year was one of misfortunes for Manila. The Mindanaos sailed out on a marauding expedition, and went in sight of Manila, pillaging and burning some villages, and taking some Spaniards captive. It was necessary to send a fleet against them, under command of Gaspar Perez, who made them retire.

That year, on the fourth of October, occurred the dangerous uprising of twenty thousand Chinese, who lived in the environs of Manila. Although they were conquered and punished after two months of war, it was at a great loss to the country and to the Spaniards. In the first onset one hundred and fifty of the best Spaniards were killed, almost all citizens, although there were not more than seven hundred citizens. The island was desolated and destroyed for more than twenty leguas round about the city, which was in danger of being lost. The inhabitants who were left had to sally out, and, pursuing the enemy, finally conquered and made an end of them.

That year, of the two ships that sailed according to the permission, die flagship "Nuestra Señora de los Remedios," after having cast out a great part of its cargo, and having lost its masts, put in at Manila; while the "San Antonio," most richly laden, and with many people who, in order to escape the hardships of that city, were going to Nueva España, suffered a greater hardship—for it was swallowed up by the sea, and no one heard what became of it.

In the year 604 was despatched the general decree granting the permission to the islands, which restricted the commerce with Nueva España, as has been declared.

In the year 606, Governor Don Pedro de Acuña made the Maluco expedition, which, although it had a good outcome, was very costly for the citizens of Manila, most of whom took part in it. He took five galleons, four galleys with poop-lanterns, three galliots, four champans, three fustas, two lanchas, two brigantines, one flat-bottomed boat, and thirteen fragatas with high freeboard. He had one thousand three hundred Spaniards serving for pay, besides the volunteers and inhabitants, who were numerous. All incurred the expense that can be imagined in the expedition, without deriving other advantage than their service as loyal vassals.

That year, while the governor was in Maluco with all the force of the islands, the Japanese revolted in Manila, and the country arose in arms and was in great danger; but, after they had done some damage and caused much, they were subdued.

In the year 608, two ships sailed for Acapulco, under command of Juan Tello de Aguirre, and the flagship was wrecked in the Embocadero of Capul, one hundred leguas from Manila.

In the year 609, three ships sailed under command of Juan Ezquerra. The flagship "San Francisco" was wrecked in Japon, and the ship "Santa Ana," which went to Nueva España the following year, put in at the same island.

In the year 610, of the two ships that sailed in accordance with the permission, the almiranta returned to put in at Filipinas.

That year Governor Don Juan de Silva sailed with five ships and three galleys to attack four Dutch ships and one patache which had been before Manila for six months, pillaging all the vessels that entered and left, and holding the city almost besieged. He found only three of the ships, burned one, and captured the two others with a loss of many men; for those expeditions, although their outcome is favorable, are always a source of loss to the inhabitants, because of the many who are killed, and because of the expenses incurred in them.

In the year 611, the governor built another fleet, with which he entered Maluco — but without accomplishing more than the cost, which was heavy; and little was the reputation with which he returned.

In the following year, 612, there was nothing with which to make the despatch of the ships to Nueva España, because of the losses and expeditions above mentioned, and an advice patache alone was sent.

In the year 614, two or three ships from Olanda burned and sacked the town of Arevalo [Arrebalo — MS.] with all its [surrounding] country.

In the year 616, Governor Don Juan de Silva made the disastrous expedition to Malaca with all the force of the islands, of which mention has been made. He died there, and lost on that occasion all the sum that had been spent, which was so vast that it is affirmed that a million was left owing to Spaniards and Indians. To the extortions that were practiced for this, some attribute the ill-success of the expedition.

That year, while Don Juan de Silva was away with the fleet, the Mindanaos came with sixty caracoas, and burned a ship and two pataches which were being built in the province of Camarines, and pillaged the land, seizing and capturing many people.

That year the trading ships, under command of Don Francisco de la Serna, put back. Fearful of the enemy, one discharged its cargo twenty leguas from Manila, and carried the goods overland. The other went to the island of Cibuyan.

In the year 617, occurred the battle of Playa Honda, which was fought by the commander Don Juan Ronquillo, with seven ships and three galleys pitted against six of the Dutch. He sank the flagship, and one other ship, and another was burned. Of the Spanish ships, the galleon "San Marcos" was run aground and wrecked, as above stated. [In the margin: "In number 31."]

That year two ships sailed to Nueva España, under command of Juan Pardo de Losada, and both of them put back.

In the year 618, advice was received in España of the straitened condition in which the islands were, through so many disasters, losses, and foes; and it was determined to send them a goodly reënforcement by way of East India. The commander, Don Lorenço de Zuaçola, was given one thousand seven hundred soldiers with six huge ships, and two pataches, manned by seven hundred and thirty-two seamen and thirty religious. The fleet left Cadiz, and after sailing twelve days was, on December 26, 619 [sic], struck by so fierce a gale that the flagship and almiranta, besides three other large ships, were lost. The ship which was left, with the two battered pataches,56 returned to España. Thus deprived of the greatest reënforcement that has ever been sent to the islands, and when there was most need of it, the islands were greatly afflicted by that loss; but it was supplied by the valor of their inhabitants, who maintained themselves with their usual reputation at the risk of their lives, at the cost of their possessions, and in spite of their enemies.

In the year 620, of the two ships that sailed under command of Don Fernando Centeno, the flagship was lost, thirty leguas from Manila, through the fault of the pilot, whom they hanged there, while the almiranta put back to Manila.

In the year 625, Governor Don Geronimo de Silva made an expedition, taking for it five galleons (two of which were of 1,400 toneladas), one patache, and two galleys. There were 2,269 soldiers, 152 pieces of artillery, and five champans, with food and ammunition in as great abundance as if they had sailed from Sevilla to Lisboa.

In the year 631, the ship "Santa Maria Madalena," while already laden with its cargo in the port of Cavite, and about to sail, went to the bottom—drowning fourteen persons, and losing all the cargo aboard it, as it remained a fortnight under the water. The ship "Santa Margarita," which was left alone, sailed out, but put back with the losses of other times.

In the year 634, the trade of the Filipinas with Japon was suppressed by the efforts of the Dutch. That was a great loss, and it is not known that it has been revived.

In the year 635, as the city of Manila was so ruined and poor, it had no wealth with which to lade the ships of their permission, and hence the ships did not sail to Nueva España.

These are the chief instances of which our knowledge can make relation, and in which Manila and the islands have suffered misfortunes; and those disasters have been so many that of all the sixty-five years since its foundation only fifteen are free from loss and disaster; and some of those disasters are so great that the prosperity of other years was unable to make up for them. From all of them can easily be inferred the proof of the two propositions—namely, the services of their citizens, and the small profits in their commerce, if, as the former are qualified by valor, the latter are proportioned to the losses, risks, and hardships that they endure in order to maintain it.

Number 94. Fifth point: in which is explained the commerce of the islands, according to its parts

For the last justification and the final point, this commerce of the islands with Nueva España will be explained. It has two parts, one the coming with the merchandise, and the other the return voyage with the returns [from the merchandise] in silver. Regarding both will be stated what profits they produce, and whether it will be advisable to suppress or restrict the commerce, or how illegal acts can be prevented.

Number 95. Trade of the islands necessary in Nueva España, because of their goods

In regard to the first part, which pertains to the merchandise, the trade of the Filipinas is so necessary today in Nueva España, that the latter country finds it as difficult as do the islands to get along without that trade; and its lack cannot be supplied with merchandise from these kingdoms. The wares taken to Acapulco are plain and figured velvets, satins, and damasks; grograms, taffetas, and picotes; headdresses and stockings; silk, loose and twisted, in skeins, that reeled on spindles, and woven; thread; tramas,57 plushes, and other silk stuffs and textiles. Of cotton, there are sinavafas,58 fine glazed buckrams [bocacies], glazed linen [olandilla], fine muslins [canequies], and semianas; and of cotton and silk, beds, curtains, coverlets, quilts, and other pieces. [They also carry] civet, musk, and amber; gold and pearls; crockery-ware, cabinets, and articles made of wood, and other things; and the products of the islands themselves, of which mention has been made [In the margin: "In number 15"]. But the bulk of the commerce is reduced to the silk and cotton textiles; for there is but little else that is rare or elegant, or that has much export. From the skeined silk, and the silk thread, and trama are manufactured in Nueva España velvets, veils, headdresses, passementeries, and many taffetas, which were taken to Perú when there were ships that went to Callao, and to other parts of the Indias — where the black, brown, and silver-colored goods that are sent from Sevilla do not arrive in good shape, because the sea rots them. It is known that the skein silk of China is more even and elegant for delicate and smooth fabrics than is the Misteca59 which is produced in that kingdom; besides that, there is less of the latter kind than is necessary in the country. By this trade and manufacture, more than fourteen thousand persons support themselves in Mexico, La Puebla, and Antequera, by their looms, the whole thing being approved by royal decrees. Of the cotton textiles, linens [lienzos] are used in Nueva España more than any other stuff, as they are so cheap that they sell for one and one-half or two reals per vara. Therefore, they are desired by the Indians and negroes; and when these are lacking, even though there should be an over-supply of the linens of Europa, they do not want them or use them, as those are dear and not so much used by them; and they get along with their own cloths from Campeche or La Guasteca, and others that they weave. Hence the importation of these linens (which are brought from China) is now proposed as an expedient measure; if that be administered at the account of the royal treasury, it would gain annually more than one hundred and twenty thousand pesos, as is apparent from a decree of November 20, 606.

Number 96. Distinctions in products from the islands, and their qualities with respect to those of España.

All these products that are trafficked from the islands are divided into six [sic] classes. The first is of silk, in skeins, thread, and trama. The second, the silk textiles. The third, the cotton textiles. The fourth, the products of the islands. The fifth, other small wares and articles that are brought. Of these, the last class amounts to but little, and is not harmful to the commerce of España, as it is composed of rarities and foreign products. The fourth class, namely, that of the products of the islands, by that very fact ought to be exported—a claim that is founded on justice; since it is not usual to prohibit to any province its own trade, and the exportation of its products wherever they may have a sale, even though foreign commerce be denied to it. Besides, this sort has the characteristic of the third, namely, that these wares are so cheap that their like cannot be supplied from España, as has been said, on account of the great difference of their prices. [In the margin: "In number 95."] Hence, the wares of these kingdoms would not be used any more, even did those of the islands fail; nor less, even if there were an over-supply. For the Indians and negroes care only for the linens of China and Filipinas, and, if they do not have them, they get along without them; for they have no wealth to give eight reals for what costs them one and one-half reals. One thousand bales of linen which is shipped from Sevilla in each trading fleet always finds a sale, and no more can be carried [to Nueva España]—because that would create a lack in España, and it would, moreover, be too advantageous to the foreigners, to whom almost all this commodity belongs.60 Two thousand bales of cotton textiles exported from Manila are also consumed [there]; and the fact that there is less or more does not cause any considerable loss in the linen made from flax and hemp, nor does it involve much money; for the two thousand bales of cotton are worth one hundred and fifty thousand pesos, while one thousand of fine linen are worth more than one million.

Number 97. Damage caused to the [sale of] Spanish silks by those of China

The second and first classes of goods are those which may cause more damage, because they come in conflict with those same commodities that are exported from España. Since the latter are dearer, and the former cheaper, while the people are increasing daily, and the wealth decreasing, necessarily they desire the goods that have the more moderate price, even though it is not of the same quality. But this damage, which is the only one, is not such as is imagined. First, because the prohibition of sending textiles to Perú causes a much smaller quantity to go to Acapulco than formerly. Second, because on account of the danger from the piracies of the Dutch, few silks are shipped from China to Manila, and those cost so dear that it is not the product in which there is greatest profit; nor can so much be bought, since he who formerly bought two or three boxes with one thousand pesos, now buys one. Thus the merchants make the bulk [of their exportations] in cotton linens, and in the products of the islands. Third, because Nueva España is now so full of Spaniards, and they have so little money, that one can understand of them in regard to the silks, what has been said of the Indians in regard to the cotton textiles—namely, that if they find those of China, they use them, and if not, they get along without them. Where this is most true, and where it ought to be considered, is in the mines—where the aviadors61 do not and cannot use the cloth from Castilla because of its quality and value; but that of China, as it is cheaper and more durable and serviceable. Consequently, with one thousand pesos' worth of it they maintained their mining operations longer than they could with five thousand worth of that from España. From that it follows that if [the supply of] it were to fail, the mines would necessarily decrease; and that would redound to the greater damage of the royal treasury, and to that of the country, your vassals, and commerce, than what is suffered today, even though what is stated be considered as accurate and true. If there was an over-supply of textiles when there were fewer people, and now much less rather than more is imported, and there are more consumers, there can be but little resulting damage to the goods that are carried hence. Fourth, because the silk in skeins, as already said, is what is consumed; and, if it should fail, more than fourteen thousand persons who are employed and supported by its manufacture would perish. [In the margin: "In number 96."] Fifth, because this [export from España] is already very little, since a great quantity of the silk used by the looms of Granada and Toledo was formerly taken to Sevilla; but, since the year 618, that has been decreasing so much that the workmen of that trade, through lack of silk with which to work, have gone to Nueva España. The cause that lies at the root of this injury is found in the navigation from China to Manila, in which passage the silk is plundered by the Dutch; they carry it to their country, and send it to Castilla by the hands of third persons, and sell it at a great profit. It would be better to have it carried, as formerly, from Manila by way of Mexico, the vassals of this crown thus gaining the profit that its enemies gain. This is a matter of no slight importance, and one which has been advanced as a measure for securing a gain of one-half million for the income of the royal treasury—as appears from a decree of February 16, 602, which was sent to Filipinas; and from the memorials furnished in the year 621 by Oracio Levanto, who tried to make a contract for it.

[XCVIII.—Ex. his.] The damage caused by the silver that is sent to the islands is not at the charge of their inhabitants.

Fourth, in regard to the second point, which concerns the silver that is carried from Nueva España, it is not denied that it may be damaging and prejudicial to bleed that kingdom on that side; but it is denied that the excess in this is that which is alleged—as has been proved. [In the margin: "In number 83."] And if this be conceded, it ought to be noted that this commerce was granted in favor of the citizens of the islands, and not of others; and since most of them are poor, and cannot maintain a commerce of such value as those of Nueva España wish, the residents of Mexico have entered and gained control of a great part of the commerce, under [cover of] the permission granted to the citizens of Manila, and aided by certain persons. The violations of law have resulted from that; for, as the Mexican exporters make those consignments and carry the returns for them—in violation of the royal decrees, and in opposition to the inhabitants of Manila—they are hidden and kept not only from your Majesty's employees (or they endeavor to keep these under obligations, so that they will not denounce them), but from the citizens of the islands, who are not guilty in that. On the contrary, the inhabitants desire and endeavor to obtain a remedy for this, because of the damage that it causes them, not only in usurping their permission from them (as it has in fact been usurped, by good or evil means), but because, if more silver than what their inhabitants carry goes in the Filipinas ships, as that which exceeds [the permission], it belongs to the exporters of Mexico. Such money is sent for investment, and to be returned on the first voyage, and those who have it in charge try to buy on their arrival; and to shorten the time of their return, they will force prices in that place so high, that what is bought from the Chinese for one hundred will immediately advance to two hundred. Since the inhabitants have scanty means and considerable expense, in order that they may therewith support themselves their profits must be great; but on account of such proceedings their profits come to amount to nothing, and they become ruined. Consequently, the whole profit is made by the inhabitants of Mexico; and, as they have more money, and are not burdened with the obligations of the islands—their expeditions, wars, and reënforcements—their profits, although smaller, are larger for their commerce than for that of the citizens of Manila; the latter lose, not only in the purchase, for the Mexicans increase the prices of the merchandise, but afterward in the sale which they make in Nueva España. There they are compelled to sell more cheaply, in order to return immediately, or to take silver at high interest—which is not done by the inhabitants of Mexico; for they remain in their houses and sell as they choose; for they sell slowly, and by that means make up the excess of the price in Manila. The citizens of the latter place cannot enjoy that advantage, and hence return ruined, or with so little profits from so long voyages that, at the end, they scarcely realize the principal with which they commenced. Besides, as the greater part of their possessions are those on which the duties are paid, as they come registered, while the others are concealed and unregistered, by that fact also their costs increase and their profits are diminished.

Number 99. Intention of the inhabitants of the islands in regard to the excesses of the commerce

Therefore it is to be noted that it is not, and cannot be, the intention of the inhabitants of the islands to have the illegal acts that shall have been committed in that commerce remain unpunished, or that liberty be given for the continuance of these and the commission of greater transgressions. They are honest in this, as they ought to be in obeying and observing the royal orders and mandates, which they reverence and respect with so much more obedience, love, and good-will, as the distance which separates them [from España] is greater, and it is more difficult for their great services (for they are great) to be seen and valued, and for them to obtain the rewards and favors which they deserve. What they solicit with the humility of vassals of so Catholic a monarch, and represent under the arguments of expedients and good government which they propose (subject in everything, to what should be of greatest service to your Majesty), is, that the past be punished in such manner that the penalty be not equal for those who have not been equally guilty—and if any have been, it was rather because they have been carried away by their need and hardships than for the sake of the profit of their business; since whatever they have acquired in their business (which, according to the wealth that they possess, is known to be little), has been spent and intended to be spent in your Majesty's service, in ministering to and maintaining those islands, at the cost of their blood and possessions. They ask that, at present, attention be given to what is hidden and concealed;

and that this be corrected and reduced to the amount that is permitted and ordered, without the inhabitants being proceeded against or punished for what they have done through ignorance, until it shall be known in the islands what they ought to do, and new orders issued. For the future they petition that the increase of duties on the goods within the permission be avoided, whether it be silver or merchandise; that there be no innovation in the appraisals of it; that their boxes be not opened or appraised in a different manner from that which has been observed, followed, and kept—since, as has been seen, they pay more than they are able, although not as much as they owe. [In the margin: "In number 91."]

Number 100. Summary of what is alleged in this memorial

Therefore they once more represent to your Majesty what is contained in greater detail in this memorial. The charges made against their commerce, inasmuch as these were based on malicious reports and on less knowledge than was required by the matter, have disturbed, changed, and altered it, so that it is in danger of being lost or suspended (which amounts to the same thing), and with it all the Filipinas, whose importance is so well known. That can be understood from the strong arguments advanced for not abandoning them when they were less necessary than now, when the fact of that importance has been established by so decisive a resolution. To this can serve as new motives the extraordinary manner of their discovery; the greatness of their territory, and therein the notable and especial greatness of the city of Manila—which, as the mistress of so many seas, and capital of so many archipelagos, is the second pole of this monarchy; and the estimation in which their qualities are held, both for the nature of their lands and from what has been acquired from their commerces, which, if they are small as regards their own products, [in their beginnings—MS.] are most opulent as regards those of foreign lands. That is facilitated by their remarkable situation, which, as it is the center of so many islands and powerful kingdoms, is, if not in advance of all of them, superior to many, as it is the key of the ancient and ever rich commerce of the Orient. That commerce, after so many changes, came into the possession of Portugal, and through the Filipinas was communicated to Castilla. It has been usurped in part by the enemies of this crown (who now go to search for it, and carry it on in various ports of its origin), against whom India and the islands are defending and maintaining it. The islands especially protect the commerce of China and that in cloves, as they are now lords of the islands of Maluco—which they recovered after they had been lost, and which they preserve, although infested [by enemies], at the cost of the blood and the possessions of their inhabitants. They are exposed always to the raids of powerful opponents, who in order not to lose what they have had the good fortune to acquire, the Oriental trade and that of Maluco (which is of the greatest value), spend the most of what they gain in forts, presidios, and fleets, that they may resist the Filipinas. If the islands are important for that reason, not less important are they for the effects that result from their preservation. These effects are the promulgation of the Catholic faith, and the extension of the gospel preaching through so extensive regions, and so remote kingdoms of pagans and Moors — which in spite of the northern heresy, has been received by some, while others are ready to receive it; the assurance of safety for India, which has doubled its strength because of the nearness of the islands, which on all occasions reënforce it; the prevention and hindrance of the enemies from the trade in which they most wish to be absolute masters, and which they would obtain were it not for that valiant resistance, and that fortified camp; the relief of the Western Indias from their raids, which because of this diversion have rest; and finally, the maintenance of the reputation of this crown, in the most remote part of its domain. And since, in order to obtain these and other effects, it is sufficient that the Filipinas be maintained in the force and renown that they have at present, for that only two methods are to be found, which consist either in spending from the royal treasury the amount necessary for them, or in giving them a commerce such that all the cost of the islands may be derived from it. Each method is impossible alone, for the expense of the islands is considerable, and the amount that they contribute is not sufficient, as those of Maluco are dependent on them, while the royal treasury is exhausted. The commerce ought not to be opened so widely that its duties supply all [the cost of the islands], because of the injury that this would cause to the commerce of España, which is more important. The only remedy comes to be (and it is that admitted by experience) the union of both these means, each sharing a portion of the expense. With this the royal treasury will be relieved, the commerce permitted, and the islands maintained. In order to provide a guarantee for this obligation, it is advisable to favor the inhabitants of the islands, who have attended and are attending to their defense (as that is the chief part of their preservation) with so abundant aid and so liberal expense. For this, taking a middle course between the damages and the advantages, the restricted commerce with Nueva España, without which they cannot live, is permitted to them. And although results from that concession the withdrawal of a quantity of silver (which if it came to these kingdoms could enrich them more), and its passage to the foreigners, besides the bringing of merchandise from which results a less consumption of the goods of these kingdoms: as this is not the only cause that weakens the trade of the Indias, but there are others very different from it, it is necessary, in order that that trade be not ruined, that this of Filipinas be preserved, but not more than in the quantity that is sufficient for its maintenance, and that is not harmful.

Thus has the commerce been given its present form, conceding it alone to the inhabitants of the islands, restricted as to the amount of its merchandise and the silver for its returns, by imposing on both the latter and the former a fixed and determined quantity, as also on the ships which are to carry it. That is the condition least damaging to each part which, attentive to the state of so many kingdoms and the mutual relations of so many provinces, it has been possible to arrange. Although great illegalities have been ascribed to this permission, which are not lacking in any part of the world, and are found in all commerces, and are tolerated—either because it is impossible to correct them, or because it is not advisable to reduce them to the full rigor of the orders—those that are found in this commerce are not greater than those of others; for62 neither the silver nor the merchandise which is hidden can exceed the amount permitted so greatly as has been represented, as has been [herein] stated. If there is any violation, there are sufficient precedents so that it ought to be tolerated, and the greatest reason [for so doing]; for it is impossible for that commerce to last in any other way, or to have capital with which to maintain it. [This is true], not only because of the duties that are paid, which are heavier than those of Sevilla; but because of the great amount that is lost in it by the risks, expenses, and hardships of its navigation, and by the special disasters that the islands and their inhabitants have suffered, and are liable to suffer—which are such and so many, that it is a wonder that they are not destroyed, ruined, and deserted by the onset of their disasters, losses, and diminutions, which it seems that the loyalty, the valor, and the constancy of their inhabitants have opposed. Besides that, their commerce is no longer what it was formerly; nor does it cause the damage that is noted; nor is it such that it can be done away with, without the downfall of the islands, the suffering of Nueva España, peril to Eastern India, the loss of its commerce, a greater infesting of the Western Indias, and the sorrow of these and those kingdoms for the result of this cause, as it is common to them all, as is proved. Therefore, the procurator-general of the islands, reducing all their affairs to this memorial, petitions your Majesty to grant them favor in the affairs and points which he will request in a separate memorial.

Don Juan Grau y Monfalcon

1 In the present translation we follow the printed original—using the copy belonging to the Academia Real de la Historia, Madrid—as per the above title-page. Our transcript was collated with the manuscript copy in the Biblioteca Nacional, Madrid, which may possibly be a contemporaneous copy of the original manuscript of the Memorial; but this manuscript (which bears

pressmark MSS. 8990, Aa–47, of which it occupies folios 273–350), which appears to have been done hastily, bears the mark of inaccuracies that make the printed Memorial preferable. Where the difference is considerable, the reading of the manuscript is inserted in brackets after the other reading, and signed "MS." These variations are here noted mainly as a guide to those who may use that manuscript. In almost every case the number of the paragraph is omitted in the manuscript, as are also sometimes the marginal headings of the paragraphs, and most of the other marginal notes. Reference has also been made in the translation to the published edition of the manuscript Memorial in Doc. inéd. Amér. y Oceanía, vi (Madrid, 1866), pp. 364–484, which has been edited somewhat; and to an evident reprint from the printed edition of 1637, in Extracto historial (Madrid, 1736), folios 215–264. Matter taken from the latter is signed "Ex. his."

2 Avería was the tax or duty levied on goods shipped from Spain to America, or from America to Spain, to meet the expenses of the naval convoy to protect the fleet from pirates. See tit. ix of lib. ix, Recopilación de leyes de Indias which treats of the avería, entitled, "Of the tax, administration, and collection of the duty of avería." — Edward G. Bourne.

3 Note in margin of Extracto historial: "Note: The numbers cited in these margins refer to this same memorial."

4 At this point the manuscript and printed original both contain a partial reduplication, as follows: los vexinos y cargadores de Filipinas, que sin reconocer — es digo por solo no verse sujetos á denunciationes. It may possibly be regarded as a parenthetical expression added for the sake of force, and is translated: "the citizens and exporters of Filipinas, who without recognizing — it is, I say, for the sole purpose of not becoming liable to denunciations." This clause is dropped in the Extracto historial reprint.

5 See Vol. xvi of this series, pp. 225–227.

6 The manuscript at this point contains a duplicate or confusion of words, as follows: Reyes tienen vnos Estados, porque los han menester, y otros digo el embiarles ministros della aunque los. This proves the manuscript only a clerical copy, as does also the fact that it is copied in the same hand as other manuscripts of this same collection; and it shows the carelessness with which this copy was made.

7 The progress made by the Mahometans in the eastern part of Asia was very slow. The inhabitants of Malacca were converted in 1276, those of the Moluccas in 1465, and those of Java in 1478, and those of the Celebes one year before Vasco da Gama rounded the cape of Good Hope. Nevertheless, after 1521, many of the inhabitants of these islands began to be converted to Catholicism. — See Doc. inéd. Amér. y Oceanía, vi, p. 375, note.

8 Empeño: This transfer, as may be seen from the treaty of Zaragoza (vol. 1, pp. 221–239), was part of the sale by Spain to Portugal of the spice-trade, right of navigation, and islands then in dispute between the two crowns; but various stipulations were made regarding it, so that the Maluco Islands were, in a sense, held as a pledge for the observance thereof.

9 This word is lacking in the manuscript.

10 At this point occurs a doublet of nine words in the manuscript — simply an error of the transcriber.

11 See this decree in vol. III, pp. 250, 251.

12 See this decree, with illustrations, in vol. IX, pp. 211–215.

13 See Vol. iv, p. 108.

14 This is the date in the original printed edition, but both the manuscript and the reprint in the Extracto historial give 1626.

15 At this point there is another lapsus calami by the transcriber of the manuscript, resulting in another reduplication.

16 Both the manuscript and the Extracto historial reprint say May 16.

17 See Vol. XX, p. 257.

18 This word is omitted in the manuscript.

19 Singapore signifies, in Malay, "place of lions" — although it would be more apropos to call it "the place of tigers," which are so plentiful there (Doc. inéd. Amér. y Oceania, vi, p. 383, note).

20 This sentence is very blindly worded, but perhaps indicates, by anticipation, the point made in section 40, post — where India and the Philippines are mentioned as the "extremes" of the Spanish empire in the Orient. Or it may refer to the alternative presented near the end of section 2.

21 Grau y Monfalcón evidently made use of Leonardo de Argensola's Conqvistas de las Islas Malvcas in this review of Oriental commerce.

22 Referring to Ptolemy Neus Dionysus, surnamed Auletes ("the Flute-player"), who ruled over Egypt from b. c. 80 to 51. One of his daughters was the famous Cleopatra VI, who so infatuated the Roman Cæsar and Antony.

23 This date in the manuscript is 1457, which is misprinted 1417 in the reprint of 1866 (Doc. inéd.).

24 See Sir Henry Middleton's Voyage to Bantam (Hakluyt Society's publications, London, 1855); that voyage took place in 1604–06.

25 This word is missing in the manuscript.

26 The cate is equivalent to 1.8 English pounds; 87 pounds equal one quintal, 100 catés one pico, and 40 picos one koyan (Doc. inéd. Amér. y Oceanía, vi, p. 390, note).

27 See the description and prices of precious stones found in the appendix to Duarte Barbosa's East Africa and Malabar (Hakluyt Society's publications, London, 1866), pp. 208–218.

28 Apparently referring to some plant of the genus Strychnos, several species of it having the reputation of curing the bites of serpents. Blanco says (Flora, p. 61) that he himself has witnessed several cures by this means.

29 A dried fruit, resembling a prune, which contains tannin; formerly used in medicine, now mainly in tanning and dyeing. It is the product of various species of Terminalia.

30 The manuscript is mutilated at this point, and contains only the first part of this name, "Vera."

31 The manuscript reads "29."

32 Apparently an error for "November;" see vol. xvii, p. 252.

33 Cf. Heredia's list (1618?) of Dutch factories and posts, vol. xviii, pp. 107–110; and Los Rios's mention of them, vol. xix, pp. 288–290.

34 Tacomma, where the Dutch erected Fort Willemstadt.

35 This word is omitted in the manuscript.

36 The capital of the island of Gilolo bears the same name. Batochina is properly a part of the island (Doc. inéd. Amér. y Oceanía, vi, p. 400, note 1).

37 The island of Amboina was discovered about 1515 by the Portuguese, and taken by the Dutch February 23, 1603. See Doc. inéd. Amér. y Oceanía, vi, p. 400, note 2.

38 This word is lacking in the manuscript.

39 See, in Vols. V and VI of this series, the ordinance of May 5, 1583, giving form to the Audiencia, the establishment of which was decreed by royal order of the above date (March 5).

40 An imaginary money used in the Indias, which serves as a standard for valuing the ingots of silver; it is differentiated from the value of the real-of-eight, or coined peso, in order to allow for the amount of seigniorage and other expenses at the mint. (Dominguez's Dict. nac. lingua española.)

In Morga's time the governor received eight thousand pesos de minas annually (see Vol. XVI, p. 188; also II, p. 97, note 43).

41 Spanish, santas; one would expect sanativas, "healing."

42 Spanish, seis mil aremilas. Mil is an obvious error, probably typographical; and aremilas is apparently a misprint for acémilas, "mules."

43 Comitre: an officer in the galleys of that epoch, who had charge of the working of the ship, and the punishment of the rowers and convicts. See Doc. inéd. Amér. y Oceania, vi, p. 421, note 1.

44 This word is omitted in the manuscript.

45 This word is lacking in the manuscript.

46 Cf. financial statements of the Philippine colonial government found in Vols. VI, pp. 47–49: XIV, pp. 243–269; XVI, pp. 188–193; XIX, pp. 248–250, 292–297.

47 The manuscript is much confused at this point, reading y assi el Real instead of y assi al Perù — the idea of the copyist evidently being "Accordingly the royal [Council] concedes one ship annually to Nueva España," etc., which does not make sense with what follows.

48 Annuity assigned upon the revenue of the crown.

49 Grau y Monfalcón leaves out of account the expeditions of Loaisa and Villalobos.

50 This word is lacking in the manuscript.

51 Spanish, angeos; i.e., Anjou linen, because it was obtained from that duchy; a coarse, heavy cloth of the poorer quality of flax. The linen of Rouen was fine.

52 These words, lo mas, are omitted in the manuscript.

53 See Cíeza de Leon's account of the mines of Potosi, in his Chronicle of Peru (Markham's translation, Hakluyt Society's publications, London, 1864), pp. 386–392. He says that he himself saw (1549) the amount of the royal fifths, 25,000 to 40,000 pesos each week; and that these for the years

1548–51 amounted to more than 3,000,000 ducados. Cf. Acosta's description, in his History of the Indies (Hakluyt Society's publications, London, 1880), i, pp. 197–209; he reckons the fifths as 1,500,000 pesos (of 13¼ reals each) yearly. Both writers state that much of the silver was never reported to the royal officials.

Humboldt makes the statement (*New Spain*, Black's translation, iii, p. 372) regarding the yield of Potosi from 1624 to 1634, that it was 5,232,425 piastres (or pesos; of eight reals each)—as translated, "average years," which presumably is intended for "yearly average."

54 See Vol. XV, p. 293.

55 Here occurs, in the manuscript, a later sentence copied in the wrong place.

56 This word is omitted in the manuscript.

57 Trama: a kind of weaving silk.

58 Sinabafa: material of the natural color, i.e., unbleached.

59 Evidently meaning the silk produced in Misteca (Miztecapan), a province of Nueva España, now part of the state of Oajaca. This industry appears to have been introduced there in consequence of a suggestion by the viceroy Montesclaros in 1612 (see Vol. XVII, p. 219).

60 Apparently meaning that as linen must then be imported into Spain, to make good this deficiency, an extension of their market for this commodity would thus be secured by the French and Dutch, its chief manufacturers.

61 Aviador: a term used in Nueva España to denote the person who supplied others with articles to work the silver mines.

62 This word is omitted in the manuscript.

Documents of 1637

Sources: The first, third, and fourth of these documents are obtained from MSS. in the Academia Real de la Historia, Madrid; the second and seventh, from MSS. in the Archivo general de Indias, Sevilla; the fifth, from Barrantes's *Guerras piraticas*, pp. 303–310; the sixth, from Pastells's edition of Colin's *Labor evangélica*, iii, pp. 757–758.

Translations: The first of these documents is translated by Arthur B. Myrick and Emma Helen Blair; the second, fourth, and sixth, by James A. Robertson; the third, by Helen E. Thomas; the fifth, by Alfonso de Salvio; the seventh, by Emma Helen Blair.

Defeat of Moro Pirates

A relation of the battle with the fleet from Mindanao, and the victory of the Spanish, off the coast of that island and the cape known as Punta de Flechas, on the day of the blessed Saint Thomas the Apostle, December 21, 1636.

Tagal, a chief of Mindanao,1 who was entitled Captain-general of Corralat on sea and land, had performed exploits in his service for many years, both in wars waged with the Goloes and in various incursions, and on all these occasions came off with good fortune. In the past year of 636, in the beginning of April, he asked Cachil Corralat, king of Mindanao, to give him four caracoas, with which he would go over to the islands of the Castilians, and spend nine months plundering them—urging that he would return rich, with his ships laden not only with Vissayans but Castilians; and that he would bring him the God of the Christians a prisoner; and other inducements. Corralat gave him the vessels, and with them he went, in the said month of April, to the chiefs of Taguima and Jolo, urging them to accompany him. They excused themselves, saying that they were near neighbors of the Spaniards, and desired no wars with them. No one accompanied him from those islands, but he, with the four joangas, entered among the islands of Cuyo and Calamianes, and the coast of Mindoro, where he remained almost eight months, robbing and inflicting enormous damage. He plundered the churches of Cuyo and Calamianes, profaning the vessels and holy vestments, breaking the holy images, and capturing the ministers in these islands. He seized three Augustinian Recollect fathers, and captured the corregidor of Cuyo2 and another Spaniard. The Moro committed and uttered many blasphemies against our Lord and His saints, and the holy images and consecrated things, calling out in a loud voice that Mahomet had taken prisoner the God of the Christians. Having seized a chalice, with the paten that belonged to it, they used the latter for a plate for buyos, and the chalice to spit in. They made a hole through the linen cloth on the image of Christ our Lord, through which a man would thrust his head, wearing it as one would a scapulary, suspending it mainly over the breast and shoulders. They also kept the choristers' mantles, in order to wear them when they entered Mindanao. Returning, then, with much booty and many captives, their four large caracoas and three smaller vessels, seven in all, laden with the plunder which they had seized, the Moro dared to go where his sins carried him, to pay for his arrogance and madness. Although he had a large force, he did not choose to pass between Jolo and the island of Basilan, or Taguima, as he had done in coming; but he actually passed, in the darkness of night, before the fort at Sanboangan, in the strait which is made by the said island with Basilan, for a distance of a league and a half, more or less, from the fort. This was astonishing audacity; and if, for our sins, he had returned unhindered to Mindanao, they would have lost all fear of that fort and the royal arms. He actually passed the strait without being noticed, and at dawn arrived at a place where he could not be seen by our people. The day on which he passed before our fort was a Wednesday, December seventeenth, on the evening of the Expectation of our Lady, about eight o'clock. The next day just as Father Gregorio Belin3 was preparing to say mass, there arrived a Lutao Indian, who has always displayed fidelity to the Spaniards; and told him, as above, how that night the enemy had passed near there on their return, and that it would be easy to go forth in pursuit of them, because they were heavily loaded and weighed down, for they had been at sea for eight months. Beside this, the Mindanaos had a superstition or idolatry according to which all those who are returning to their land victorious are obliged to proceed to a hill that is encountered after doubling Punta de Flechas,4 and at the point. Each man brings from the ships one of the lances that they carry, made of bamboo hardened in the fire; and these are usually hurled into the ground on this hill, because it is of soft stone. The Indian said that this superstition was so infallible and established among them that on no account would they omit going together to this place; and thus it was necessary that we should come to blows with them. The father placed the whole matter before Sargento-mayor Bartolome Diaz Barrera, governor of Sanboangan, and Sargento-mayor Nicolas Gonzales— who is an excellent officer, a captain of infantry in the garrison there. These men, overcoming many difficulties, prepared, in two hours, with incredible promptness and diligence, a fleet of six ships with one hundred infantrymen and one hundred and fifty volunteer Bisayan warriors, with their cannon and all necessary supplies; and the said governor detailed Sargento-mayor Nicolas Gonzales to pursue the enemy. The latter set out with his fleet, with such energy that although some of our vessels were mere rafts, and all had but scanty equipment, and let in much water, he allowed nothing to hinder him, but [kept on his course], overcoming many difficulties. On the first day he sent back to the fort one of his six vessels, because he saw that it was falling behind the rest on account of leaking badly; and with only the five remaining he pursued the enemy, with remarkable persistence, for three days and three nights.

On the morning of St. Thomas's day, Father Belin, at Sanboangan, felt such impulses to expose the most holy sacrament that he was almost unable to restrain himself; and, although he could hardly overcome the difficulties arising from the inconvenience of the sacristy, he exposed [the body of] our Lord, in supplication for the fleet. The governor was piously present, and the people adored the Lord with supplications. At that very time (as has been carefully investigated) our fleet discovered two of the enemy's ships near Punta de Flechas, one rather small and the other very large. The smaller vessel, on account of its lighter draft, was able to run ashore—all those who were able fleeing, and leaving the ship, their captives and arms, and many other things in the hands of our men. Aboard the large vessel was a chief named Anpay Apuy; with terrible fury and determination he attacked our capitana, fired three shots at her, and pierced her with one. But [the men of] our capitana with great gallantry and valor boarded her, and discharged several shots. The Moros would not surrender, so almost all of them were killed; even those who escaped by swimming attacked our almiranta, which was assisting the capitana. Many Christian captives were rescued, with a large amount of plunder found at Punta de Flechas. Our people sighted four other vessels at the place where they practiced their superstition, where they were casting their lances of burned bamboo. As soon as the enemy saw our fleet, they tried to escape by lightening their ships of the captives aboard them. Two vessels which they had drawn ashore were captured, but the other two escaped on account of their lightness of draft, after receiving several volleys from our fleet. The darkness of the night helped them, as well as their having thrown overboard nearly all that they carried. At that place many of their Christian captives were recovered. At this time, in the middle of the night, a strange thing happened, almost prophetic of the misfortune to those Moros, and apparently a presage of their fall and destruction. There was an earthquake, so sudden and so terrible that it was plainly felt upon the sea; and a rumbling which sounded as if some aperture of hell were opening. All our soldiers were thoroughly terrified at so frightful rumblings and quaking, and fancied that they heard voices, or terrible yells; so they armed themselves with their rosaries, Agnus Dei's, and relics, commending themselves to our Lord. During this earthquake, the hill where they superstitiously shot their arrows or lances fell into the sea, where it can still be partly seen. It is to be hoped that when it fell, or began to fall, it carried with it the pride of these Mindanao Mohammedans. Our fleet at midnight sighted the enemy's capitana, which was standing out to sea with another little ship which served it for a lanpitao, as they call a boat for reconnoitring, or a tender. The sargento-mayor, who had ever conducted himself as a prudent and experienced man, did the same in this case, ordering every one to keep quiet and await that vessel which was coming into their hands, on its way to their place of worship, to shoot their arrows there. They were hoping that that flagship—which was a large one, and carried more than one hundred and twenty rowers—was heavily laden with captives, booty, and stores. At midnight, our men heard the enemy's vessel near us, whereupon our flagship went to attack the enemy's, followed by our almiranta; and our men boarded her at the stern. Seeing that they would not surrender, a cannon was fired at them, which Carlos (a good artilleryman and a good Christian) had loaded with ordinary balls, an iron bar, and a lantern full of musket-balls. It swept almost all the men from the bailio, and a captive who was aboard that flagship said that this shot killed twenty men. This artilleryman made several other good shots, and in the meantime the infantry kept up a continuous fire, so that it is said that most of our men fired more than thirty shots apiece. Twenty-four picked musketeers were stationed on our flagship alone. Finally the [Moro] ship abandoned resistance and was boarded by Sargento-mayor Nicolas Gonzales—who killed with his own hand two men who still continued to resist. Some leaped overboard, but it was impossible for them to make their escape, for the high waves and the strong wind carried them far out to sea, so that they presently drowned. Father Fray Francisco de San Joseph, of acknowledged piety, died here, well content that he had seen the side of the Christians victorious, and witnessed the valor and courage of the leaders and soldiers of our fleet, for they behaved well and honorably.5 The sargento-mayor, beside his usual valor, received assistance from the Lord. Although he had very poor health, yet from the moment that he hastened to go forth until the final fortunate outcome he enjoyed perfect health for all the hardships which he underwent before and during the battle. All this made the good father say that he was very content to die, and especially because he had not seen the abominations, blasphemies, and shameless acts of that rabble. There was one sick, Tagal, who was the leader of the enemy's fleet, and on this occasion he ended his evil life, to commence payment for his atrocities, blasphemies, and daring. On the other hand, a younger brother of his who was mortally wounded asked anxiously for holy baptism, protesting that he believed the Christian religion to be the true one, and that he had always had a pious leaning to it. They instructed him in the Christian faith, and after baptism he died, our Lord taking only this one to heaven out of all that number of dead Mindanaos—three hundred, more or less. Five ships in all were captured from the enemy. Of the four large vessels one only escaped, although our men kept up a continuous fire at it, and pursued it for a long time. Seventeen shots were fired from the cannon, to say nothing of the continuous musketry fire. The powder for one of the cannon was blown up by a shot, and they lightened ship as much as possible by throwing overboard captives who had been cut to pieces, in order to make their flight more rapid. One hundred and twenty of our people were rescued and fourteen Mindanaos who desired to receive baptism were taken alive. According to their account the rest of the Moros, full of rage and showing their teeth, fought to the death. A large amount of gold and many other things of value were found among their plunder. The soldiers, as good Christians, declared all the church property they found—among other things, a gilded lunette, a chalice and paten, three chorister's mantles, and ornaments and images which had been misused. One ship was seized, because it was needed for the men who were crowded in the others; also two cannons with ladles [pieças de cuchara], two culverins, and thirty muskets and arquebuses; with campilans and lances, and much cloth. The victory did not cost the life of a single Spaniard or Indian.

This victory has been of so much importance because it has terrified Mindanao and Jolo, and has been a strong incentive to the resumption of peace. The day when the fleet sailed, there was a juanga of Joloans at Sanboangan which was seen going out, and a little while afterward another was seen entering which came from Zibu, carrying Captain Becerra; the rest of his company, consisting of thirty infantrymen, were in five vessels, which entered with great gallantry, all of which is to the credit of our side. Hundreds of Indians came out from the shore, from Sanboangan as far as this place,6 to meet the ship which bore the news, with demonstrations of great joy; they brought presents and refreshments for a father who was aboard the ship. The same thing happened along the shores of these our islands. The inhabitants of Sibugay—which is the storehouse for Corralat, who cannot get along without that town—and others of his subjects have offered tribute. Thanks to the Lord, and to the most holy sacrament which appeared in public—and, as it were, on the field of battle—and to the most holy Virgin Mary, our Lady, on whose day the expedition was prepared and sailed.

The Joloans, by the agreement which they made in the time of Captain Juan de Chaves through Father Vera and the queen (although it was in the interim government of Licentiate de Mana), made raids against the Camucones, and, it is said, they have carried away more than six hundred [of those people] at one time. They have sold many [of these captives] in Sanboangan, and they are bringing a number of them here in a champan. Father Belin says that he has sometimes talked to the Joloans, asking them to give up the body of Father Vilancio. They answer that they would like to preserve it, because it is holy; and they say that it is uninjured. We are very glad [to hear this], although we do not mention it to those outside until we know about the matter with more certainty.

The father prior of the Recollects came the day before yesterday from Cagayan. He says that those who have come there from Mindanao say that Corralat is quite destitute [*three words illegible*]. The ruler of Buayen and his sons-in-law are making war upon him, in company with a brother of that Gogo whose execution Corralat had ordered, because he had corresponded with the Spaniards at Sanboangan. The peasants, and the people who dwell inland, are molesting him, and he scarcely trusts even his own men. He possesses no mounted cannon, and no arms in good condition. The Mindanao prisoners say that he has not even means enough to arm three good caracoas.

They write from Oton, that they are hourly expecting the lord governor, because he has written that he would leave Manila on January 26. He orders the pataches laden in Sanboangan to wait for him, and the galleon and galleys to sail.

1 Montero y Vidal says (Hist. piratería, i, p. 162) that Tagal was a brother of Corralat.

2 These religious were Fray Francisco de Jesús María, missionary in Cuyo; and Fray Juan de San Nicolás, and Fray Alonso de San Agustín, of Linacapán in Calamianes. See sketches of their lives, captivity, and deaths in Luis de Jesús's Hist. relig. descalzos (Madrid, 1663), pp. 284–293. Cf. "The martyrs of Calamianes," in Prov. S. Nicolás de Tolentino agust. descalzos (Manila, 1879), pp. 184–190. The corregidor (alcalde) captured at that time was Diego de Alabes.

3 Gregorio Belin (or Belon) was born at Madrid, March 15, 1608 (probably; misprinted 1628 in Pastells's and Retana's Combés, col. 699); entered the Jesuit order in 1625, and was ordained a priest January 6, 1633. In 1640, while in Cebú, he left the Society.

4 Punta de Flechas is the headland marking division between the great bays of Illana and Dumanquilas on the southern coast of Mindanao, and is at the south end of boundary line between the provinces of Cotabato and Zamboanga. This cape was anciently known as Panaon.

5 See Combés's account of this battle (Hist. Mindanao, cols. 234–238), and that of La Concepción (Hist. Philipinas, v, pp. 304–310). The latter states that the priest who died in the battle was Fray Francisco de Jesús María, the Recollect captured in Cuyo; he was on Tagal's ship, and was fatally wounded by the Spanish guns.

6 This letter was probably written by Pedro Gutierrez, from Dapitan—of the Jesuit residence at which place he was rector in the preceding year—which was at that time the chief of the Jesuit missions in Mindanao. It is located almost at the northwest point of that island.

Auditorship of Accounts in Manila, 1595–1637

Sire:

The Council, on examining in the hall of justice the [records of the] official visit which Licentiate Don Francisco de Rojas made of the Audiencia and royal officials of the Filipinas Islands; and having examined therein charge three made against the said royal officials regarding the general account for each year to be taken from them by an auditor of accounts [contador de cuentas]—namely, that they have not given him sworn statements; and, in particular, that they refused to give a sworn statement of the amounts that ought to be collected, and of other things which the auditor of accounts ordered—commanded me to make a comprehensive report from what should appear in the records of the visit, and in the other papers resting in the secretary's office concerning the matter; so that, having been examined in the government where they are considering whether it is advisable or not to appoint one for life to that office of auditor of accounts in those islands, and with what conditions, the advisable measures may be taken. In fulfilment of that command, having attended to that matter as was fitting, I have drawn up this paper, in which, as briefly as possible, and as was required by the gravity of the matter, I have compiled what treats of it, dividing it for greater distinctness and clearness into the four following points.

Point 1. Of the beginnings in those islands of the office of auditor of accounts, and of the variations and changes that have occurred in it, down to the present.

Point 2. Of the litigations that have occurred between the royal officials and the auditor of accounts, in regard to the manner of exercising the duties of that office.

Point 3. Of the disadvantages, as seen from the records of the visit, that arise from the existence of that office in those islands.

Point 4. Of the advantages that are found for the existence of that office in those islands, and what has been enacted and decreed in the Council regarding it, up to the present.

[Point 1]

Book 7, folio 284, verso. In regard to the first point, I presuppose that, as appears from the certification of the government notary of those islands, there is not in it the particular reason of an order from his Majesty for the governor of the islands to appoint an auditor of accounts, as all the governors have done for many years past. What appears is, that in years preceding that of 1595 (although it does not appear when this practice was first inaugurated), the governor made an annual appointment of an auditor of accounts, in order that he might audit the general account of the royal officials for the preceding year — as is mentioned by the governor Don Luis Perez Dasmariñas in the first perpetual title that he gave as auditor of accounts, in the year 595, to Bartolome de Renteria, who was the first to whom it was given with this title. The governor says the following in regard to it:

"Inasmuch as his Majesty has ordered the governor of these islands to audit the account of the royal official judges of the islands annually, by means of an auditor of accounts who should be appointed for that purpose, and to send each year the report that he should make to his Majesty, as has been done; and inasmuch as I am informed of, and see, the disadvantages and dangers that result to the royal estate of having the governors appoint, as is their custom, a new auditor [contador] for the said accounts each year, in order to give him that profit that is due him for other services: there is no one in that calling as competent as is necessary. Thence it results that the said accounts are not audited with the clearness and completeness that is advisable, or in the good order and style in which an expert auditor would leave them, and who would learn by experience and by special acquaintance from the times when he should have audited them before, or by his knowledge through the condition of other accounts that he might have audited, the condition of the royal estate. Such a person will try to understand the royal treasury thoroughly, while he who audits the accounts once will do it more carelessly. All that carelessness would cease, as would many other disadvantages which experience has shown;

and we could achieve the results that are desirable for the service of his Majesty by appointing an auditor to audit the accounts every year, without changing or removing him for another, but allowing him to hold the said office continuously."

The title continues with the appointment of the said Bartolome de Renteria as auditor of accounts, as long as it may be the will of his Majesty and of the said governor in his royal name; and orders that the uncertainties, additions, and results [*resultas*] that shall arise be communicated to the said governor, so that they may be concluded and executed with his decision. The title assigns him a salary of five hundred pesos of common gold, payable from the royal treasury.

Book 7, folio 235. His Majesty despatched a royal decree in the year 596, ordering the establishment of the Audiencia of the said islands. In that provision were inserted the ordinances pertaining to this point, namely, the sixty-seventh, the sixty-ninth, and the ninetieth.1 They read as follows:

"Ordinance 67. Item: My president shall, together with two auditors [oidores], audit the accounts, at the beginning of each year, of the royal officials who shall have had charge of my royal treasury for the past year. They shall conclude it within the months of January and February; and when they are completed, a copy of them shall be sent to my Council of the Indias. I order that if the said two months pass, without the said accounts being completed, the officials of my royal treasury shall receive no salary until they shall be concluded. Each of the auditors who shall be present at the auditing of the said accounts shall have a gratification of twenty-five thousand maravedis, provided that that salary or gratification be not given them—and it shall not be given them—except for the year for which they shall send the said accounts concluded to my royal Council of the Indias."

"Ordinance 69. *Item*: I order that when my president and auditors commence to audit the accounts of my royal estate, in accordance with the provision in regard to it, they shall go first of all to my royal treasury, and weigh and count the gold and silver and the other things that may be there, and take account of it [*In the margin: "Sic."*]. Then they shall begin the accounts, and, having finished them, shall collect the balance within the time ordered by the said decree. [*In the margin:* "I do not find any account, in the records of the visit, of this provision which is cited."] The amount collected shall be placed in the chest with three keys; and orders shall be given that the balance from the past year shall not be made up from what shall be collected during the time in which the accounts shall be audited."

"Ordinance 90. *Item*: The said fiscal shall be at all the meetings which shall be held outside the ordinary Audiencia by the president and auditors, whether of justice or pertaining to my royal estate, with the officials of it, either for matters of government, or in any other manner."

Book 7, folio 239. In a royal decree of January 25, 605, directed to the royal officials of the said islands with the ordinances of their offices, the two following touch on this matter:

"Ordinance 29. The accounts that you shall be obliged to give of what is in your charge during the administration of your offices, shall be given annually in the accustomed manner. For that purpose, you shall deliver as an inventory to the person who shall audit them, all the books and vouchers pertaining to them, and those that shall be requested from you, and that shall be necessary for the clear understanding of the accounts. You shall continue the administration of your offices with other similar and new books. The accounts shall be balanced in the presence of my governor, and of an auditor of my royal Audiencia who shall be appointed by the governor and the fiscal of the Audiencia. Should any doubts and additions result from the said accounts, the said my governor and auditor shall adjust and decide them, so that they may be balanced and completed."2

"Ordinance 42. You shall send annually the final account of the receipts and expenditures of my royal estate, declaring the same in its distinct heads. In case that an auditor of accounts appointed by the said my governor shall audit your accounts, he shall be obliged to have them made out in accordance with the aforesaid, for the said end."

Book 7, folio 2. August 24 of the same year 605, his Majesty despatched a royal decree, ordering three tribunals of the exchequer to be established in the three cities of Lima, Santa Fe [de Bogota], and Mexico, so that the accounts of all the provinces of their [respective] districts might be audited in each one. Its beginning is as follows:

"Don Felipe, etc.: Inasmuch as the accounts of the income and duties that belong to us and which we are to receive in our kingdoms and provinces of our Western Indias, as king and seignior of them, have been and are audited by the persons who have been and are appointed for it by our viceroys and presidents of the audiencias of the said our Indias, and by the corregidors and governors of some districts of them, who have been and are appointed for it; and inasmuch as they are sent to our royal Council of the Indias, so that they may be reviewed and examined therein; and inasmuch as the persons who audit the said accounts do not possess the skill and experience that is required for such an employment, and the accounts, as they are not furnished every year, do not show the accuracy, clearness, and distinctness that is necessary — whence have resulted many disadvantages and losses to our royal estate, as has been shown by experience: in order that such may cease now and henceforth, and the necessary precaution be exercised in everything, we have decided, after conference, examination, and discussion of the matter in our royal Council of the Indias, and in other meetings of ministers of great intelligence and long experience, that there shall be, and shall be established tribunals of the auditors of accounts who live and reside ordinarily in the said our province, so that they may audit the accounts of whatever pertains to us in any way, or that may pertain in the future to all or any persons into whose possession has entered or shall enter any of our possessions, of which they must and shall inform us. In order that this may be done as is fitting to our service, we have decided, and we will and command, that the following order and form be kept and observed."

The said decree proceeds, by ordering in its first section that the said three tribunals be founded, in each of which there shall be three auditors [contadores], who are to be called and styled "auditors of accounts." They shall attend to their business by virtue of letters and warrants sealed with the royal seal. Each tribunal shall also have two officers known as "arrangers of accounts" [ordenadores de cuentas] and other things that pertain to this. The following declaration occurs in section twenty-two:

"Furthermore, the said our auditors of accounts shall audit and conclude the final account of the said our royal officials and treasury of the said our Yndias for the preceding year, in the year immediately following, without protracting or extending it under any considerations — except that of our royal officials of the province of Chile, and of the persons into whose possession enters the money which we order to be supplied from Piru for the expenses that must be incurred there; and that of the Filipinas Islands, which, as they are so remote and out of the way, must be audited every two years. All the said our officials of the said our royal treasuries in the said our Western Yndias shall be obliged to go, or to send persons with their powers of attorney and adequate documents, to render their accounts before the said our auditors of accounts."

Book 7, folio 28. The ordinance of the above section does not seem to have been observed; for on May 16, 1609, a royal decree was despatched which declares that inasmuch as certain doubts have resulted from the foundation of the three said tribunals, in regard to the exercise of the said offices and their jurisdiction, and other things, the following is declared and ordered anew. And in the said decree many of the ordinances contained in the above-cited decree of the year 605, are declared by sections. Section twenty-four, which concerns this point, reads as follows:

"Section 24. Having examined and considered the difficulties which have been represented in regard to [the officials] being able to go to give the accounts to the said tribunals, for the treasuries of the provinces or islands which are very remote and over seas, I have decided and resolved that the accounts of the provinces of Chile and the Philipinas Islands shall be audited as heretofore, in accordance with the ordinances of the audiencias, notwithstanding any rulings of the said ordinances for the auditors of accounts in regard to sending someone to give it at the tribunals. The accounts which shall be thus audited in the said provinces of Chile shall be sent to the tribunal of accounts at Lima, and those of the Philipinas Islands and Maluco shall be taken to that of Mexico. At the beginning of each year, my officials of those treasuries shall send the lists and muster-rolls of the soldiers to the said tribunals."

Book 7, folio 247. In conformity with the above-cited section, the tribunal of accounts of Mexico despatched a decree in the year 612, ordering the royal officials of the Philipinas to observe and keep it. Notification was given to them, and they obeyed it in the same year.

Book 7, folio 305. It appears in the fulfilment of the said royal decree, and of section twenty-four of it, that the governor of Philipinas gave the title of auditor of accounts and results [*resultas*] to Francisco Lopez Tamayo, October 6, 610, in the following words:

"Inasmuch as his Majesty has ordered that the office of auditor of accounts be again established in this city, so that the accounts of the royal officials of all the royal estate and other royal possessions that ought to be given might be audited, etc."

The title proceeds, appointing him for such time as may be the pleasure of his Majesty and of the said governor in his royal name; and the latter assigns him an annual salary of one thousand pesos of common gold, to be paid from the royal treasury in accordance with the resolution made at the preceding meeting of the treasury on September 30 of the said year.

The above-mentioned tribunal of accounts of the governor and two auditors has punctually fulfilled its duties; and, as well as the said office, still exists — although there has been a change in regard to the title of "auditor of accounts," as will be stated later.

Point 2

In case that your Majesty may be pleased to order that this office exist, will you be pleased also to ordain and determine the manner and form in which it is to be exercised, in order to avoid the differences and encounters that there have been and that may occur between the auditors of accounts and the royal officials. I shall relate in general terms the litigations that they have had hitherto, and the decisions therein of that Audiencia and the tribunal of accounts.

Book 7, folio 252. The first instance of litigation that I find was for the year 620, when the auditor of accounts claimed that the royal officials ought to deliver to him, not only the books and papers that he asked, but also the account in orderly form, in order that he might audit their general account of the preceding year. The royal officials answered thereto that they had never rendered that account, and that they were not bound to do so, but only to deliver to him the books and papers necessary for the verification [of accounts]. The tribunal decided in favor of the royal officials.

Book 7, folio 261, et seq. The second instance of litigation was in the year 625, the auditor of accounts claiming that the royal officials must deliver to him all the books, vouchers, and papers of the treasury for which he asked; and that he could take them to his house, without any time-limit in which they must be returned. The royal officials claimed the very opposite to the above. Therefore, the Audiencia decreed an act on January 2, 626, ordering the auditor of accounts not to take the said papers from the treasury, but to audit the said account there. The auditor of accounts (at that time Luis de Vera Encalada) having entered a petition, the Audiencia enacted on the twenty-seventh of the said month and year that, notwithstanding the above-mentioned act, the said auditor of accounts, in consideration of the ill-health that he alleges, may exercise his duties in his house; but that he may not demand any paper by act from the royal officials except in virtue of the act from the tribunal of accounts for this purpose which proceeds, in which he is under obligation to ask for the papers which shall be necessary. From those which shall be ordered to be delivered to him, he shall select what shall be necessary, and shall return them to the treasury in accordance with the ordinance.

Book 7, folio 344. The third instance of litigation was at that same period, on the question whether the auditor of accounts was to audit the accounts of private persons, who should have to account for royal revenues, or whether he was to review those concluded by the royal officials. The Audiencia ordered that the said auditor of accounts should not audit accounts of that class.

Book 7, folios 77–79. After the year 628, the said tribunal of accounts ordered by an act that the auditor of accounts could make additions to and draw up results [resultas] from the accounts concluded by the royal officials, provided he do it in a separate blankbook without making notes in the royal books.

The fourth instance of litigation was in regard to the question whether he was to be entitled "auditor of accounts" [contador de cuentas] or "auditor-arranger of accounts" [contador ordenador de cuentas]. The royal officials claimed that it should be the second, saying that the name "auditor of accounts" belongs only to those of the three tribunals of Lima, Santa Fe, and Mexico, according to the provision of August 24, 605, and the ordinances therein cited. The auditor of accounts claimed that this name belongs to him by virtue of his office, and because he has always been so called. The ordinances give him that name, as appears by ordinance forty-two given above, and in the warrants despatched by the governors. The Audiencia decreed an act February 14, 626, ordering that he shall not be called "auditor of accounts," but "auditor-arranger of accounts of the royal treasury;" since the auditing of the accounts does not belong to him, but only the arranging of them, so that the president and auditors, the judges of the accounts, may audit them, and conclude and remit them, as is ordained. Thus was he styled until the visitor altered it.

The last and most acrimonious lawsuit was in regard to the form of the sworn relation which the royal officials must give to the auditor of accounts, in order that he may audit the general accounts of each year. Upon this point arose the charge in the visit, the examination of which was the cause of my being ordered to compile this paper. In that contention, the royal officials have claimed that they do not need to give a sworn statement of the amounts that ought to be collected; but that the auditor of accounts must charge himself with that duty in the general account of each year. In case that the royal officials have to give a sworn statement, [they claim] that it is to be only of the debts incurred during their time; and that they do not need to give a general sworn statement, but only a statement of those kinds of royal revenue which are received into that treasury, and are current through their administration — and not of other things which, although they belong to his Majesty, do not enter into that treasury; and which are disbursed before they enter it, and pass through other hands. They allege that in these islands a very different account of the royal revenue is usual from that furnished in other provinces. They availed themselves, for all three points of this claim, of the same sections of the ordinances on which the charge was founded, namely, the sections 14 and 22 of "tribunals of accounts, the decree of the year 605," and section 20 of the decree of the year 60 [sic] explanatory of the tribunals — which, copied word for word, are as follows:

"Book 7, folio 5, section 14. Item: We ordain and command that at the time and when the said accounts are to be audited and completed, and before anything else, both the said our royal officials and other persons — of whatever estate, rank, and condition they may be — who may have received, and have had or have, the duty of receiving and collecting our revenue, must deliver — and they shall deliver — to the said our auditors of accounts, sworn statements, signed with their names, of all that they have received, and all that has been delivered to them, as well as what they have disbursed and distributed. They shall take oath, in the form required by law, at the foot of the said sworn statements, that everything therein contained is accurate, faithful, and true; and that they have not received more maravedis than those entered in their accounts, and that they have [actually] paid out all that which is entered therein as spent and disbursed. They shall bind themselves, with their persons and possessions, that if at any time it appear and be found that they have failed to enter anything of what they have received, or have entered as disbursed any sum in excess of what they have honestly and truly paid out, they shall pay such sum, together with a fine of a sum three times as large—to which we declare them immediately condemned, and order that the penalty be executed on their persons and possessions. One-third part shall be given to the denouncer, one shall be placed in our exchequer, and the remaining third shall be given to the judges who sentence and decide the matter."

"Section 22. Furthermore, the said our auditors of accounts shall audit and conclude the final account of the said our royal officials of the said our Indias for the year preceding, in the year immediately following, without delaying or extending the time, under any consideration whatever—except that of our royal officials of the province of Chile, and of the persons in whose possession enters the money that we order to be supplied from Piru for the expenses which shall be incurred there; and the accounts of the Filipinas Islands, which, as those islands are so remote and out of the way, shall be audited every two years. All the said our officials of the said our royal treasuries which we possess in the said our Western Indias, shall be obliged to go, or to send persons with their powers and sufficient authority, to render their accounts before the said our auditors of accounts, except those who shall audit the accounts of our royal officials of the imperial city of Potosi, which shall be done as will be declared hereafter. And in the said accounts that shall be audited and concluded for all, entry shall be made of all the said our incomes and duties, which pertain and ought to pertain to us in any manner, in the said year as abovesaid, notwithstanding that they may say and allege that they have not collected nor can collect it; and the balances of their total shall be struck. If they shall present sufficient evidence from which it appears that they made the efforts necessary at the time when they were obliged, and that they were unable to collect it, they shall be given a brief respite from paying such balance, which, as above said, shall have been struck against them, which time shall be long enough for them to collect it or place it in the said our treasury. And should they, upon the expiration of that time, not have executed it or presented sufficient evidence that they have made the efforts necessary for its collection, they and their bondsmen shall be proceeded against by the full rigor of law, in order that they may place and deposit the amount due in the said our royal treasury. In regard to this action, the necessary executions and investigations shall be made, and by maravedis of our treasury. If it shall appear from the evidence that they shall present, that they have made the necessary efforts, and have been unable to collect, and that they have discharged their duty in this regard, the amount of their accounts shall be received on account, and the said our auditors of accounts shall make the new efforts that appear expedient for its collection, until it shall have been paid into the said our treasury."

"Section 20 of the explanatory decree. Book 7, folio 16. By section 22 of the ordinances of the said auditors of accounts, and by other royal decrees, is ordained the manner in which my royal officials of my royal revenues, and of the rest of my estate which is in their charge, with obligation to collect those revenues, or show sufficient efforts, shall be held responsible. I have been informed that the said auditors of accounts undertake, when they audit the accounts of the said my royal officials, to proceed according to this order; but that the said my royal officials are generally accustomed to appeal from some things, and bring a suit. That causes delay and other troubles, for the correction of which I ordain and command the said auditors of accounts to audit the accounts of the said my royal officials, charging them with all my incomes and the other property which must enter into their possession with obligation of collecting it, or else proving [that they have made] sufficient efforts for what shall not have been collected, in accordance with what has been enacted by the said ordinances for auditors [contadores] and other decrees; and in no manner shall the said my royal officials be allowed to appeal to the law until what has been ordained regarding this matter be observed and executed."

Book 7, folio 87. On those three sections the visitor based his charge and the royal officials their rebuttal. The visitor ordered that, notwithstanding what they alleged, the royal officials should give a sworn statement of the collections made and of those still due, for the general account of the year 631.

In charge 3. The disadvantage and loss to the royal treasury alleged by the visitor, because the statements are not so given, is that that has resulted in there being more than sixty thousand pesos of royal revenue to collect, of which results [resultas] have been made in the visit against the said royal officials, besides others that are being made.

Point 3

In regard to the inconveniences from having this office or tribunal in those islands, I do not find that the royal officials of the islands, who are the ones who could best make such a representation, have made it. They have only opposed the jurisdiction and authority that the auditor of accounts has possessed or claimed to possess for the exercise of his duty; and they declare that the tribunal of accounts of those islands, which is composed of the governor and two auditors [oidores] is the one that truly holds and exercises this ministry of the auditing department of accounts, and that the auditor [contador] whom they call "auditor of accounts" cannot be that official, and cannot be so called, but only "auditor-arranger of accounts." They say that it is not fitting for one man alone to be superior to the tribunal of the royal officials, for thereby is lost their authority and the superiority and influence that they ought to have for the efficient management and exercise of their duties; and that the expenses incurred with the said auditor of accounts and his clerks ought to be dispensed with, for the said reasons. In this regard what appears from the records of the visit is that Governor Don Juan de Silva, in a treasury meeting held in the year 610 (Book 7, folio 301), resolved to assign to the auditor of accounts and results [resultas] (joining those two offices, which had up to that time been divided) a salary of 1,000 pesos of common gold per annum, payable from the royal treasury, for the work of both offices. Until that time, it appears that the auditors of accounts had had only one official notary of accounts, with 250 pesos of salary per annum. By the said resolution it was raised to 300 pesos; and the clerks were increased by three, each with 200 pesos salary per annum—in consideration of the fact that there were many accounts in arrears to catch up with, and that the said two offices were joined into one. Other appointments resembling the one aforesaid were made in the persons of Pedro de Leuzarra, in the year 618, and Luis de Vera Encalada, in the year 620. At this time the said chief official notary of this exchequer was given a salary of 450 pesos, without its appearing when or why this increase was granted; and that same practice was continued. In the year 626, Alonso Garcia de la Vega was appointed with the title of "auditor-arranger" (Book 7, folio 65), in accordance with the act of the Audiencia above mentioned. In the year 629, Juan Baptista de Zubiaga was appointed [In the margin: "Memorial, folio 266, Book 1, folios 49, 128"] with the title of "auditor-arranger," and four clerks, of whom we shall treat at the end of this paper, its proper place.

Against the statements of the royal officials, in regard to its being possible to avoid those expenses, the auditor of accounts, Luis de Encalada, stated in the year 625, in the suit that he had with them, that they could not be avoided, for the tribunal of accounts, consisting of the governor and two auditors [oidores] cannot personally arrange or audit them, both because of their occupations and because it is outside their profession; and their only duty is to dispose of the uncertainties and results [resultas] which may be proposed to them by the auditor of accounts.

[Point 4]

Papers of the secretary's office. In regard to the advantages in having this office or tribunal, it seems that Governor Don Alonso Faxardo, in a letter of August 10, 619,3 petitioned your Majesty to have intelligent persons sent as clerks; and informed your Majesty that he had appointed Pedro de Leuzarra, a trustworthy person, auditor of accounts, because of the incompetency of Francisco Lopez Tamayo. The Council, upon examining that letter, decreed, November 17, 620, that persons be named for that office, and that it was to be filled from that time thenceforth by his Majesty; and accordingly the appointment by the governor must cease.

That decree does not appear to have had any effect; for since that time and until the present, as has been seen, the governors have filled that office, notwithstanding that the Council gave that advice in the said year, and your Majesty granted the office to Alvaro de Revolledo. As it was then believed that the salary of this office was 500 pesos, the said Alvaro de Revolledo petitioned that it be increased to 2,000 ducados or to 510,000 maravedis, the same as that of the royal officials of those islands, so that he could exercise the said office with greater authority. No decision was made on the petition, and the said Alvaro de Rebolledo was afterward appointed to the accountancy of San Miguel de Piura, with a salary of 300 pesos ensayados.

The tribunal of accounts of Mexico state, in a letter of June 27, 625, that they have seen the necessity, from what they have examined of the accounts of the said Filipinas Islands, of sending a person to visit them who can adjust affairs pertaining to the expenses of the royal estate of those islands, and lay down a system [of conducting them] for the future. The person who must go should be of the ability, authority, and qualifications that the matter demands. He should be highly compensated and honored, in order that his office be respected and the end in view obtained. It is the most important action for your Majesty's service, and has most need of reform.

It appears that the said Alvaro de Rebolledo again petitioned, in the year 626, that his warrant be despatched to him, with the salary that your Majesty might be pleased to grant him, so that, its value being known, he might be able to fulfil his duties. February 19, 626, it was decreed by the Council that he should be heard. Thereupon, the Council ordered the viceroy to investigate this matter, and to submit a relation of whatever had happened in regard to the office of auditor of accounts of Manila, and whether this office is necessary, whether it be for life, and what are its qualifications and duties; and of the tribunal of accounts. In obedience to this order, the viceroy, Marquis de Cerralbo, in a letter of May 22, 627, states that what he understands is that it is necessary that this office be permanent, and that very suitable persons trained in the tribunal of accounts and the other duties of the royal estate, should be found [for it]; and that it will be advisable that the official who should exercise it be approved by the governor of Filipinas.

The tribunal of accounts of Mexico, in a letter of May 28, of the same year 627, sent a report regarding the aforesaid which had been drawn up, by order of the viceroy, by one of the auditors [oidores] of the tribunal, Gaspar Bello de Acuña. In this it is declared that it is necessary that not only should the accounts of the royal treasury in Manila be audited, but also the accounts of all the royal estate which should be in the keeping of any person whatever; for this was a thing that has never been customary there, or had regular course, because of the resistance offered by the royal officials. The said accounts are of much more importance than any others; and it is therefore important to appoint a person who is thoroughly competent and reliable to inspect everything pertaining to the royal estate of the said islands; for the accountants hitherto appointed have been remiss in their proceedings. That has arisen from the poverty of the country, and from all being united there; or because those who try to proceed with any show of thoroughness in your Majesty's service do not find aid in those who can give it in a matter that is of so great importance; and because this office, from what is understood of the condition of the royal estate in those islands, is subject to ordinary occupation and residence, and has a salary of one thousand pesos per annum. Since not more than one is appointed, he will need a clerk to help him in the methodical arrangement of the said accounts, and what is dependent on them. For the said office of accountant, a fully competent person, and one of abilities, will be needed. He should be well equipped, and honored with the necessary writs of prohibition for matters pertaining to his office, and with the privileges that may pertain to it. It is advisable that he should be sent as visitor of all things that concern the royal estate, to audit the accounts that are to be audited, and review those that are concluded, notwithstanding the visitor-general appointed; for the latter cannot have the intelligence, experience, and method which your Majesty orders to be exercised in such matters — which are understood only by those who have gained their knowledge in the chief bureau of accounts of those kingdoms. Such a person can be appointed with a time-limit, and, at the expiration of that time, he may return; and another man of skill and experience may remain as the ordinary and usual one, with the title of "auditor of accounts" for your Majesty; and he should receive the ordinary salary that your Majesty cares to grant him, and have a clerk to help him.

The Council, upon examination of the above-mentioned reports, decreed on December 6, 627, that the papers that occasioned them should be collected, and taken to the Council. From that time, it does not appear that anything pertaining to this matter has been done in or out of the Council until the year 631, upon the arrival of the visitor, Licentiate Don Francisco de Rojas, at the said islands. He having found Juan Baptista Zubiaga holding the said office of auditor-arranger of accounts and results [*resultas*], by the appointment of the governor in the year 629, ordered the said Juan Baptista to cease to exercise his duties, and to bring the papers in his charge to the visitor's office; and ruled that there the said Juan Baptista and Diego Ortiz de Vargas, auditor [*contador*] of the visit, should together review all the accounts of the royal treasury and estate, with four other clerks. They were to receive the following salaries: the said Diego de Ortiz de Vargas, 2,000 ducados; the said Juan Baptista, 1,000 pesos, the same as he had received before [when exercising his office]; to one clerk 400 pesos, to another, 350, to another 300, and to the fourth 200.

Later, at the end of the visit in the year 633, the said visitor gave the said Juan Baptista de Zubiaga the title of "auditor of accounts and results" [resultas] with a salary of 1,000 ducados per annum, increasing his salary [In the margin: "Memorial, folio 266"] because of the extra work which he would have in collecting [the amounts due from] the results [resultas] which remained drawn in his possession. He was to get a confirmation from your Majesty for the increase, namely, from the 1,000 pesos which he received before to the 1,000 ducados assigned to him by the visitor, within six years. Besides the above, he was to have two clerks to assist him and commission to audit all the accounts, both general and private, pertaining to the royal estate. [In the margin: "The title is to be found in the collection of papers for the claim of this man in regard to the confirmation."]

He made rules in regard to its execution, and ordered them to be obeyed and observed, and to be inscribed in the royal books for that purpose. Although the royal officials were opposed to both things, the visitor ordered them to obey the enactment. Because the said royal officials refused to inscribe the said ordinances in the royal books, he fined them five hundred ducados apiece, which remained in the royal treasury. He had those ordinances inscribed in the books, getting the books for that purpose from the royal treasury, for the royal officials refused to do it [In the margin: "Memorial, folio 266"]. In the report made for your Majesty by the said visitor in the year 634, regarding the visit, he states that he thinks that those islands have the greatest need of a tribunal of the bureau of accounts, so that the accounts of the royal treasury may be audited there annually for the preceding year, and results made of all for which warrants have been improperly issued, and that has failed to be collected, thus avoiding the delays which have occurred hitherto. It is very necessary to have not only the said auditor of accounts appointed by him in the said bureau of accounts, but also a greater force of men and more authority in the said bureau of accounts. If that course had been pursued hitherto, it is undeniable that so great a quantity of funds would not have been badly administered, lost, and uncollectible. In his opinion, those islands have much greater need of a tribunal or a bureau of accounts than of an Audiencia, president, and auditors [oidores].

By a certification given by the said auditor of accounts and of the visit, Juan Baptista Zubiaga, it appears that the results [resultas] drawn up against the royal officials and other private persons during the visit amounted to six hundred and ninety-five thousand and sixty pesos.

The governor of Filipinas, in a letter written to your Majesty August 10, 634,4 declares that it will be advisable that your Majesty be pleased to send an auditor of accounts, and that such auditor should be a person of authority, who shall receive an adequate salary; and states that he who is holding that office ad interim was a servant of one of the auditors [oidores] of those islands, and thinks more of spending his time in maintaining his friendships than in attending to what is necessary. He thinks that with the above appointment, and the correction of some recent ordinances, the condition of affairs would be improved.

A report made from the secretary's office having been examined in the Council on September 26, 635, regarding what appeared to be there on this matter, it was ordered that your fiscal should examine it; and that, after also examining what advices had been received concerning it and the letters of the visitor, he should inform the Council in regard to it all. The said your fiscal declared that the ordinances and papers sent by the royal officials had come without authentication; and therefore, until they should come with that requisite, he had nothing to say.

This defect no longer operates, for the above-mentioned ordinances have arrived duly authenticated, in the body of the [records of the] visit; and the officials, in a letter in which they set forth the objections to those ordinances, have sent some authenticated papers for the proof of their statements.

On February 20, 637, the papers on the matter having been examined in the Council, it was ordered that they be taken to your fiscal, with the rest of the papers concerning the visit that touch the royal estates and its accounts — so that, upon receiving his statement, the advisable decision may be made as to whether it is best to send an auditor of accounts to Filipinas, or not. It does not appear that the said your fiscal has as yet answered. This is the condition that appears from the above-cited records; and your Majesty will ordain the measures that seem best to you.

1 Arts. 67 and 69, here cited, are respectively 60 and 62 in the original document (May 5, 1583) founding the Audiencia at Manila—for which see vol. v of this series, pp. 294, 295; cf. duties of fiscal, p. 302. These differences of numbering, and some additional matter in No. 67, show that considerable additions to the old decree were required at the reëstablishment of the Audiencia.

2 This ordinance is contained in the first part of ley x, titulo xxix, libro viii, of the Recopilación de leyes. See Vol. XVI of this series, p. 193, note 251.

3 See the letter by Fajardo, here referred to, in Vol. XVIII, pp. 247–279.

4 See this letter in Vol. XXIV, p. 301.

The Conquest of Mindanao

Letter from Father Marcelo Francisco Mastrili,1 in which he gives account of the conquest of Mindanao to Father Juan de Zalazar,2 provincial of the Society of Jesus in the Filipinas Islands.

Gratia, et pax Christi, etc.

I would by no means have expected, Father, your Reverence's command to inform you of our expedition to Mindanao, had you known that the letters which I wrote to Father Juan de Bueras from Lamitan had remained at Sanboanga; because, since I recounted in them, with much detail, all the events of the conquest of Mindanao, I asked him to read them to your Reverence, so that, without fatiguing yourself with my separate letter, you might know what had happened. And now, having in obedience to your command, departed for Taytay, I will here relate to you faithfully as much as I can remember.

Your Reverence of course knows how Don Sebastian Hurtado de Corcuera, governor of these islands, having determined on the expedition to Mindanao, called a general council of war, in which all were of adverse opinion, saving only his nephew, Sargento-mayor Don Pedro Hurtado de Corcuera. In spite of this, constrained by desire for his own glory, and for the honor of the two Majesties, the human and the divine, he resolved, notwithstanding the contrary opinion of the entire council, to persevere in his pious intentions. On the day, therefore, of the Purification of our Lady, February second of this year 1637, having with all the soldiers attended confession and communion in the chapels of the palace, he ordered them to embark in eleven champans, which were already provided for this purpose. Father Juan de Barrios and I embarked in the flagship with his Lordship, and Sargento-mayor Don Marcos Zapata, whom he brought for a companion, and to sit at his table. The priest Don Juan, chaplain of the fleet, sailed on the almiranta, with Sargento-mayor Don Pedro Hurtado de Corcuera; and an Augustinian friar came, as confessor for the Pampangos, in Lorenço Ugalde's champan.

The previous day a letter had come from the archbishop, stating that there were eighty hostile caracoas at the island of Mindanao; so his Lordship, in order to surprise them, sailed with five champans for the opposite and outer coast of the island, and directed Captain Ugalde to skirt the inner coast, with the rest of the boats, as far as Point Nasso,3 on the shore of the island of Othon. The fact that they found no trace of enemies anywhere, stamped the report as false, and as inspired by the effort of the devil for the purpose of hindering us in our journey; for we were compelled, by taking this route, to toil for more than twelve days in order to cover the distance of twelve leguas to this Point Nasso in Othon, the brisas being dead ahead when we attempted to round the cape. One day when (an opportunity offering) we were trying to double it, the fury of the wind and the sea was so great that we broke the steering-gear, and there was great danger of the ship's foundering, and of our being drowned. I would have been drowned more quickly than anyone else, for, being at the stern, I became entangled with the sheets of the sail,4 at the time of the furious and unexpected turn which the ship (being no longer under control) gave, through the force of the wind.

So great, in fact, was the rage and pain which the evil one suffered on account of our expedition, and what he already feared [from it] that, as I afterward knew with certainty, he often complained to a certain person, speaking in an audible voice in the woods, saying: "Why come ye? What do ye seek? Who brought you here? Curses on you; I will deprive you of life, and we will have done with this!" I did not believe this at the time, as coming from the father of lies; but he taught us later, by experience, how much he did to make his word good.

Now, although all these things were enough in themselves to cause some trouble, yet the most agreeable conversation of his Lordship, with the pious division which he made of the hours of the day, left the evil one no opportunity. For, in the morning, Father Juan de Barrios and I said mass; there with his Lordship we recited the canonical hours, the office to our Lady, matins, and the prayers for the dead; in the afternoon at vespers, the same prayers, and the holy matins, and the prayers to the Virgin; in the early evening we had the Salve [i.e., "Hail, Mary"], with the public litany; and at night prayers for the souls in purgatory, usually relating some miracle, which was of great profit to many. Nor need your Reverence think that we lost any time because of the contrariety of the winds at Point Nasso that I mentioned; for orders were despatched to the Pintados Islands by the Indian volunteers, and sent to Othon with the falua5 by Adjutant Don Francisco Olozaran—who returned in a champan with the father rector of Othon, Father Francisco Angel,6 and Father Gregorio Belin. The latter was going from Samboanga to Manila to give his Lordship the news of the victory won by Sargento-mayor Nicolas Gonçalez over seven caracoas from Mindanao, which were returning, with some slaves and sacred ornaments, from plundering the islands. The father rector brought with him from Othon excellent provisions, and afterward he gave the whole fleet much better at Iloilo. His Lordship arrived at that place with the aforesaid father, in the falua, three days before we did, in order to have time to visit the fort, and see whether the boats of Captain Briones were prepared for the relief of our troops in Mindanao. On the arrival of the champans, Father Angel disembarked, to return to his mission in the island of Negros; and the father rector of Othon embarked in Captain Martin Monte's champan, with his Lordship's orders for Samboanga, which place we reached on the twenty-second of February.

Here his Lordship commanded that neither the [cannon of the] fort nor the musketry should be discharged at his approach, in order not to make a noise and thus make his presence known; and for the same reason he ordered that no vessels should go out of the river. In spite of all this Corralat soon knew of his coming, through the son of a chief of Basilan, who at that time was imprisoned in the fort of Samboanga, with orders that he was not to be released except upon urgent request by the [Jesuit] fathers, so that in this way they might secure the goodwill of the Moros. The next day general communion was proclaimed, together with an indulgence and full jubilee for the whole camp, for the first Sunday in Lent—his Lordship obliging all the soldiers to give certificates of confession and communion to their officers; and he had his own servants do the same thing, for I found him one day collecting the certificates with his own hands. All this was done with great fervor, and with many general confessions, in which the continual discourses and sermons of those days aided greatly. All received communion on Sunday with his Lordship, the blessed sacrament being exposed, and all were present later at Father Berlin's [sic] sermon. In the evening, at the time of replacing the Host, his Lordship was again present with all the soldiery, because he had appointed me in the morning to preach the evening sermon on the reverence and devotion necessary to be observed in church, in the presence of so great a Majesty. This I did to the best of my ability, at the end inspiring the soldiers for the campaign, and inciting them to battle by showing them, painted on canvas,7 a figure of Christ, whose feet and right arm the Moros had cut off; in the middle of it they had made a large hole, using the cloth as a chinina, or small mantle. This a Moro actually wore, and they killed him while he had it on, the day when Nicolas Gonçalez captured the caracoas. Father Berlin brought it with the sacred ornaments to his Lordship; and he, knowing that I had been on the lookout for some such thing in Manila, as soon as he saw it at Point Nasso, gave it to me. When I showed this image to the soldiers, and exhorted them to avenge with arms the injuries of the holy Christ, such were the tears, and so great the tender devotion and holy desire for vengeance with which they were fired, that (as they afterward told me) they would, on leaving the church, have been willing to offer battle with all the world [against them]. The effects were very marked, and much tenderness [of feeling was displayed], so that at last it was openly said that the mother who had no sons in this glorious enterprise was very unfortunate.

With this fervor and so excellent preparation, the champans departed on the trip to Mindanao,8 which is sixty leguas from Samboanga, on the third of March, and on the fourth all the rest of us set out, with his Lordship, in eleven caracoas. In all, four companies embarked, three of Spaniards, and one of Pampangos. His Lordship's company consisted of a hundred and fifty soldiers; Nicolas Gonçalez had one hundred, and Ugalde as many more, who were seamen; the master-of-camp had that of the Pampangos. I would not fail to write of what happened on Tuesday, when the champans departed. We all wished that his Lordship would not go until Saturday, that we might see whether some of the Indian scouts would not return in the meanwhile; but I did not wish to ask it from him until I had commended the matter to God. I asked the father rector to say mass to St. Francis Xavier for my intention, and I also said it. Then we withdrew into a room, and, after suitable prayer, his Lordship opened the book of the letters of that saint (which I hold to be a divine guide), pointing out beforehand the part which was to be read, and these were the words: Many times we think that our own opinion might be better; nevertheless, we must leave affairs to Him who governs them, if we wish to succeed. The will of the saint was plain to be seen, nor did I desire to contrive further speech about the arrangements with his Lordship. And truly all things were guided by Heaven in order to give him the glorious victory which he attained—to the confusion of the Moros and the undeceiving of the Indians, who now know that the Spaniards can, when they choose, fight in their territory without them.

In the gulf of La Silanga we met with a very severe and dangerous tempest, of which we rid ourselves by exorcisms and sacred relics, as is our way in dealing with things evidently planned by the evil one. Here Nicolas Gonçalez waited with eight caracoas to tow the champans through La Silanga, which is a strait of the sea two leguas long, between the great island of Mindanao and another and small island. His Lordship, with four of the caracoas, went to Punta de Flechas, so called from the ceremony and superstition of the Moros in shooting arrows at one of its rocks when they are returning to their own country, to show their thankfulness to Mahomet. Here we remained for two days, awaiting the vessels of the fleet; during this time I said mass on shore, having beforehand uttered tremendous conjurations against the evil one, as holy Mother Church is wont to do, with her exorcisms, holy water, etc. Then our people burned all the arrows, of infinite number, that were fixed on that headland, with a thousand other things—articles of food, such as fish, eggs, etc.—which, as a sign of their devotion, they are wont to leave fastened to the rock with black pegs. We set up a number of crosses in different places, and then the name of the place was solemnly changed to Punta de San Sebastian, in order that that saint, with his holy arrows, might complete the destruction of those infernal and accursed ones which for so many years have vexed us. The name was given also in commemoration of the fact that Don Sebastian [i.e., Corcuera] has been the first governor to cast anchor here and to round this cape; besides this, the marvelous fall of this rock in the night when Nicolas Gonçalez fought within sight of it, we all attribute to this saint, who desired to give to Don Sebastian pledges for the glorious campaign of Mindanao, since only that part of the rock fell which faced toward Mindanao—as we all saw with wonder. While we were here, a light vessel came from the enemy to reconnoiter our fleet; our falua gave chase, but, being very far away, could not overtake it. We, however, encountered a small boat containing four of our Indian captives who had fled from the enemy; they informed us that several Javanese ships were on the point of departure from Mindanao, laden with Christian slaves. I confess to your Reverence that this was not news to his Lordship, but he was cut to the heart by the misery of so many souls, and he at once decided to sail night and day in order to overtake the ships. This holy zeal was the sole and true reason for his pushing on without halt till he came up with them, instead of waiting for his fleet; and he was well rewarded by Heaven with so fortunate a victory, as your Reverence will see.

Now the evil spirit, who for so many years had dwelt at this Punta de Flechas, undertook to oppose us and hinder our advance. For three times, by the violence of the wind and sea, we were turned back; and the fourth time, without any contrary wind, we remained motionless for more than an hour, although our caracoa had ninety *barrigas* (as they call rowers on the Pintados Islands). Thus the work of the evil one was plainly to be seen; but, by casting a few holy relics into the sea and pronouncing exorcisms, as before, we soon passed on.

These deceptions and obstacles of the invisible enemy being overcome, we came in sight of Mindanao, without recognizing it, on Friday the thirteenth of March, with four caracoas. When I had finished saying mass—this was before dawn—his Lordship embarked in the falua, and with only six soldiers went to reconnoiter the place, to sound the rivers and harbors of the coast, and to see whether any Moro who could serve as a guide might be captured, for we had none. He pursued several of them up to their own shore, discharged two muskets at them, and nevertheless they fled up the river, abandoning their vessels. In response to these shots, the report of a cannon was heard from inland; this gave us much cause for fear, seeing that his Lordship was so bold, and we dreaded lest he had engaged with the enemy. Then we recited the litany, and other prayers; and, rowing as fast as possible, met them coming back. The governor embarked in his caracoa at eleven o'clock in the morning, and placed in order all four of the caracoas, with the two champans of our fleet—those of Captains Don Rodrigo and Ugalde, which had arrived three days before, and captured three caracoas from the enemy.9 From another direction there came, under a white flag, a letter from the Recollect fathers whom the Moros held captive there, that [our men?] should inform them of what was going on. He cast anchor near the mouth of the river, where some huts were to be seen, without knowing what village it was;10 and turning to me, said: "I will quarter my men in those cabins tonight." Then he ordered all to eat; and having sent Adjutant Don Francisco Olazaran to land with twenty-five musketeers to seize the shore, and sounding the trumpets and the drums, discharging the ship's cannon in the direction of the harbor, his Lordship disembarked, with all his soldiers—who, between Spaniards and Pampangos, amounted to seventy men. The sargento-mayor of the forces and the admiral of the fleet, Don Pedro Hurtado de Corcuera, drew up the forces on the beach, placing, at his Lordship's direction, two field-pieces in the vanguard; and these were the terror of the enemy. Here, after I had aroused and encouraged the soldiers with the [sight of the] miraculous picture of St. Francis Xavier on one side, and that of the holy Christ (which I mentioned above) on the other—the two suspended from a lance—I walked between the vanguard and the body of the troops, with Father Juan de Barrios, the Augustinian father, and the chaplain of the fleet, which line of march we preserved during the whole campaign. At the time when we were disembarking one of our captive Indians came swimming toward us from the land, and we learned from him that this was the port of Corralat; but he was in such terror of the many musket-shots which the Moros, on seeing us, fired at him from an ambuscade which they had prepared against our people, that he could tell us nothing more. And so we marched on without knowing whether in the aforesaid port there were any force of arms or soldiers; we took for granted that what had always been said of the place was true—namely, that all the defenses of Corralat were upon the hill above, and not in the town below. Yet because this was the cause of God, where human means failed, I besought His Divine Majesty, together with the saints, to illumine with especial light his Lordship [the governor], so that, leaving the open road from the shore to the town, he should march with his soldiers by the road on the right. This route compelled us to cross the river twice, with considerable difficulty for the two cannon and for the person of his Lordship, who plunged into the water with all the rest of the soldiers. In spite of all this, it saved us from two very great dangers: one of them the armed ambuscade on the left side of the road, in the thickly-wooded part of a little hill—which we could hardly have escaped, as the road was very marshy, and was blocked by reeds, fruit plantations, and houses. The other peril was even greater; all the cannon of the fort were trained in the aforesaid direction [toward the left], and could not harm us, because they could not be turned to the right. The truth is that they had trained two chambered culverins very low against our path at the foot of the fortification—which would doubtless have done us much injury, but, through their great fear and confusion, no one succeeded in firing them.

After God had delivered us, without our knowing it, from perils so great, considering the small numbers of our expedition, his Lordship was marching in the vanguard, by the road which he had miraculously chosen. We had crossed the river for the first time, and the artillery and musketry were soon clearing the field as far as a stockade near the river, where the Moros made their first stand. Here it happened that, upon his Lordship's going forward for a moment to see what enemy lay behind the stockade, four Moros set upon him with their campilans; he very swiftly faced about, to fire at them his gun, which a negro at his side always bore; and, not seeing the servant (for he had fallen a little behind), his Lordship fell to with his sword, with such spirit that the Moros, disheartened, soon fled. In spite of this, one of the Moros—Borongon, Corralat's most valiant captain—going out most courageously from the other side of the stockade, tried to prevent our men (who were now ready to cross the river for the second time) from attacking the fort, which had been descried from this first stockade. He valiantly wounded two, and, for a third, attacked Captain Lorenço de Ugalde who was leading half the troops in this direction—the rest, under Captain Don Rodrigo, marching along the right bank of the river, where a great number of Moros was now gathering. Captain Ugalde parried with his shield the first two blows of the campilan; and then, rushing in with his sword, gave Borongon many wounds in the face, being unable to reach his breast because of the arms that the Moro carried; but he forced him to retire. His retreat, however, availed but little, because of the furious musket-fire of our men; and finally Don Francisco Olaceran's sword completed the work, and the Moro captain went into the river. And now, after this man's death, our troops went on, without further resistance, to the fort. It was furnished with a new moat, and was full of arms; and it had eight pieces of artillery in bronze, twenty-seven culverins [versos], many muskets with rests [?; de pinsote], arquebuses, and other hand-arms. There was a garrison of more than two thousand Moros for the fortress and the port, as we were told by Sosocan (a Moro friendly to us, and very well informed in regard to the equipment and strength of Corralat). All this profited them little, however; for so pressing was our attack that very soon we were masters of all, and Alférez Amesquita raised his flag above the fort. Many Moros had been killed, and the rest fled badly wounded, as we learned on the following day from our prisoners. At this place we killed the commander of the fort, a grandson of Corralat—the son of one of his daughters, who had married the lord of the lake11 [country]—a very spirited youth, of whom his grandfather was very fond. He had that day vowed to Mahomet not to abandon the fort until his death, and thus he fulfilled his promise.

Seeing now our flags on the enemy's stockade, we soon, with his Lordship, crossed the river for the second time; and climbing up on the other side, I also raised my standard, that of Christ and St. Francis Xavier. We all sang the Te Deum laudamus; and, after his Lordship had given the name of St. Francis Xavier to the fort and had left Alférez Amesquita as its governor, with a garrison of soldiers, we advanced to the rear of a stockade which Corralat defended with its one cannon, and to the mosque. Here the Moros had rallied for the last time, trusting in what their captain-general [condestable] had told them, that they were not to retreat until they saw him fall. He believed, by some witchcraft or other, that our bullets could not injure him; and he had had proof of this, for once a ball had broken the bone of his leg, crippling him, but without breaking the skin or drawing blood. In this confidence, he came out with his men to defy us, but Captain Zubire at once leveled his musket at him, and sent two balls through his forehead; this was the only portion of his body uncovered, the rest of it being protected by an English shield. The wretched man fell dead on the spot, and instantly all the rest in the stockade and the mosque lost courage, left their arms, and fled with all possible speed to the woods. At this same time Don Rodrigo, marching with his detachment between the slope of the hill and the river, charged the enemy so valiantly that by force he compelled them to abandon all their ships—which, for fear of us, they had hidden two days before in a broad inlet to this same river. Here they thought the ships would be safe, because they had brought them in so quietly, and because the place was so far away from the mouth of the river.

Thus in a little more than half an hour we gained possession of all below [the hill], and we would have captured the heights above on the same day, had we had all our forces, for the Moros fled in so great fright that Corralat himself had covered his face with mud so as not to be recognized by our men. This was told us by one of his servants, a Christian, who came to us the following morning, reporting a great number of Moros wounded— especially the king of the Lake, who was suffering with a bullet-wound in the breast; he had come to celebrate some marriage, that of a cousin of his with a daughter of Corralat. From this captive, and others, we learned that Corralat had desired, in any event, to surrender to the governor, but that the Christians had not consented to this, and had persuaded him to make a defense, promising that they would fight in the front rank. This promise they fulfilled, especially the day of the assault upon the hill, for it was they who did us the most injury; but they paid the penalty of this advice, not only with the property which we took from their ships, but with their lives, which the Moros themselves took in anger at their bad advice.

After the fight, the soldiers commenced to sack the houses; and the governor, having seen all the ships as far as the river above, retired with those who had accompanied him, to the mosque. Here the first thing that was done was to take the great chair of Mahomet, with his books and other paraphernalia, and burn them. What we saw when we came to take out this throne certainly surprised us; for, before we reached the fire, two most venomous serpents came out from the feet of the chair, terrifying the soldiers greatly. And truly, nothing other than serpents and poison ought to guard the chair of the great devil of Mindanao. When the chair was burned, together with all else that savored of superstition, we consecrated the mosque to our Lady with the *Salve*; and early the next morning (which was Saturday, the fourteenth of March), having dedicated the church to God with the title of "Our Lady of Good Fortune," we commenced to say masses in it, at a very beautiful altar, which served us during the twelve days while we were there.

This same mosque, being very large and conveniently situated, served for headquarters; his Lordship and the other captains lodged there, the other houses round about being used for the soldiers—although our being on the bank of the river, very near the woods, and somewhat distant from the fort, brought it about that every night the Moros attacked us. Because of the continual showers of rain that fall at night, they might have given us a great deal of trouble (since we cannot use firearms when it is wet), if his Lordship's wise arrangements and planning had not provided for everything; for after having fortified the road to the hill with a very strong ravelin guarded by soldiers, etc., great fires burned every night around the camp. The sentinels continually called out the watchword; and all the sargentos-mayor and captains, and often his Lordship himself, made the rounds. The Moros, therefore, seeing us always vigilant, dared not attack us openly, but a few of the bravest tried their fortune in attacking us, and these were often at the mouth of the river, when our men were going to or from the fleet. One night, returning from visiting the sick, I was there in a small champan, with only Captain Rodrigo and four Sangleys—who, in their fear, not seeing the way ran the boat on a shoal. It certainly was a miracle of God that the Moros did not notice this; for, if they had, they would surely have killed us. I escaped at that place another great danger, for, not knowing that by day the Moros lay continually in ambuscade in some little huts quite a distance from the fort, I went each day among them; and it pleased God that they never saw me. When his Lordship learned of these ambuscades, he ordered the huts burned.

The vessels which were in the river the first day could not be taken to the fort until the next day, the tide being low. There were more than thirty of these ships—large, medium-sized, and small—the greater part of them laden with a thousand things, especially five or six very large vessels from Java, full of wax, oil, rice, and other articles of merchandise. All our people had the benefit of these things, except of a certain quantity of wax, which was kept for the king, together with a great number of arms. There were eight cannon of bronze, with ladles; twenty-seven versos, a cast-iron pedrero, a great many chambers for versos, and more than a hundred muskets and arquebuses; and an infinite quantity of bullets, iron, powder, arrows, and sompites, a kind of little arrow which they shoot by means of blowpipes12—so poisonous that, unless very powerful remedies are soon applied, it kills in a few hours. Other implements of warfare were found in the powder-house, which we used as barracks for the Pampangos.

The next day the rest of the champans and caracoas of our fleet began to arrive, and the governor at once appointed Captain Mena as head of the fleet for all the time while we should be at Mindanao. For governor of Fort St. Francis Xavier, he chose Sargento-mayor Palomino, who fortified it and put it in order, fencing it in on all sides, with its port-holes and defenses, and adding around it a hidden rampart with embrasures, so that it could contain two ranks of artillery and musketry. On this enterprise Don Pedro Hurtado de Corcuera worked very hard, for he is especially skilled in the

Flemish mode of fortification; and the governor himself gave the plan for the building and his hands for the work, turning the first earth with the spade.

Two days more, Sunday and Monday, were spent in making many sorties and in burning many neighboring places, Captain Rodrigo with his men traveling by land, and Captain Ugalde with his, by sea, until they reached the former dwelling of Corralat, which is called Puerto de las Savanillas.13 They burned all the houses, together with many other villages and some large ships which they found concealed in a river. The other soldiers who remained in the camp busied themselves in launching all the sunken caracoas (which were many) with which the Moros were wont to make raids; and in searching out whatever was buried. This included many chambers for versos; also iron, wax, and three bells—besides the large one which stood at the door of the mosque, mouth upward, full of water in which the Moros washed their feet before entering the mosque.

On this Sunday morning, his Lordship sent also to Samboanga a Moro caracoa full of our Christian prisoners and Sangleys, who had been coming in great numbers to the camp since the first day, especially on Saturday morning. At the same time, a boat came by way of the river with the Indian who had been our prisoner for many years, accompanied by twelve others of his household—his wife, his son, his father-in-law, etc., most of them Moros. At the stern of the boat was a large cross with a white flag suspended from it. This sight, you may be sure, drew tears of joy from us all, at seeing the spoils so valiantly snatched away from the great devil of Mindanao. I was caused some anxiety by the coming that Saturday morning of a certain Moro, who appeared, his whole body covered with mud, and came up the river in a small boat with two fowls, asking to be taken to the señor Aria (for thus they call the governor of these islands, this word meaning "king" in their language), for he wished to present the fowls to him with his own hand. Questioned as to the cause and motive for his coming, he said he was driven by hunger and necessity, because they had nothing to eat up on the hill; so would all have to come [to us] in a few days. Events showed this to be false, for a great quantity of provisions was found there later, confirming my suspicions and those of others. It must have been a trick contrived by the devil and his ministers against our captain-general, who, conducting himself on this occasion (as on others) with great prudence and diplomacy, commanded without seeing the man, that he should be handed over to Sosozan—a Moro who was friendly to us, and had come with us from Samboanga—who was to hand him over to the governor of the fort. This was done, and thus, without knowing it, we were saved from a great danger.

When matters at the fort and the port below were settled, and all the ships burned except three or four, which were kept to take back to Samboanga, Nicolas Gonçalez arrived, on Monday evening, the sixteenth, with the rest of our fleet. A great tempest had detained them after they passed La Silanga, in which one caracoa was lost, under Captain Sisneros, but only a boy was killed.

At once his Lordship arranged affairs for marching upon the hill the next day. He ordered that biscuit and cheese for four days be given to the soldiers; and Sargento-mayor Don Pedro, with Adjutant Don Francisco Olazaran, spent the whole night in making them confess — which confessions I received — not being content with their confessions at Samboanga.

At three o'clock in the morning masses began to be said, and at the end of the first his Lordship made an address to the soldiers, in which he manifested his great zeal for the honor of God and his military experience. We had agreed that afterward I was to display [the images of] the blessed Christ and St. Francis Xavier; but, to confess the truth to your Reverence, I had no heart for it; and therefore I decided not to do so — as it were, a presage of what was to happen to us that day.

When his talk was finished, his Lordship sent Sargento-mayor Nicolas Gonçalez with Father Melchor de Vera (who had come with him from Samboanga), with a hundred and twenty Spaniards, thirty Pampangos, and eighty Indians to carry the packs, to cut off the enemy's retreat from the hill, and to descend by the same path to attack them. He assigned Captain Castelo to the advance-guard, and Captain Bererra with two famous spies (one a Moro, the other a Christian) to the rear-guard — ordering them to sound their trumpets beforehand, so that his Lordship might attack at the same time from the other direction, and thus they could surround the Moros. After Nicolas Gonçalez had gone, the governor drew up his troops, putting Captain Rodrigo at the head of the rest, and giving to each of the half-pay captains a troop of soldiers. The flags, a piece of artillery, the ammunition, and the provisions were with the body of the troops, and in the rear-guard were the Pampangos; Sargento-mayor Don Pedro was in the advance-guard, with Captain Don Rodrigo; Sargento-mayor Palomino remained in the camp with a goodly number of soldiers, and with the father rector of Othon as chaplain.

The troops were drawn up, and at six in the morning we commenced our march very gayly. After going a legua and a half, we came upon a large town at the foot of the hill, very beautiful and quiet, full of fruit groves, bananas, and sugar-cane — but deserted by the Moros on the previous night, as far as we could infer from the houses, and from the fire which was still consuming the king's fortified house; they had fired it, doubtless, for fear that his Lordship would entrench himself in it, it being very well fitted for that. However, he ordered the adjutant, Don Martin, to fortify another house on the bank of the river with a good barrier,14 a cannon, and a garrison of Pampangos, to guard the packs and cover the retreat of the soldiers. Then the rest of us crossed the river to reconnoiter the enemy's position; the water was breast-high. A little later, we crossed another creek, and commenced to climb a ravine full of coarse grass. Here his Lordship halted, and, seeing another road farther down, asked the guide whether that road also led to the hill. He said "yes;" but, upon being asked which was better, replied that both were very bad. Then his Lordship (a special light from heaven illuminating him) said: "If, in the opinion of this Moro who is guiding us, both roads are bad, I prefer going by the other rather than by this one by which he is taking us." So he commanded the advance-guard to turn back and go by the other road. Your Reverence will soon see the special providence of God, and the protection of my glorious saint. At the other road (by which the Moro was leading us) there were aimed three pieces of artillery, which could not be seen; and one of them might at least have destroyed the whole vanguard. When our chief gunner discharged the bronze cannon, which stood between two large iron ones, he found that it contained two great cannon balls, two crowbars, and three hundred musket-balls, with a double charge [of powder]. Having escaped this danger we proceeded by the other road, by which, having crossed the river and the creek for the second time, we arrived at the foot of a hill. Here we halted, and his Lordship sent some of the advance-guard ahead to inspect the road, since from what could be seen at the beginning of the ascent it seemed very bad. They went to examine it, and soon word came back that after the first turn the road was better, so we all went up. The truth is that the overflowing courage, spirit, and desire for fighting which possessed the soldiers, those of the vanguard especially, made the road seem good to them; as a matter of fact, it was narrow, rough, and very dangerous on account of terrible precipices on each side. We had made two or three turns, up the hill, thinking to find some place where we could halt, when from two stockades on the right side of the mountain the Moros commenced to fire upon us. A cannon ball came toward me, grazing me; but it was prevented by divine Providence from inflicting any further injury than leaving its mark in the shape of a hole in my cassock. May God grant that by this wonderful escape I am reserved for some other and more glorious death!

We all felt sure that there was no other stockade besides these two which we saw, when, at the third turn of the hill, the advance-guard came upon another, which we had not been able to see. They commenced to fight bravely from below it, but because the position of the stockade was very strong, and that of our men very cramped—hemmed in by formidable precipices, and exposed to all the guns and other weapons of the enemy (especially sompites, bacacayes, and stones)—no sooner would some of our men gain the little open place before the stockade than they would fall dead or wounded. For this reason, after having fought a good two hours, the fort could not be taken.

During this time the four priests who went up the hill—Father Juan de Barrios, the Augustinian friar, the chaplain of the fleet, and I—remained at this place, confessing the wounded and encouraging the others. On the whole march, so far, I had not chosen to unfurl the standard of the holy Christ and St. Francis Xavier; but at the time of the battle, my fervor and zeal being aroused, I did what the Holy Ghost bade me, and was thus constrained to give the banner to a soldier—who at my order went on ahead, further up the hill, to guard the person of his Lordship, who had left me in order to reconnoiter the stockade from a nearer point. A ball came, which pierced the canvas of both the sacred pictures, but without touching the figures; at that time the saint was facing the stockade, and it has been positively learned (how, I know not) that that ball was intended by the evil one to kill a great personage, and the saint who stood before him saved him from it.

I, seeing that our affairs were in such straits, offered on my part an earnest prayer to the saint; and afterward I said aloud to his Lordship that he ought to make a vow to the saint that he would build him a chapel at San Miguel. To this he replied with much spirit and generosity, "Yes, Father, and it shall be made very rich and very beautiful." I thought it best to designate that church, because it was that of the saint to whom St. Francis Xavier, when he was living, felt most devotion and love. I cannot deny that my heart was much troubled at this time, although not for fear of the bullets, which flew about us like mosquitoes, and made a terrifying noise in the trees; for I can truthfully assert to your Reverence that I felt no trace of fear during this whole campaign, thanks to God, although I found myself in the greatest straits and perils of my whole life; and His grace comforted and aided me greatly in this emergency. Forever blessed and hallowed be His holy name, que attingit a fine, usque ad finem fortiter, et disponit omnia suaviter,15 who hath brought me by so many circuitous ways to a position so in accord with my life-long desires. Thus, what distressed me on that day was not fear, but the sight of the bravest and most gallant soldiers either dead or wounded; nevertheless, it consoled me much to see them enter the battle with the names of Christ and St. Francis Xavier on their lips, and die uttering the same words. Over many was laid the standard containing these two images, which even bore some spots of blood. Some were praying with their reliquaries and kissing them, others beseeching me for general absolution to prepare them for so glorious a death—obtained in avenging the injuries done to the holy Christ (this was the common formula, as it were, of all)—and others at last, whom I could not reach, declared their sins publicly giving tokens of the great grief and contrition which they felt. There was one of these, in particular, who said three times: "Sirs, tell such-a-one to pardon me; for money was given me in Manila to induce me to murder him in time of battle, and I should have murdered him had not God brought me to this condition." Truly, the depth of his contrition touched me greatly—only this one thing he had not confessed the night before; then I confessed nearly all the rest, and they received the sacrament with the utmost devotion.

Among the first wounded was Captain Ugalde, who had two bullet-wounds in his arms, and Sargento-mayor Don Pedro Hurtado de Corcuera, with a musket ball which went through his right leg; so that this valiant cavalier, being no longer able to be upon his feet, remained for a long time upon his knees, encouraging the soldiers, although he was in great danger of being killed. He was in the very spot where they had wounded Don Rodrigo de Guillestigui, who was a most distinguished soldier; for he fought continually, and remained all the time in the ditch of the stockade without coming out, even when he had a considerable wound. Alférez Amesquita succeeded in hoisting our flag over the fort, but with the utmost danger; for they nearly hurled him down, with a spear-wound in his head and several sompites in his throat. Our men were fasting, and, besides that, laden with provisions and arms, and wearied by the march (which had been more difficult than long); but, like lions, they caused the Moros much more fear in their death than if the port had been taken without bloodshed. The Moros were terrified, too, by seeing our soldiers thus obstinately keep up the battle in a slaughter-house—for this place deserves no other name. And your Reverence may be well assured that a million of Spaniards could never have gained the height; for I believe that no one can possibly picture or imagine the strength of that place unless he were present at the attack. The truth is, that they passed from courage to rashness; for, by not ceasing to fight, they changed his Lordship's orders (or else they heard them backwards) [as if he were] commanding the leaders to rally instead of ordering a retreat. Then they counted on gaining the victory through the soldiers who were coming up behind (though most of them paid for this over-confidence with their lives), and were for a long time deceived with this hope. However, the real reason why the governor did not sooner order the retreat was that he was waiting for the instant when Nicolas Gonçalez should attack from above on the other side, for the latter had no more than three leguas to go; but, having found the road very bad, and being himself far from well, he could not get there till night. With these hopes, and with very many false tidings of victory, which were very often given, his Lordship waited, and urged on the soldiers for full two hours in a very dangerous place, exposed to all the weapons of the enemy; but, seeing many dead and wounded, he pushed his way forward, and, with great danger to himself (and to all of us, if any mishap had befallen him), reached the little open space in full sight of the stockade. There he stood, in a furious storm of bullets, stones, bacacayes, and sompites, which killed and wounded many at his side—especially his armor-bearer, through whose helmet and skull they sent a bullet. Now, having reconnoitered the place for more than half an hour, and seeing that it could not be taken by storm from this road (as a half-pay officer had told him a little while before), he expressed his annoyance at those who sought with lies to detain him and involve him more deeply, and ordered the retreat to be sounded.

The enemy might, indeed, have done us much injury when we commenced the retreat; for the dead numbered eighteen, the wounded more than eighty, and the few who remained were very weary, and hampered by the aforesaid wounded men. Besides this, the road was precipitous, and more difficult to descend than to climb. But God our Lord, by the intercession of my glorious saint, blinded the enemy wholly; and the courage and prudent management of his Lordship gave them no time to attack us. With the utmost courage, he went along as if nothing had happened, brandishing his naked sword—encouraging all; holding back the soldiers, so that they should retreat gradually; with his face always to the enemy, sending the men down; and having our drums and trumpets sounded, until we reached the house which Adjutant Don Martin had fortified. When all were there, we saw on one side a great number of Moros coming down a defile to prevent our retreat to the camp. A few cannon-shots were fired at them, and they quickly hurried back to the hill. His Lordship wished to halt here and await the attack by Nicolas Gonçalez, but the smallness of his forces compelled him to retire, which he did, the drums beating, as before, until we reached the camp. The wounded were placed, for that night, in a cabin in front of the mosque; and in the morning we transferred them to the champans, burying three who had died. Many were of the opinion that his Lordship ought to retire that evening to the fort—a safer place, in case of attack—but he was not willing to display any weakness before the enemy, and so that night passed in great anxiety; for, if the Moros were to come down, it would at least endanger the wounded. We learned from some of the captives that they really intended to attack us; but that, thinking the governor (for whom they mistook Captain Martin Monte,16 on account of his distinguished presence) had fallen on that day, they felt it necessary to give thanks first to Mahoma for so great a victory, with many ceremonies and revels which they held that night, with the heads of our dead — as we ourselves guessed from the great number of lights which we saw at the same time on the hill. After this assault, when we retired at nightfall to the camp, the governor wrote to Nicolas Gonçalez, telling him of what had happened; and ordering him that if, by his position and the state of his troops, he thought he could take the hill, he should attack vigorously alone; but, if he thought that he could not succeed, he should contrive an honorable retreat to the camp, where they would arrange everything. He gave the letter to Sosocan to send, but no one dared to take it, so it came back to the secretary.

Very early the next morning, I was saying mass, when cannon-shots and volleys of musketry commenced to be heard from the hill — a sign that our men were fighting. The whole camp was in a tumult, and his Lordship ordered Don Pedro to march with all the able-bodied men by the same road that they had followed the previous day, in order to divide the enemy's forces, assuming that Nicolas Gonçalez was already engaged. I kept on with the mass, although with much difficulty, because of the many tears which the noise of the cannon called forth; and since the mass that I was saying was for our dead soldiers, I implored their blessed souls to obtain from God for us the victory for which they had spent their blood the day before. After mass, we said the full litany, and all engaged in prayer; it was an impressive thing to see the governor on his knees with tears in his eyes, his hands raised to heaven like Moses of old, praying for aid, and that the victory might come to his troops. Less than an hour had passed when two soldiers came with the news of the victory, and soon Father Melchor arrived with the enemy's flags. I will not write of the embraces, the merrymaking, and the joy in our camp, for your Reverence can imagine it better than I can describe it. His Lordship at once gave a banner to the soldiers who had brought the news, and by him he sent [the promise of] an encomienda to Nicolas Gonçalez.

Father Vera related to us the story of the taking of the hill, as follows: They marched all day Tuesday the seventeenth, the day of our attack, not because the way was so long, but so bad, as I have already said, and because Nicolas Gonçalez had to travel in a hammock. He was actually so weak and ill that, as he afterward admitted to me, his sword served him for a cane the day of the fight; and a boy had to support his arm, which he could not lift for the weight of his shield. They had various encounters with Moros, but, in order to avoid noise, the order was given not to fight; and so on the way they killed only the cachice [i.e., kasis] of Corralat, whom they found hidden in a thicket. They halted that night and fortified themselves in a height which overlooked the hill; and early on the morning of Wednesday (the day of St Joseph's vigil and of the glorious angel Gabriel) Nicolas Gonçalez had urged on the soldiers, and told them that since there was no avenue of retreat open to them, there was nothing for it but to gain either the hill or heaven. They made a valiant attack upon the enemy, who were awaiting them behind a huge tree lying across the middle of the road—having no other stockades or ditches on this part of the hill, for they could not imagine that we would attack them there. They held their ground, fighting, for a time; but Captain Castelo, who was leading the vanguard, having crossed with some soldiers to the other side of the log, forced them to abandon their position. Then he followed them with his troops, without difficulty or danger, on the rear as far as the stockades and forts, till he remained master of two of these with four pieces of artillery and the king's strong-house where he kept his treasure. Many Moros were killed, not only by our shots, but by rushing down in a furious and headlong flight through a very narrow ravine which was at the entrance of this very stockade where they expected us—falling, by a just judgment of God, into the very snares which they had laid for us. At the same time Captain Castelo met some Moros who were coming to join the others—the garrison of the third stockade, which we had attacked the day before with our vanguard; and, with the same ease, he compelled them to flee and fling themselves down, he remaining master of the fort and its arms, which were muskets with rests, arquebuses, campilans, etc. The relatives and the men and maid-servants of Corralat, with many of his people, who were taken prisoners on that day, said that the night before he had put under his feet a monstrance containing the blessed sacrament, which he had stolen, saying to all that there was nothing to fear, for he had the God of the Christians already under his feet; and that, considering the great strength of his fortified hills and stockades, and the large quantity of provisions that they had, they would be quite safe, unless it rained men from heaven. But when, the next morning, they brought him word that our men were attacking from the rear, he said to his wife: "The Spaniards have chosen a bad place for me" (reflecting that, as I have said, he had no defense for guarding the rear of the hill); "however, be of good courage, and wait here for me, for I am going to do to these what I did yesterday to the others." He went, and his wife, seeing that we were coming in, urged her women to fling themselves down with her, so as not to be captured. They, being more sensible, refused to do this,17 and so they became our slaves; while the poor queen, with a child which she was holding in her arms, flung herself down and remained hanging from a tree. This was a cause of regret to us all, on account of the kind disposition which she possessed, according to the report given us by the father rector of Dapitan, who knew her to be very friendly to our Christian captives—sending them food secretly (especially to the religious), and reproaching her husband when he maltreated and abused them. After the queen had flung herself down, Corralat, with a bullet-wound in one arm, came in search of her; and, seeing her already dead, he fled by one of those declivities, without being recognized, to some hamlets four leguas from the hill, where they say he is now recovering.

None of our men died, thanks be to God; only seven or eight were wounded, and they are now well. Don Rodrigo—who had set out that morning, as I have said, with the other troops—learning en route of the victory, sent the soldiers to Nicolas Gonçalez as reënforcements, and himself returned to the camp.

Now your Reverence will see whether we could ever have taken the camp by starvation, as they said we could; it contained grain-fields, banana patches, a brook of very pure water, and six or seven thousand baskets of rice—which for them was very extensive provision. Nicolas Gonçalez fortified himself with his troops in two places: Captain Bezerra, with fifty soldiers, occupied the king's house which had been set aside for his Majesty [the king of Spain], and Nicolas Gonçalez remained with the rest of the forces in the principal stockade where the artillery was; while they burned all the other stockades, and the houses, rice, and grain-fields, and brought down the four pieces of artillery. This they did in two days, to the admiration of all—even of the gunners, who held it to be impossible. Those men would have abandoned them, if his Lordship had not remained firm in his intention of not going until the cannon came down—not wishing Corralat to say that the Spaniards could not bring down what he had taken up, although he did it with two thousand Indians, in six months, and our men did it in two days with four rowers [barrigas].

I cannot deny that the joy of that day was very great, but the death of the two Recollect fathers distressed us greatly—his Lordship having tried to the utmost of his power to deliver them from the Moros. Although they had captured three at Pintados, one of them was killed by our own men18 under Nicolas Gonçalez, on the day when he surprised the enemy's fleet at Punta de San Sebastian, formerly Punta de Flechas. One the Moros killed on the day when we gained the lower port, because, when they were fleeing with their wives and captives to the upper fort, this good servant of God being unable to travel very fast on account of having been ill, they killed him with a shower of blows; and then hanged him, dead, from a tree so that we should see him from the camp. But, because we were at a distance, we could not, although we saw him, get possession of his body—especially as they took it away early the next day; and we were unable to find out what they did with it. The other father they killed on the hill, through rage, on the day that Nicolas Gonçalez won the hill—although he did not die until the following day, in the mosque below the hill, before the altar. It comforted him greatly to see already blessed, with the title of Nuestra Señora de la Buen Succeso ["Our Lady of Success"], the building which a little while before had stood there dedicated to Mahoma. Five fathers whom we found at the camp were present at his death; and the next morning we buried him in the sea, not being willing to leave his sacred body to the hands of the barbarians. When I was washing him to prepare him for burial, I was astounded at the great number of wounds and cruel campilan blows with which they had mutilated his whole body; and then I wondered at his patience and endurance. The soldiers too admired the great zeal of this holy man, because, when they found him thus wounded in a corner of the fort, he did not complain, but immediately asked if there were any wounded soldier for him to confess. When he was told that he must not fatigue himself, and that we had brought a Jesuit father for that very purpose, he was greatly rejoiced, and asked to have him brought so that he might confess to him; Father Melchor de Vera came up at once.

When, they brought him down to the camp, I was with the sick on the fleet; they told me (but not till evening, when I returned) that his Lordship had performed acts of kindness for the father, in keeping with his devotion — helping to bring him in and place him in the bed, giving him food with his own hands, washing the blood from his wounds, and comforting him with tender and loving words, especially when the surgeon commenced to treat him. Inasmuch as his clothing adhered to his wounds by reason of his having passed a day and a half without attention, the pain of pulling the garments away was very great; and, when he winced a little, his Lordship was at once at hand with the story of the passion of our Lord, and found it so efficacious that, as he afterward declared to me, the father did not utter another word, nor offer any other resistance, but exhibited the patience of a glorious martyr. I confess that I washed his wounds after his death more with tears from my eyes than with water from the river, in holy envy of the glorious way in which he had ended his pilgrimage. Before he died, I begged him to beseech God for a like death for me, or even a more painful one, in defense of His holy law. The holy man promised it, and I hope by his intercession to obtain it — although not because I deserve it, unless in return for the relief I gave his glorious wounds in the last four absolutions which I gave him with my special consolation. Surely those are fortunate fathers who have been able to show to the world, by their blood, the zeal and divine love which they bear in their bosoms.

After burying the father the next morning, Friday, March twentieth, two days after the victory, we went up the hill with his Lordship; but so great was the stench from the dead Moros in the ravines (although many still lived, judging by the cries and groans of many persons which were heard) that, almost as soon as we had reached the top and had looked at the king's house, we returned to the camp. His Lordship then commanded that with the exception of the church ornaments, and the arms kept for his Majesty, everything should be divided among the soldiers. His Lordship did not reserve for himself or his friends even one blanca's worth—surely an action very justly applauded, certainly, and admired because it is not now practiced among the captains-general, and because it was, I believe, the first [of its kind] in these Filipinas Islands; and it confirmed the opinion that all held of the governor, as a wholly disinterested gentleman. An enormous amount was found and divided; they say that there were many cabinets full, and very heavy; what is certain is, that the whole of Corralat's treasure was here, and whatever he had plundered during so many years. Your Reverence does not need to be told that the soldiers came back well satisfied, and many very rich. The campaign brought them great profit; and truly they deserved it all, for they all fought most valiantly. A great chest was filled with the ornaments of the churches—sacred vessels, such as chalices, patens, monstrances, censers, chrismatories, etc.—which we have now most carefully returned to their owners; so that your Reverence was enabled to fill four floats with these ornaments, in the solemn procession which his Lordship held in Manila on Trinity Sunday, in thanksgiving to God for the victory. It troubled me, however, on the day when we climbed the hill, that I had not time to search for my beads, which I had lost on the day of the assault—when, to placate the wrath of God, I tore my cassock hastily down the middle. But the next day God chose to console me; for, on my return from visiting the sick at the camp, his Lordship gave me my beads. He had recognized them in the hand of a soldier who had found them on his way down the hill, and had given the man I know not how many pesos for them. They certainly were worth it, because they were made from the stake at which the martyrs in Japan were burned; and because they had touched the whole body of my most glorious patron saint Francis Xavier, at Goa; these are the reasons why I prize them so highly.

Six whole days were spent in distributing, or burning and destroying, everything in Mindanao; and thus on the twenty-fifth of March, the day of the blessed Annunciation, we started on the return trip to Samboanga. But the governor would not set sail before returning thanks at that very place to His Divine Majesty for so great a victory. He therefore arranged a solemn procession with the blessed sacrament, from the mosque to the fort—himself at the head, carrying the image of the holy Christ and of St. Francis Xavier, patron of the expedition, and wearing the white robe of his order, in which he had received communion. The soldiers with their muskets, and the artillery at the fort, gave eight royal salutes with ball — which aside from doing honor to the procession, served to clear the two little hills of the ambuscade, which, without our knowledge, the Moros had laid to prevent our embarkation. We found this out by means of the large number of dead bodies which Captain Juan Nicolas discovered a little while after, when, returning from the Bugayen River, he wished to see the place where we had attacked Corralat. When the procession was over, we set fire to the mosque and the fort; and the troops commenced to embark in good order, in the small champans of the fleet. Then Sargento-mayor Palomino was sent with five caracoas and a hundred Spaniards, with Father Melchor de Vera, who knew the language very well, to search for Moncay, king of Bagaien [i.e., Buhayen][19] and the real lord of the island of Mindanao; this Corralat, though his relative, was but the tyrant. Bagaien is twelve leguas from the fort of Mindanao. [Palomino went] to make a treaty of peace with him whereby he should become a tributary and vassal to his Majesty. While we were setting sail, one of our Indian captives appeared on the shore. The falua brought him off to our champan, and he told us how he had fled from the enemy's grain-fields where they had kept him during those days; and that, passing through one of the ravines of the hill, he had found a vast number of dead Moros.[20]

Two or three hours after leaving Mindanao, we met Captain Juan Nicolas and Father Gutierrez,[21] father rector of Dapitan, who with forty ships and order for Sargento-mayor Palomino, in which he commanded that officer that, notwithstanding his previous instructions, he should make use of all the troops sent him to capture Moncay, or at least disarm him. After this we continued our course, and on Passion Sunday we reached Samboanga. The fleet and the army received their captain-general, returning victorious, with a royal salute; and Father Gregorio Belin, in his cope, with the Te Deum laudamus. I, after accompanying them as far as the official buildings, went to arrange the hospital for the sick; for although I had attended them at Mindanao and on the journey, and assisted them with all that his Lordship provided, yet, on account of the discomforts of the ships in which they had had to be shut up, and because of the lack of fowls, they arrived in a very weak condition. I set out at once in search of beds — even taking those in the [Jesuit] house. I collected in one room as many dainties as I could find, for the refreshment of the sick; and I shut up in our corral all the fowls which had come to Samboanga from Othon, which private persons had given his Lordship, and he had turned over to me for the use of the wounded. With these provisions I remained in the hospital, to minister by night and by day to the bodies and souls of the sick, encouraged by his Lordship's visits. By means of all this care, and by the confession and general communion in which all took part on Palm Sunday, the majority of the men, thanks to God, were quite well by Saturday in Holy Week, at which time we left Samboanga.

Truly anyone who saw the number and grievous nature of the wounds could not deny that it was a miraculous thing that out of eighty wounded only two died, aside from the three who succumbed on the night of the attack; for all the wounds contained poison, and many of them, moreover, were very deep and serious. Thus we saw the effects upon our sick of the sompites, bacacayes, and bullets—which, although they were all deadly weapons, we found on the hill [that we attacked], placed in a jar filled with poison. It is true that I availed myself of some very effective antidotes which they gave me at Manila; but the true remedy was to mix with them a little of a relic of St. Francis Xavier—which, in conjunction with the faith of those who were ill, worked wonders. Captain Maroto tested their virtues well, for he was already black in the face, and in his death-agony, when he called me to confess him and to administer the sacraments. Better still was Alférez Amesquita, who ejected through his mouth three sompites which had pierced his throat three days before, during the attack. But best of all was the case of a sargento in the same company, to whom I gave extreme unction in great haste, because he had a bullet-wound in his stomach and most of his food passed out through the wound. There are many others too, who, grievously injured at Mindanao, are now going about Manila. Only Alférez Romero and Menchaca died at Samboanga, and that was because they would not let themselves be cured.

During this time, the governor was awaiting the return of Sargento-mayor Palomino and of Captain Juan Nicolas from Bugayen. In place of resting on those days, he went in person among the soldiers, working in a ditch which he had ordered to be dug to bring to the fort a stream of fresh water, which it lacked; and now they send word from Samboanga that, by the grace of God, the water has reached them. Before putting his hand to any other work he desired, like the devout gentleman that he is, to thank God a second time for the victory, with a fiesta in honor of the blessed sacrament. And because he lacked neither the valor nor the piety of that great captain, Judas Macabeus, he ordered that the next day the funeral honors should be solemnized for his dead soldiers—although, unfortunately for these festivals, it devolved upon me to preach at both. He also published a long bulletin of gifts, offices, and rewards for those who were wounded in the campaign; and in this way so attached all the soldiery to himself that now they talk of and concern themselves with nothing else but their captain-general—even the very seamen declaring that they do not wish to avail themselves of the privilege of crossing to Nueva España, because they would miss next year's campaign.

In this way several days were spent, until our fleet from Bugayen arrived—on Wednesday in Holy Week; and the next day, with three caracoas came the brother of the king as ambassador, to treat with his Lordship and confirm the peace negotiated by Sargento-mayor Palomino. The latter had done so because he was not able to execute the second order, which Juan Nicolas carried, who had come too late, bringing it when Moncay had agreed to as many conditions as we could desire—even to stating publicly to his followers that he wished to be the friend and vassal of the king of España, and that whoever did not desire the same must quit his villages. In accordance with this, the ambassadors offered five things to the governor in the name of the king his brother: to surrender all Christian captives; to pay tribute to his Majesty; to receive the Jesuit fathers, so that they might publicly teach his subjects the law of Jesus Christ; that if the governor wished to maintain a fort with a garrison of Spaniards in Moncay's country, he would treat them as brothers; and that he would be the friend of their friends, the enemy of their enemies. Consequently, he would do all in his power to put a stop to Corralat's doings, dead or alive, and to deliver him into the governor's hands. His Lordship received the envoy in great state, seated in a chair, surrounded by the most brilliant of the army, in elegant and splendid array. The ambassador sat on one end of the same carpet, astonished at the magnificence of our captain-general and his soldiers. The captain-general commanded the governor of the fort to entertain the envoy at his own house, and sent later, for his delectation, some cocoanuts and chickens. He gave him some very beautiful pieces of silk; but for a captured sargento whom the ambassador gave back in the name of the king his brother, he said that he would give nothing, because that soldier was a vassal of the king of España. The ambassador was importunate that he should send Moncay something, at least some of his own weapons. His Lordship replied that up to this time Moncay had been an enemy, and that, as such, nothing was due him; but that he must begin to give proofs of his friendship, by immediately sending us his captives, etc.; and then he would very soon experience the governor's liberality. He offered him two thousand pesos if he delivered up Corralat dead, and four thousand if alive. This news was received by the Moro with great pleasure, on account of the greed for money which possesses those people; so that I am sure, considering this, that Corralat's days are few. On Saturday in Holy Week, his Lordship being ready to embark, he came to dismiss the ambassador, and to receive the documents and articles of peace, signing them in the envoy's presence. At the end, while his Lordship, to do honor to him at the final farewell, was embracing him, the Moro told him most gratefully that at the end of four moons (they designate months thus) he would come to see him at Manila—news which consoled me greatly, because of the facility that it will afford your Reverence to send workers to so abundant a harvest.

Then all the artillery was discharged, the fleet responding; and, when his Excellency the governor had embarked, we set sail for Manila, and the ambassador for Bugayen. At the same time Captain Juan Nicolas and Captain Juan de León departed with a company of a hundred Spaniards and a thousand Indians, with the command that, after having accompanied the ambassador of Bugaien to his own land, they should go on and make the circuit of the island of Mindanao, as far as Dapitan, destroying and burning all the villages that would not submit to our arms. The father rector of Dapitan, and the Augustinian friar who had come as confessor for the Pampangos, were chaplains for this fleet.

On the same day Father Gregory Belin with Captain Sisneros departed from Samboanga for the island of Basilan, for a reason which I will explain to your Reverence. This island—lying in front of our fort, and two leguas away from it—has three or four thousand tributarios who pay to the king of Jolo, although they have always desired to be tributary to his Majesty. The chiefs of the islands came lately to render their obedience to the governor; he thereupon commanded that the governor of the fort should protect the aforesaid tributarios, and defend them from Jolo, until the next year, when he would subject Jolo also by force of arms to the same tribute. When this was proclaimed, two hundred Joloan chiefs, with all their households, came to a near-by island, intending to cross over and live in Samboanga and be our vassals. But they wished to know his Lordship's pleasure; so the aforesaid captain with Father Belin went to assure them of their safety and take them to the fort, where, he trusted in God, they would now be well instructed and become favorably inclined to holy baptism. Because his Lordship had no fathers to send to Basilan, he wrote to Father Francisco Angel that, by virtue of the very far-reaching grant which he has from your Reverence, he should at once cross from the island of Negros to Samboanga. Here the governor of the fort would give him soldiers for his body-guard, and all else necessary for the promulgation of the holy gospel in the aforesaid island—where, as I have said, he had already gone most joyfully, as the father rector of Othon informed me; for the principal motive of his coming from España to these Filipinas Islands was the mission to Mindanao. But that father could not minister alone to the whole island; besides, at Samboanga there are but two fathers—Father Melchor de Vera, who on account of his frequent attacks of illness can scarcely take care of everything at the fort which his Lordship entrusted to him, as a person well skilled in such matters; and Father Gregory

Belin, [who is busy] in caring for the whole garrison, of which he is chaplain. So the many villages of Moros that are in the vicinity of the fort, such as La Caldera, etc., have no one to instruct them. The king also of Sibuguey (a river [whose valley is] much more fertile and abundant than La Panpanga) himself came, while we were in Mindanao, to the governor to ask for terms of peace and for priests. His son has come now, with the [Spanish] galleons from Terrenate, to be educated in Manila; and in like manner the other chiefs are coming every day, since the miserable downfall of the principal king of these islands, Corralat, who held almost all in tyrannical subjection, and as tributarios. Even the king of Jolo sent Dato Achen (his especial favorite, and the most gallant and valorous captain that we have seen among the Moros) with letters to his Lordship, to confirm the terms of peace which his wife herself had come with our captain, to negotiate the year before—excusing himself for not having come in person by saying that he was expecting a fleet with which the king of Burney was coming to make war on him, being an ally of his enemies the Camucones.

May your Reverence's charity recognize what an abundant harvest offers in Mindanao, and how destitute that field is in laborers; for where, in my opinion, forty would be few, there are only two of them. Certainly this is to be regretted, for it is one of the most glorious missions that could be desired, lacking neither the evidence of great fruitfulness nor promise of most noble martyrdom. And finally, it is enough that St. Francis Xavier is its apostle, since it was he who first preached in it the holy gospel,22 as is stated in the bull for his canonization. I trust that, through the divine compassion, the news of this glorious and longed-for victory and conquest of the great island of Mindanao will move the hearts of those in his Majesty's court and his royal Council of the Indias, to send many workers this year to this glorious harvest field.

This is all that concerns our expedition to Mindanao, except the return journey to Manila—which, being long and dangerous, caused us much suffering. For if we came across any island, we had perforce to sail all the way around it; and if we wished to go in any given direction the wind instantly put itself dead ahead, with three or four baguios [i.e., hurricanes]—which are violent tempests. At the islands of Negros, Mindoro, and Marinduque it was a divine miracle, through the special protection of St. Francis Xavier, that we escaped all the dangers, especially the one that we encountered at Mindoro. Our mast broke, and a huge wave rushed over our stern so suddenly, so unexpectedly to the pilots and sailors that they, seeing it coming over the sea from a distance, hastily summoned me to exorcise it, which I did. It can assuredly have been of no other than diabolic origin, to declare as the author of so many attacks, hindrances, and contrary circumstances the great devil of Mindanao, whom his Lordship had just so valiantly wrested from his seat.

But if the work of the enemy was evident in our dangers, much more manifest and clear was the divine protection and that of our saint in these same perils—as when it saved us from some rocky shoals just off Manila, where we would have inevitably have run aground; and from a champan which sprang a leak, from which, without knowing about the leak, we shifted our quarters a day before. There are many other instances which I will not mention, that your Reverence may not be wearied. Twice we stopped on the way for provisions to refresh the sick—once at Iloilo, where our fathers entertained us; the other time at Panay, at the invitation of Captain and Alcalde-mayor Don Francisco de Frias. At last, since the winds were wholly contrary and his Lordship had suffered so much on the way, he resolved to disembark in Tayabas, with Sargento-mayor Don Pedro, his nephew, and Captain Lorenço Ugalde, both being ill and in need of a surgeon's services. From this place we traveled by land for two days, as far as the lake [i.e., Laguna de Bay]; going from there by the [Pásig] River, we reached Manila on May nineteenth. I halted at San Miguel, and the sick remained at Manila, while his Lordship went on the same night to Cavite, where the armada had orders to await him. The whole fleet, by God's protection, arrived safely within four days; and so on Sunday the governor made his entry with the pomp and magnificence which your Reverence saw. I know not whether many remarked on the events of that day, but this is the fact, that of all the champans but one was lacking—that of Captain Gabriel Niño de Tabora, which was carrying some large cannon of the enemy's; and when his Lordship reached Manila by one route, from Cavite, to make his entry, Don Gabriel Niño arrived, by another, from Mariveles. In this it seems that God chose to show His special providence by bringing all the fleet in without the loss of anything, small or great, from the spoils. Blessed and praised forever be His holy name, who through the valor, zeal, and Christian devotion of this gallant knight, has glorified Himself by granting at the same time relief to the islands, and punishment to the arrogance of these Moros. Events showed plainly the truth of the revelation which that holy servant of God received with regard to the coming of this governor, for the complete deliverance and salvation of this conquered land. May our Lord give him life and health, that he may finish what he had undertaken with so much spirit and courage for the glory of His Divine Majesty.

This is all that has suggested itself to me to write to your Reverence of this campaign of ours in Mindanao, as glorious as it was wonderful— except to urge that your Reverence at once send many laborers23 to sow the seed of the holy gospel and even to gather the harvest in many parts of the island, judging by the great readiness [to receive the faith] that I observed when I came away. Only the great lack of workers which I perceived in this province of Filipinas troubles me, for they are very few in proportion to the many missions and Christian settlements which are in their charge—and much more now than ever, since so wide a door is opening. Certainly, if God had not called me to another empire,24 I should consider myself most fortunate if I might be employed, in accordance with my obedience, in the spiritual conquest of the kingdoms of Mindanao. In spite of this, I trust in the intercession of my glorious saint, Francis Xavier, that since he was the first to labor in this island, and, although wounded, was the protector and patron of this expedition, he will not cease to prosecute the work in which he has so earnestly engaged, as we know; and that he will dispose matters in such a manner that many will come from Europe in these years to employ their labors in so glorious a mission. Therefore, since, as I have already said, I do not deserve to be chosen, I beseech your Reverence to obtain from that saint, with your holy sacrifices and prayers, this boon for me—that for the part which I have taken in the conquest of this island, he will admit me into the number of the workers in some other island, and into its spiritual conquest; so that, all of us thus working in missions near to that of this great apostle to the East, we may together enjoy his special protection and support in this life, and be admitted among his devoted and beloved ones in the life to come, which may God through His infinite mercy grant us! Taytay, June 2, 1637.

The humble servant and obedient son of your Reverence:

[MARCELO FRANCISCO MASTRILLI]25

1 Marcelo Francisco Mastrilli was born at Naples September 14 (Crétineau-Joly says September 4), 1603, and entered upon his novitiate March 25, 1618. In obedience to the command of an apparition of St. Francis Xavier which he believed he had seen (that saint also miraculously curing him of a dangerous wound), he asked for the missions of Japan. He left for his field in 1635, arriving at Manila on July 3 of the following year. At the request of Corcuera, Mastrilli accompanied him in the expedition against Mindanao; soon after the governor's triumphant return therefrom, Mastrilli went to Japan, where he was almost immediately imprisoned and tortured—finally (October 17, 1637) being beheaded at Nagasaki. See Murillo Velarde's Hist. Philipinas, fol. 81, and Crétineau-Joly's Hist. Comp. de Jésus, iii, pp. 161–163; the latter says that Mastrilli went to Japan to attempt the reclamation of the apostate Christoval Ferreira (Vol. XXIV, p. 230 and note 91), and that martyrdom there seemed to him and other Jesuits a sort of expiation for Ferreira's

sin.

2 Juan de Salazar was born at Baeza, Spain, December 26, 1582, and, while a student there, entered (October 26, 1598) the Jesuit order. His studies were pursued at Montilla and Granada, and completed at Manila, where he arrived in 1605. He ministered to various Indian churches in Luzón, and held important offices in his order, becoming provincial in 1637. He died in 1645. See Murillo Velarde's Hist. de Philipinas, fol. 142–147.

3 The southwest point of the island of Panay, now called Siroan.

4 Spanish, arpa de la vela (literally, "harp of the sail"); apparently designating the arrangement of the ropes attached to the sail, suggesting the strings of a harp; see engraving of champan in Vol. XIV, p. 223.

5 Falúa (also faluca, English, felucca); a small open boat, or a long boat with oars.

6 Francisco Angel was born at San Clemente, Spain, April 14, 1603; and at the age of fifteen he became a Jesuit novice. He reached the Philippines in 1626, and spent a long and arduous life in the service of the missions there; a large part of his work was in Mindanao and the adjacent islands. He died at Catbalogan, February 24, 1676. See Murillo Velarde's Hist. Philipinas, fol. 353 verso.

7 This image had been taken by the Moros from the Recollect church on the island of Cuyo. "It was a titular [i.e., an ¡mage of the titular (or patron saint) of that church] of our father St. Augustine, and on a linen cloth represented the holy doctor, with Jesus Christ on one side, refreshing him with the blood from His side; and on the other the Virgin, offering him the ["virginal," as La Concepción words it] nectar from her royal breasts." Thus Luis de Jesús, in his Historia religiosos descalzos (Madrid, 1663). The figure of St. Francis Xavier was conjoined with this one, later, by the Jesuits, to incite the soldiers.

8 Retana says, in the preface to his edition of Combés (col. lvi) that the ancient divisions of the island of Mindanao were four: Butúan, Zamboanga, Mindanao (or district of the Moros), and Caraga. Colin states (Labor evangélica, p. 42) that "the district of the Moros begins at the river of Sibuguey, and extends along the discovered coast, always to the south, for more than sixty leguas, until it encounters the beginning of the jurisdiction of Caraga.... Its furthest part is the bay of Tagalooc" (i.e., Davao, according to Pastells, in his edition of Colin, i, p. 43). The river above mentioned "discharges its waters into the bay of Dumanquilas" (Retana and Pastells, Combés, col. 761).

9 The Ventura del Arco transcript is here somewhat differently worded; and according to it the sentence would continue thus: "(and by another caracoa,

which carried a white flag, a letter to the Recollect fathers whom the Moros held captive there, that they should inform them [i.e., our men?] of what was going on) should cast anchor," etc.

10 This place was Lamitan, Corralat's seat of government and court. The height to which that chief retreated after the capture of Lamitan was named Ilihan, according to Montero y Vidal (Hist. piratería, i, p. 168).

11 Probably referring to Liguasan, a large lake southeast of Cotabato, which forms a reservoir for the waters of the Rio Grande of Mindanao—which river seems to have been the headquarters of the piratical Moros of that island. The fort captured at this time was located at the mouth of that river.

12 Sarvatanas (or zarbatanas): a word of Arabic origin, here applied to reeds or canes through which are blown poisoned darts—the sompites (or sumpitans) of the text. (See Retana and Pastells's note in Combés, col. 783.)

13 Sabanilla, diminutive form of sabana (English, "Savannah"); a name given by Corcuera's Spanish soldiers to the fortress which was constructed, under the direction of Father Melchor de Vera, at that point in Mindanao, south from Lake Lanao. Puerto de la Sabanilla was anciently called Tuboc, on account of the springs that flow there ... which form the river now named Malabang. The etymology of this last name indicates the formation of land by the deposits made by the river, which may also be seen in the delta of the Rio Grande of Mindanao. (Retana and Pastells, in Combés, col. 760.)

Tuboc is the name of a modern pueblo on the eastern shore of Illana Bay.

14 Spanish, empuyado, from empuyar, meaning "to fasten with sharp spikes." There seems to be no satisfactory English equivalent as a name for the defensive contrivance that has always been employed by the Malays in the use of sharpened stakes (usually of bamboo) driven into the ground, point upward, and planted thickly in the spot to be defended; sometimes these are placed at the bottom of a trench and hidden by leaves, forming a dangerous pitfall. The use of empuyado in the text suggests the possibility that the Spaniards adopted this device to guard some exposed approach to the building, fearing Malay treachery—a conjecture strengthened by the presence of the Pampango auxiliaries, who probably were accustomed to the use of this sort of defense. See Vol. XX, p. 273.

15 i.e., "who attains His ends with power even to the end, but disposes all affairs with gentleness."

16 Combés says (Retana's ed., p. 251) that Monte was slain in the conflict.

17 Luis de Jesús says (Hist. relig. descalzos, p. 290) that other women fol-

lowed the queen's example, in order not to become captives of the Spaniards. Combés, however, states (Hist. Mindanao, col. 252) that the queen and her children escaped as did Corralat; and that the earlier accounts were incorrect, based on hasty or mistaken reports.

18 This was Fray Francisco de Jesús Maria. The one slain by the Moros was Fray Juan de San Nicolas; Luis de Jesús says (p. 289) that this was caused by his rebuking Corralat for his profanation of the sacred articles which he had pillaged from the churches, whereupon the priest was slain by the enraged heathen. The third, Fray Alonso de San Agustin, was attacked at the same time, according to the above historian, and left for dead, but managed to make his way to the Spanish camp.

19 The name then applied to the region situated some twelve leguas up the Rio Grande from its mouth, lying around the south-west part of Lake Liguasan. Retana and Pastells say (Combés, col. 750) that Buhayen signifies "the place where crocodiles live." Combés says (col. 271) that Moncay was generally supposed to be a mestizo, the son of a native "queen" and a Spaniard.

20 See accounts of this campaign in Combés's Hist. Mindanao, cols. 238–257; Murillo Velarde's Hist. de Philipinas, fol. 82–86; La Concepción's Hist. Philipinas, v, pp. 310–328; Montero y Vidal's Hist. piratería, i, pp. 165–173.

21 Pedro Gutierrez was a Mexican; he was born at Colima on April 24, 1593. He was sent to the Jesuit college at Valladolid, Spain, for his education, which resulted in his entering that order, in May, 1611. In 1622 he arrived in the Philippines, and labored long in the Visayas. In 1629 he was assigned to the residence at Dapitan, Mindanao, from which he soon undertook the conversion of the savage Subanos, and later of the Lutaos of Mindanao, with whom he achieved notable success. He visited the captive Vilancio in Jolo, and tried in vain to ransom him; but he gained the goodwill of the Joloans. He aided in the establishment of the Spanish fort at Zamboanga, and accompanied the Visayan fleet sent to Mindanao to reënforce Corcuera. In 1638 he went with Corcuera's expedition to Jolo, and afterward with others to various parts of Mindanao. He filled important posts in Bohol, Zebu, and Mindanao; and died at Iligan, July 25, 1651. See Murillo Velarde's account of this missionary's life, in Hist. de Philipinas, fol. 198 verso–207.

22 "Colin and Combés say that he crossed from Ternate to Mindanao, about the year 1546; although Garcia says that he went there later, on his way from Japan to India. The former statement is more credible." (Murillo Velarde, Hist. de Philipinas, fol. 74 verso.)

23 In Pastells's edition of Colin (iii, p. 796) is published the following letter from Corcuera to the king, obtained from the Sevilla archives:

"I gave your Majesty an account last year of the need that the Order of the Society has for priests to act as ministers in the missions, now that I have gained two islands for your Majesty, that of Mindanao and that of Bassilan. I have petitioned them to place ministers there, in the parts where they are so necessary, and they have commenced to do so. As they are few, they cannot give me as many as I want, although they are doing all that they can to coöperate with me, taking religious from other parts in order not to let so great a work cease, and one in which they will so well serve our Lord and your Majesty. This order renders much aid, Sire, and with great affection and love. I entreat your Majesty, with all humility and earnestness, to be pleased to command that at least thirty or forty priests be furnished to them; with that aid they will be able to give me the ministers whom I ask, and chaplains for the galleons of Terrenate and other parts — as they are doing, serving your Majesty without self-interest, and checking, by their teaching and good example, the loose conduct of the seamen and soldiers. It seems as if God has been pleased, ever since we undertook to fear God in these islands, as your Majesty had ordered, to give us so many successes and victories, from which the arms of your Majesty gain the luster and credit that is proper."

24 Referring to Japan, the field to which Mastrilli was assigned.

25 In Pastells's edition of Colin (iii, p. 768) is printed the following letter from Mastrilli to the king, dated July 8, 1637:

"I have (clad already in Japanese garb) written a long letter to your Majesty this same day, bidding farewell to your Majesty, and declaring that, whether alive or dead, I shall ever be your Majesty's vassal, and most desirous of the increase of your empire and monarchy; and among the executioners and tortures of Japon, and much more, if I die I shall be, in the heavens, an eternal intercessor. I left two things to request from your Majesty by special letters: one for forty priests of the Society of Jesus to come to these Philipinas Islands, about which I have already written a letter; and the other, which I beg from your Majesty in this letter — namely, that you favor with your royal munificence the schools of our Society in this city of Manila, and in especial the college of San Joseph, by erecting in it twenty fellowships, as your Majesty has done in the colleges of Peru and Mexico. This is the last thing that I petition, with all possible earnestness, from your Majesty, in whose royal hands this letter will be placed when this matter is discussed in the Council, so that your Majesty may order it to be accomplished. May our Lord preserve your royal person, and give you the years and happiness that we all desire and need."

Events in Filipinas, 1636–37

Pax Christi, etc.

Father Diego de Bobadilla:

I shall give your Reverence an account in this letter, although very briefly, of what happened in these islands after your Reverence left them; for many are writing long relations of special matters.

The father rector of the college of Manila, Francisco Colin,1 arrived at Manila at the end of July, and was received with great rejoicing by all in general, both by the inmates of the house and by outsiders and by the orders; and throughout the year he has had the same acceptance. He has aided the governor by his counsel; but he who has shown the greatest joy and happiness is the archbishop, who is receiving much help from him. His Excellency has been notably won over, and has shown us extraordinary favors. He gave us the mission of Quiapo, which we had so much desired because of its nearness to Santa Cruz. He continued the Tuesday sermons during Lent in our house, and honored our church on the day when the indulgence of the seven altars was published. On that day he dined in our refectory, and on all occasions has shown himself truly a father to us. On account of the said indulgence, the number of people who come to our church has greatly increased.

Father Marcelo Mastril, he of the miracle of our father St. Francis Xavier, arrived here with four other Italian fathers, on the day of our father St. Ignatius, 1636, in a galliot, aboard which was a knight of the Order of Christ, who came as captain-general of Macan; he brought, as his auditor, another knight of the same habit. The matter occurred as I shall relate. Two galleons left Goa for Macan. In the second was that Polish father, the relative of the king of Polonia [i.e., Poland]. While passing through the strait of Sincapura, they met three Dutch vessels. The ship of the captain-general of Macan took to the sea, and taking the best direction, escaped the Dutch vessels; and the first land that they struck was the mouth of this bay. The other ship was captured by the Dutch. Two days later another galliot arrived from Cochin, carrying a Portuguese father named Figueredo,2 en route to Maluco. When that ship passed, the Dutch had already left. One would not believe the joy with which Father Marcelo was received; for the miracle had already become known, as I had brought many of the pamphlets from Madrid.3 All looked at him as at a man brought back to life; all were eager to learn of the miraculous occurrence from his own mouth; and in order to satisfy the whole city, he preached on the day of our father St. Francis Xavier, in our church at Manila. Many people were there. He preached very eloquently, and called forth tears from the audience at the narration of the miracle. The devotion of the people toward the saint has been greatly increased. They have all copied his pictures from a painting which the father had painted in Portugal, and which he says greatly resembles the pilgrim figure in which he saw the saint. The Portuguese found here a patache from Macan; and consequently, their people went [thither] by the last of October, in the patache. In their galliot went the captain-general. Father Marcelo tried to proceed on his trip to Macan; but, when he came to embark, Don Sebastian [Hurtado de Corcuera] pressed him strongly to remain this year, for ends that he said were very important for the service of God and of the king; and accordingly the father did so. The four Italian fathers who had accompanied Father Marçelo embarked in the patache, and with them Father Juan de Barrios, who took as his companion Brother Alonso Bernal. Father Juan de Barrios was going to negotiate matters of importance on behalf of the governor with that city. They left this port, and scarcely had they coasted along for forty leguas from this island, when so furious a storm struck them from the north, in which direction they were sailing, that they had to return. The galliot was saved, but the patache was driven ashore twelve leguas from here, on All Saints' day, suffering about twenty-five drowned. Among them were two priests—one a secular, and the other a friar. The rest escaped, although they suffered considerably. None of the money which they were taking to Macan was lost. The captain-general went to Macan later in his galliot, taking three fathers with him. Father Marcelo was in Mindanao at that time, and another father in Marinduque, and accordingly they remained here. It has been learned from Chinese ships that they arrived safely. This month of July Father Marçelo embarked in a Chinese ship, whose owner gave bonds that he would land him in a place where he could get to Macan. May God grant him a safe voyage. He has left these islands greatly edified by the shining examples of admirable virtues that he has given, and all have universally regretted his departure. Don Fray Diego Aduarte came from Nueva Segobia to endeavor once more to unite the new congregation of San Pablo with the ancient province of Rosario. He returned without concluding anything, and died shortly after his arrival at his bishopric.

A pilot and three other sailors—all Dutch—escaped from this port The Indians of Yndan killed the three sailors, and captured the pilot, who confessed and was awaiting the gallows. But Don Sebastian pardoned him, and promised to send him to Terrenate or the island of Hermosa, if he wished; or, if he preferred to serve the king again, to give him employment. He chose to serve the king, and was very grateful. The three Dutchmen whom your Reverence left in our house were converted to the Catholic faith. They came to this port, and were given places as sailors. One of them was one of those who ran away and was killed; the other two remain quiet. Two pilots and sixteen Spanish sailors fled in a champan; and another champan, with twenty soldiers, was sent in their pursuit. The latter encountered a large champan at Playa Honda, and tried to reconnoiter it, believing that it was the one in which the men had fled. The other champan, which was full of Chinese, prepared for defense, and fought; they wounded the [Spanish] commander and other soldiers with clubs, stones, and fragments of crockery ware. Six of the Sangleys were killed, and others wounded, whereupon they surrendered, and were brought to this port, where liberty was given to those left alive. Nothing was heard of the other champan. But it is already known, by way of China, that they arrived at Macan.

Another large gang of sailors were afterward discovered, who had a champan in the river of Cañas4 in order to flee. They were caught, and some of them were punished, although mercifully; as a result, those flights have ceased. A friar came here, clad as a secular priest, who had been punished and exiled by the Inquisition at Goa. He attempted here to flee to Cochinchina with a number of negroes—one of whom was the one whom your Reverence left in the office of the procurator for the province, and a good interpreter. They were caught, although by chance, while within the river, and are in prison.

The island of Hermosa

Last year a champan left there for Manila with seventeen Spaniards aboard. A Franciscan friar who had been for two or three years in China was also coming, who was still wearing his hair long. His name is Fray Antonio.5 They suffered great storms and hardships, and at the end of twenty days they found themselves before the fort owned by the Dutch in that island. They were captured and sent to Jacatra, and from thence to Maluco, with orders that they be set at liberty—but only on condition of a signed statement from the governor of those forts that a like number of Dutchmen would be returned to them when opportunity offered, which was done. They came with the galleons that carried the reënforcements. I saw here Fray Antonio, who is a native of Balladolid and who was still wearing his hair long. I have lately heard it said that he has returned to China with other friars. He affirms that it is very easy to enter Ucheo, and that a hold has been obtained among the people; and that it is openly known that they are Europeans and priests, without anyone molesting them. He said in regard to Jacatra that the Dutch have deeply offended the emperor of Java; and that no Dutchman leaves their fort without the natives cutting off his head. That prince has begged aid from the viceroy of India, in order to drive the Dutch thence. He told, us also that while he was there, a fleet sailed for Ambueno, where the natives had revolted, with the intention to reduce them by force. The relief ship which went last year to the island of Hermosa was, while returning, wrecked at Ilocos by the strength of the currents. No one was drowned. There is nothing else to narrate concerning that place.

Maluco

The relief ships for Terrenate sailed in January of this year. Their commander is Hieronimo Enriques Sotelo, who sailed in the galleon "San Luis." As admiral goes, in the "San Ambrosio," Don Pedro de Almonte, who came from Acapulco as captain the year before. Don Alonso de Acoçer was commander of the patache which came from Acapulco as almiranta; and Rafael Ome was commander of a galley which had just been finished on the stocks, named "San Francisco Xavier." Father Marcelo Mastril said mass in it and blessed it, on the day of its launching. A number of large champans went also. The Dutch were awaiting them with two galleons; but seeing our fleet, they retired under shelter of their fort of Malayo. The supplies having been disembarked, a feat never before performed was accomplished — namely, the galleons and galleys went out to fight with the Dutch ships where they were stationed. Our ships did some damage to them, and also to the fort of Malayo. Our almiranta also received some damage, but only one sailor was killed. Considerable reputation was gained by this attack. The Tidorans, our allies, were very proud and happy; and their king sent presents to the commander and admiral, together with his congratulations. The galleons and the patache returned; they brought no cloves, for there had been no harvest. The galley remained there, with another stationed at those forts. After the departure of the galleons, the two Dutch ships left, and during a calm were attacked by the two galleys. One of them came near being defeated; but, a wind springing up, they escaped by the favorable opportunity thus afforded. On that occasion, Don Agustin de Cepada was commander of the old6 galley. He has two brothers who are in Mexico, and your Reverence will find another brother in our professed house at Madrid. The above was learned from a champan which came after the ships of the relief expedition. In another champan, the last to leave those forts, came news regarding the king of Manados, forty leguas from Terrenate. Manados is a point of Macasar. He had sent to request help from the governor [of Terrenate], Don Pedro de Mendiola, against some who had revolted against him. He also sent his son and heir, some sixteen or seventeen years old, to be educated among the Spaniards, and asked for fathers to baptize his vassals. The youth is being instructed in our house, together with the prince of Siao, who is of his own age. The aid [which he asked] was sent, and Father Pantaleon, of our Society of Jesus. Another contingent of Dutchmen from Malayo deserted to us, and were brought here by the relief galleons.

Camucones

Many caracoas sailed out from this enemy this year. Committing depredations, they went in among these islands so far that they reached and pillaged Palapag, outside the Embocadero, and passed the cape of Espiritu Santo. They captured in Baco, in Ybabao, more than one hundred Christians. There they separated into two divisions, one of which went to Albay. The corregidor, who was Captain Mena, of the Order of St. George, sailed from the island of Manila to attack them, with some Spaniards and six Franciscan friars. They pressed the Camucones so closely that they drove ashore seven of their caracoas at Capul, where they freed many Christian captives, and some Camucones were slain by the natives. The enemy abandoned three other empty caracoas on the high sea, after their crews had been transferred to other caracoas in order to get away faster. Of our men, a musket-ball wounded only one friar, who died later. The father provincial went to visit Pintados, and passed in sight of the Camucones, as was learned afterward from a captive who escaped. But they did not pursue him, as they thought that it was an armed war caracoa of the Spaniards. The other division [of the Camucones] returned to the channel, and, coasting the island of Ybabao, entered Bangahun, where they captured more than one hundred Christians. Those two things have left us very full of wrath, both on account of the captives, and because we see that there is no place, however remote it be, that is safe. A caracoa of soldiers from Zibu fought with this division, and some damage was inflicted on them; and some of the Camucones were killed, and some captured. On returning to their own country, the Camucones suffered a great reverse from a furious gale, while they were coasting along Panay. Three caracoas were driven ashore; and of those pirates who escaped alive, many are in galleys in this port. Having crossed over to the Calamyanes, while they were sailing in much confusion some Spaniards captured two caracoas there, and delivered twenty captives from our mission of Mindoro. Fifteen caracoas were voyaging together, and while coasting along Paragua, two days before arriving at Burney, they met thirty caracoas of Joloans, who for some little time have been hostile to the Borneans. The thirty caracoas from Jolo attacked the fifteen, and captured them all. They took captive in them more than one hundred and fifty Camucones alive, and more than one hundred Christians. The latter were ransomed at a moderate price at Sanboangan. I have seen some of our missions, where I heard all about the affair. It is feared, however, that the Camucones will make a raid this year also. Accordingly, Don Sebastian is sending twenty-five soldiers to our missions of Catbalogan, etc., so that, aided by other Spaniards who are going there in some caracoas—which the Indians have built at their own cost, and which are large and good—the Camucones may be opposed and even chastised.

Mindanao

The captain-general of Cachil Corralat, one Tagal, left Mindanao with eight good caracoas7 to pillage these islands. He remained among them for a matter of seven months, at full ease, committing many depredations. At Cuyo he captured Don Diego de Alabes, who was corregidor there. He also captured the father prior of Cuyo, an Augustinian Recollect, and two other friars; and although they had hidden themselves with all their ornaments and chalices, that did not avail them, for the enemy knew not how to find them. Tagal went to Mindoro, and everywhere he pillaged a great quantity of goods, and took a great number of captives. He left Don Diego Alabes in Mindoro, so that he might come [here] to get his ransom and that of the three Recollect fathers. They demanded two thousand pesos and thirty taes of gold — the latter amounting to more than three hundred pesos in addition — for each person. Don Diego arrived exhausted with his hardships, from which he died shortly after his arrival at Manila. He narrated most insolent acts of Tagal, who blasphemed greatly, and who threatened that he would enter this bay and pillage and burn its coasts. Don Sebastian already bore in his breast the resolution to go to Mindanao, and this occurrence increased further his desire to humiliate that enemy. When the so great ransoms were proposed to him, he answered that he would like to raise them, but that until he should go, he would not discuss this point. Even before anything had been ascertained, he sent Bartolome Dias de la Barrera as governor of San Boangan, and Nicolas Gonsales as captain and sargento-mayor. They set out at the beginning of November, and shortly after their arrival [at Zamboanga] they learned that Tagal had passed on the inside8 of the island of Taguima with eight caracoas9 laden with captives and spoils. Although the pirates were one day in the lead, the Spaniards made haste, and inside of two hours equipped six caracoas;10 and Nicolas Gonsales sailed in pursuit of the enemy, thinking that, as they were so heavily laden with booty, he could overtake them.

This happened, for he met them at Punta de Flechas. It was called so because the natives believed that a great war divinity was there, who considers it a grateful sacrifice for them to offer him arrows; and this is the reason why they land at that point when they go out armed and on their return, discharging many arrows in honor of the divata or idol whom they adore there: Nicolas Gonsales and his men fought valiantly; they killed Tagal, and captured the flagship and three other caracoas. The other caracoas escaped by taking flight. Many Mindanaos were killed, and only twenty were captured alive. In the flagship was the father prior of Cuyo, who was so badly wounded by our balls that he died two hours after the defeat. A brother of Tagal was also mortally wounded. He very anxiously begged baptism of the father; and, after his baptism, they both died. The other two fathers were in the caracoas which escaped. There were one hundred and thirty-two Christian captives liberated there, and some others were also killed by our balls. Not one of our men was killed. A remarkable circumstance occurred at the time of the fight—namely, that there was a great earthquake at that time, which caused in that height prodigiously loud roaring sounds, which terrified both our men and the enemy. The Spaniards drew out their rosaries and reliquaries, and, holding them in their hands, begged God for mercy; and the cliff fell into the sea. That was an announcement of the fortunate victory which Don Sebastian was to have afterward, who gave this point the name San Sebastian, both for his saint, and on account of the arrows with which that saint was martyred. Among the spoils was found a large sheet on which was painted a figure of the Christ, and before him St. Augustine kneeling. The Mindanaos had cut off one arm of the Christ, and had beheaded St. Augustine, in order to be able to make a mantle of it after their fashion—mocking, and saying that they were carrying the God of the Christians captive. They spit in the chalices, and committed other outrages, and uttered other great blasphemies. Before receiving this news, Don Sebastian left Manila with twelve champans, in which were embarked his company, as well as that of the sailors of the port of Cavite, and another company of Pampangos. He chose St. Francis Xavier as patron saint of his expedition. With him he took Father Marcelo de Mastril, which was the reason for his detaining the latter; he also took his confessor, Father Juan de Barrios. He left on February 2, and passing by Oton, landed at the city and fort, where he learned of the victory of Nicolas Gonsales, and saw the mutilated Christ. His desire to take satisfaction for the insults offered to God increased with this sight; and, pursuing his voyage, he arrived at Sanboangan February 22.11 There in a very brief time, Don Sebastian arranged his voyage to La Mitan, as the chief village of Cachil Corralat is called. Although he had, it is true, been advised at Pintados that Captains Juan Nicolas and Juan de Leon, who were going with eighty Spaniards and one thousand volunteer Indians to take part in this war, had not even yet arrived, nevertheless with his champans and other oared vessels of Sanboangan (in which went as captain Nicolas Gonsales, who was sick), he immediately set out, leaving orders for the volunteers to follow him when they arrived. On account of the contrary weather, the vessels were unable to go in a body; and hence Don Sebastian de Corcuera arrived first, with only seventy Spaniards in a few champans. The Moro Corralat had heard of the arrival of the governor, and talked of submission; but he was dissuaded from it by six Javanese trading vessels that were stopping there. Although those vessels were already laden and about to sail, they offered to remain and aid in the defense. Thereupon they all took position ready to receive the

Spaniards and to fight with them. They had a fort in the village with good12 pieces of artillery and a matter of ten versos, and many muskets and arquebuses. Don Sebastian, thinking that the rest of the fleet was delayed, had two field pieces disembarked; and with fifty Spaniards, the remainder being left in the ships, he made an attack upon the enemy. It was a matter which was regarded as a miracle, that with so few men he should conquer so many Moros. He gained the fort and the village, and sent the people in flight to the hill, which they had fortified. There was a great slaughter of Mindanaos, but not one Spaniard was killed in this fray. Father Marçelo was carrying the standard, which was placed on a spear — the mutilated Christ on one side, and St. Francis Xavier on the other, back to back. There they found about three hundred ships, great and small, and a great amount of property. The governor set a guard over it; and, the Moros having fled to the hill, the Christian captives continued to come in, and the rest of the fleet arrived. The governor purified the mosque, and a solemn procession was made through the village with great pomp as a thank-offering; and mass was heard in the mosque. This village has a sheltered hill which the Indians call Ylihan; it is a natural fort. The Moros had in it some pieces13 with ladles, and sixteen or seventeen versos and other firearms. The ascent is very narrow, so that it is difficult to mount it single file. At its sides are steep precipices and heights. There Corralat had taken shelter with all his men, and, confident in his arms and the ruggedness [of the place] was proudly awaiting the Spaniards. At his rear was a rough and very secret ascent, which did not alarm our commander; for, six days after the surrender of the village, Don Sebastian had despatched Nicolas Gonsales with spies and good soldiers around by the rear, while his Lordship was resolved to attack from the front, which was one and one-half leguas from the village. Nicolas Gonsales set out, although very much impeded, and Don Sebastian marched with his men, after leaving a guard in the village. The plan was to attack at the same time from both sides. On coming to the hill, the vanguard immediately attacked, with over-confident spirit. But as it was so well defended, and the Moros were behind works, while the Spaniards were in the open, and there was no path by which to mount, the Spaniards began to fall dead and wounded; while the Moros received no damage, until the arrival of Don Sebastian, who made them retire. About twenty valiant Spaniards were killed. The Moros, encouraged by this, were more careless of the other approach, by which Nicolas Gonsales mounted the following day, and gained the eminence before he was perceived. When they were discovered, Corralat hastened to the defense, but he soon turned and fled, having been wounded in one arm. The others fled with him. His wife, with a child in her arms, threw herself over a precipice, as did many other people; and thus the hill was won for the king our sovereign. Two Recollect fathers14 were found, all mangled with wounds that they had just received; one of them was already dead, the other lived two days. Don Sebastian was immediately advised of the result, and mounted the hill. The booty found there was immense. The houses were burned; the artillery and versos were taken down the hill. With those below, they numbered twelve pieces with ladles, twenty-seven versos and falcons, and one hundred and twenty muskets and arquebuses. Many Moros were captured, and many Christians set free. La Mitan and three other neighboring villages were burned, and their boats were burned, with the exception of some that were taken to Sanboangan. This enterprise concluded, the governor returned with all his fleet, having first sent Sargento-mayor Palomino to Cachil Moncay—an own cousin to Corralat and his keen antagonist, and a son of the great pirate Silongan—offering him friendship, and asking that he would try to get Corralat into his power. Don Sebastian met the volunteers under Juan Nicolas at sea. He ordered them to follow Palomino in order that the treaty might be given greater encouragement. Shortly after the arrival of Don Sebastian at Sanboangan, they returned with a brother of Moncay as ambassador. Moncay offered to pay tribute, and to free all the Christian captives in his lands. Upon the conclusion of these matters, Don Sebastian returned to Manila; of his triumphal entrance therein, with the thank-offering to God for the victory, and the honors made to the dead, I shall say nothing here, as I wrote a special relation of it which I enclose herewith.15 Don Sebastian ordered Juan Nicolas, with the eighty Spaniards and one thousand volunteer Indians, to return to La Mitan, and to sail round the island as far as Caragan, committing all possible hostilities upon the people tributary to Corralat. He did this admirably, pillaging and burning many villages, beheading many of the people because they defended themselves, capturing others, and burning a great number of ships. In consequence Corralat has been greatly humbled, and all those Moros are fearful. News was received later that Moncay is sending us a number of captives, and others of the captives held by Corralat are also coming.

Xolo

What has somewhat disturbed the satisfactory course of affairs is Xolo. It is an island which is even nearer to Sanboangan than the [village of] La Mitan belonging to Corralat. That Moro has held as his tributaries the people of the island of Taguima and Basilan,16 which is four leguas from our fort of Sanboangan. After the many plundering raids which he has made among our islands, he was very desirous of peace. A letter was written to him, saying that peace would be considered; and among other conditions which were imposed on him was one, namely, that he should evacuate [the island of] Taguima (which was to be tributary to the king), and that ministers of the gospel should be established there in order to baptize the natives. In fact, Father Francisco Angel had been sent thither, so that he might administer to them the holy sacraments. To this he replied that he did not want peace, and with this declaration and action the Joloans have fortified themselves. Dato Ache, who is the greatest pirate of that island, has gone to Cachil Corralat, in order to unite with him against the Spaniards. As a result, the chiefs of Taguima and Basilan—who were apparently very contented, and were on very friendly terms with us—have retired; and Father Francisco Angel writes that he has not been able to go there. The chiefs of the mainland of Mindanao, who were dancing attendance on the Spaniards at Sanboangan, have become somewhat impertinent. But Don Sebastian is preparing for the chastisement of Xolo, and intends to go in person by the end of December to conquer it, as he did the opposition of Corralat. May God grant him a good voyage and a happy outcome. If this Moro is humbled, all the island of Mindanao will be very peaceable.

Japon

Since ships have come neither from that kingdom nor from Macan, we have not had any letters giving a detailed report of events. But we have learned from Chinese ships that the Portuguese of Macan went to the fairs in that country, and made great profits. It is also said that the emperor has ordered the Dutch that they shall not be permitted at any time or place to harm the ships of Macan that sail to Japon. A renegade mestizo priest—of a Portuguese father and a Japanese mother—gave as his opinion that, in order to extinguish more completely the Christianity of that kingdom, they should exile all those who had any blood of the Portuguese or Castilians. That was done, and they were delivered to those from Macan, so that these people might be taken to their city, and there be kept until further orders. They ordered that renegade also to go to Macan, since he was also concerned by this. He begged them to send him to Jacatra with the Dutch, and his request was granted. It has also been said that a cousin of the king,17 who is seignior of five kingdoms, is making war on him, and that many Japanese are following him.

Various

A letter was received from the father of the Society of Jesus who is in Camboja, a short time ago. He says in it that the Dutch have established a factory in that kingdom, which has certainly given us much anxiety. The island of Tabuca lies midway between Mindanao and Maluco; I have been told by the father guardian of St. Francis, who came from Terrenate, that on arriving at it on his way hither, to take in a supply of water, the chiefs of it told him that three caracoas full of men tributary to Corralat had just arrived; that they were fearful because of what had happened to their seignior, and that they were trying to send a despatch to Terrenate in order to establish friendship [with the Spaniards], and to request priests to baptize them. The commander of the galleys, Antonio Carreño de Baldes, died at this port; and that post of commander was given to Nicolas Gonsales, and he is at the same time governing the port.

Don Francisco de Balderrama, although so young a lad, went to Mindanao with Don Sebastian; and, while near his Lordship, it happened that a musket-ball struck the governor's page (who was at his side) in the flap of his helmet. The ball went in his cheek and came out through his mouth, and struck Don Francisco in the breast, knocking him down immediately. However, he received no hurt; for on examining him, it was found that the ball had passed through his clothing and shirt, and had struck in some altar-linens which he carried next his breast through devotion, without its having left any mark on them. That is esteemed as a miracle. This is what has occurred to me to write your Reverence. I shall be careful to do the same, God helping, every year, providing that your Reverence writes me of occurrences there. May our Lord preserve your Reverence, and give you a prosperous voyage, etc. Cavite, July 23, 1637.[18]

JUAN LOPEZ[19]

[1] Francisco Colin was born at Ripoll, of a prominent Catalonian family, in July, 1592. At the age of thirteen he was sent to Barcelona for his education; he there entered the Jesuit order, February 14, 1607. After his ordination he spent several years in preaching, in Gerona, Cardona, and other places; and afterward was an instructor in the college at Zaragoza. Desiring to labor among the heathen, he entered the Philippine missions, arriving at Manila June 28, 1626. About that time, the Jesuits attempted to found missions in Formosa and Jolo, to which task Colin was assigned; but, these proving abortive, he remained at Manila, occupying a chair in the Jesuit college, and acting as confessor to Governor Niño de Tavora. After the latter's death, Colin became rector of the college, and soon afterward was sent (1634) to the new mission of Mindoro, where he spent three years. Recalled to Manila, he was rector of the college until he was chosen (1639) provincial of the islands—an office which he held a second time, according to Pastelle. The latter years of his life were spent in literary work, preaching to the Indians, and religious exercises; he died on May 6, 1660. Among his writings the most important is his Labor evangélica (Madrid, 1663), part of which will be presented in subsequent volumes of this series. See sketches of Colin's life in Murillo Velarde's Hist. Philipinas, fol. 259–267; and Pastells's edition of Labor evangélica (Barcelona, 1904), pp. 225–230.

2 Antonio Figueredo was born at Ourem, Portugal, in 1586, and was admitted into the Society in 1603. He was sent to the Indias, and ministered at Salsette; he was rector of Chaul and of Tana, and of the residence of San Paolo Vecchio at Goa, where he died May 8, 1650. See Sommervogel's Bibliothèque.

3 Evidently referring to the vision and miraculous cure which are referred to ante, in sketch of Mastrilli's life, note 76.

4 Probably meaning the stream that falls into the sea nearest to Punta de Cañas, a point on the southwest coast of Bataán, which is the small province of western Luzon that encloses the western side of Manila Bay.

5 An evident reference to Fray Antonio Caballero (or Santa María, his name in religion), a noted laborer in the Chinese missions. He was born in April, 1602, at Baltanás, south of Valladolid, and entered the Franciscan order March 24, 1618. He spent four years (1629–33) in Manila, and then went to China. (His first convert in that country afterward became a Dominican friar, and was finally (1674) consecrated a bishop, the first of his nation to attain that dignity—and, according to Dominican authority, the only Chinaman ever consecrated, up to 1890, as a bishop. This man's Chinese name was Lô, and he was baptized as Gregorio López; he was sent to pursue his studies in the college of Santo Tomás at Manila, where he received holy orders. He died at Nanking in February, 1690, at the age of eighty; see account of his life in Reseña biográfica, i, pp. 433–436.) After regaining his liberty, on the occasion mentioned in our text, he spent some two years in Manila; and went in 1639 to Macao, to act as vicar of the convent of St. Clare there. In 1644 all the Spaniards residing in Macao were exiled by the Portuguese, and Fray Antonio, with those nuns, sailed (October 10) for Manila. They were driven by a storm to a port in Cochinchina, and obliged to remain six months in that country, where they were hospitably treated; in May, 1645, they arrived safely at Manila. Four years later, Fray Antonio returned to China, where he labored until his death—which occurred at Canton, May 13, 1669—having suffered imprisonment, exile, and many privations. He left many writings (some in Chinese), mainly referring to the missions in China. See Huerta's sketch of his life and labors, in Estado, pp. 406–413.

6 In the original manuscript the word "new" has been crossed out and "old" written above the line.

7 In the margin is written: "Others say with 7."

8 In the original manuscript the word "outside" has been crossed out, and "inside" written above the line.

9 In the margin occurs the note: "Or with 7."

10 Marginal note: "One of the 6 left [the fleet] because it was heavy."

11 In the original manuscript the date "March 1" has been crossed out, and the above date inserted above the line.

12 In the original manuscript the word "five" is crossed out and "good" inserted above the line.

13 In the original manuscript, the figure "7" is crossed out, and "some" added above the line.

14 Marginal note: "One was said to have been killed in Mican the day of the assault."

15 It will be found directly following the present document.

16 Both these names are applied to the same island, Basilan being the modern appellation. It is the largest island of a group of the same name; numbering fifty-seven, nearly all of them very small.

17 Meaning the shogun Iyémitsu, who reigned until 1649. He was an able and far-sighted ruler, who adopted many political and economic measures of great importance. See Griffis's account of his reign, in Mikado's Empire, pp. 285–287.

18 This letter is published by Barrantes in his Guerras piráticas, pp. 289–303; he states that it was written to Fathers Diego de Bobadilla and Simon Costa, while they were traveling to Rome, but he incorrectly gives the writer's name as Francisco Lopez, while Retana (Bibliog. Mindanao, p. 21) as incorrectly ascribes it to Alejandro Lopez. In Barrantes's version, a postscript dated September 15 is appended to the letter, describing the gift of money offered to the governor by the Chinese on this occasion. This same statement will be found in "Events in the Filipinas, 1637–38," post.

19 Juan Lopez was born at Moratalla, Spain, December 27, 1584, and when fifteen years old entered the Jesuit order. In 1606 he departed for the Philippines, where he held numerous positions of trust in his order, and was for a time a commissary of the Inquisition; he was also sent to Rome as procurator of the Filipinas province. He also labored in the missions of Pintados and in Mindanao. Lopez died at Manila, September 3, 1659. See Murillo Velarde's Hist. Philipinas, fol. 269 verso, 270.

Corcuera's Triumphant Entry into Manila

An account of the reception given in Manila to Señor Hurtado de Corcuera, when he returned triumphant from Mindanao.1

Yesterday, a little before eleven a.m., we left Cavite in a row-boat with Don Sebastian, and reached Santiago at one p.m. A short time before our arrival, some Japanese Christians came out to meet him, in two champans — the sides of which were entirely surrounded with shield-shaped forms of white linen cloth adorned with green crosses; they bore also many white flags, with fresh flowers; and they welcomed his arrival with blasts from the trumpet that they carried. The governor received them very cordially; and they, falling behind, accompanied him. We landed2 at the house of Amaro Diaz, where the military headquarters were located. From that place Father Juan de Barrios and myself went to our house, where we found the father provincial Father Juan de Bueras, Father Roa,3 and father Marcelo [i.e., Mastrilli], who had all come to the reception, (but before I give an account of it, it is to be known that a quarter of an hour after the arrival of Don Sebastian, there came the champan of Don Graviel Niño, the only one who was missing.)

At the head [of the troops] marched Nicolás Gonzalez with his famous and victorious company of the buff doublets; around his shield-bearer walked many other pages, carrying the weapons that Don Nicolas had taken away from the Mindanaos in the naval battle. We gave him a thousand congratulations for his notable success. This company was followed by that of the sailors under the command of Alférez A. Mezquita. They marched in two files, and between these went first the friendly Indians and Sangleys who had been delivered from captivity to Corralat; and indeed the sight of some of these Indians, of both sexes, moved us to compassion, as they walked carrying their rosaries. At a little distance behind them, in the midst of the same company, came the Mindanao captives, of both sexes; the women and the children were not bound, but the men marched in chains and shackles. This company was followed by a large body of men who carried the weapons taken from the enemy: shields, breastplates, campilans, spears, and two war-trumpets which seemed to be of Dutch make. Then came the company of Pampangos4 who also took part in the expedition. Captain Carranza followed, on horseback; and as he is the captain of artillery, he was in charge of the carts with the firearms taken from the enemy. In three of these carts were the muskets and arquebuses; in one were the culverin-chambers and three small church-bells, and in another followed twelve or fourteen small culverins; then came a large falcon which could easily be taken for a culverin, and five or six gun-carriages, each carrying two small pieces and some falcons. These were followed by large artillery pieces, one by one, which the natives dragged with ropes; and the last and largest of these was drawn by four horses. All these weapons were accompanied by the artillerymen; and directly after them came six boys, carrying six flags taken from Corralat. Behind these marched the company of the governor with great splendor; Don Sebastian himself rode before them on horseback, in plain attire, and almost treading upon the flags of the enemy. Behind him came his shield-bearer, carrying his helmet, on which was a large tuft of white plumes; his chaplain and his secretary followed, also on horseback. As the governor was seen advancing toward the city, a salvo of artillery was fired from the forts at the Bagunbaya gate; and as he entered the city, a merry peal of bells rang from our house, the wind-instruments began to play, and the choir sang a festal song [villancico]. All the inmates of our house5 stood, clad in our priestly mantles, waiting for him under a fine triumphal arch, handsomely adorned with silk and with scrolls containing verses. There we gave him welcome, and congratulated him on the victory won; to which he responded very courteously. As the governor came under the arch, Don Josepito de Salazar,6 elegantly dressed, came out from behind some screens which were on a platform, and recited a poem7 written by Brother Liorri, in which he extolled the victory, thanked and congratulated the governor and his soldiers, and ended by saying that according to the name Corquera—that is, corda quærens ("seek for breasts and hearts")— he had found them in all of us who were there, since we held him in our hearts, and wished him all prosperity and happiness. The governor listened attentively to this address, and at the end he turned toward the fathers and thanked them.8

Then the procession marched to the square, where a squadron of six companies, under arms, was awaiting it. All of us, in order to see the affair, went to the balconies of the master-of-camp, Pedro de Heredia, arriving there in time to see the governor alight before the great church, where the royal Audiencia and the ecclesiastical and secular cabildos awaited him. He entered the church and, humbly prostrated on the floor, offered a prayer of considerable length, attributing his entire success to God. Again he mounted his horse, and approached the squadron; there, hat in hand, he addressed both captains and soldiers with great display of kindness; and the army answered him with a general salute, while the standard-bearers lowered the flags. Then he proceeded to his palace; but when he was descried from the fort of Santiago, its warden, General Don Fernando de Ayala, saluted him with a volley from all the artillery of the fort. The six companies of the camp followed the governor's company; and thus ended this magnificent triumph, which has greatly delighted people of all nations. The master-of-camp, Pedro de Heredia, regaled us with a bountiful and choice repast, with several kinds of conserves; after which we returned to our house, thanking God for having seen what we have desired to see during so many years. The multitude of people who filled the streets, windows, and balconies could not be numbered; and words cannot tell the tender feelings which the joy and the sight of so grand and new a spectacle caused in every heart. There was scarcely a person from whose eyes the joyful tenderness of the heart did not draw tears. At night all the walls around were illuminated, as well as many other places both within and without the city. Many sky-rockets were fired, and at about ten or eleven o'clock at night the soldiers in masquerade went through the streets on horseback with many torches, to display their joy; both men and horses were elegantly and splendidly adorned. May God send us many days like this, on which Christ Jesus may triumph over his enemy; and may He preserve your Reverence, etc. Manila, May 25, 1637.

Last night, May twenty-sixth, the city masquerade came out; it was so large and magnificent that, from whatever side it was viewed, it made a fine appearance. All the windows and balconies were brilliantly illuminated. Before the door of our church huge bonfires were built, and we ourselves went down to see the procession a little nearer. This took place about nine o'clock at night.

For those who died in the war, the governor caused solemn funerals to be held in the new military church, on June fifth. Eight altars were erected, and, beginning before dawn, masses were said at these altars to which office all had been invited, both the secular clergy and those of the orders; and this lasted throughout the morning. To each priest who would accept it, a gratuity of a peso was given for the mass celebrated, but many refused to take this. At the proper time was celebrated a mass followed by a sermon, at which were present all the city, the clergy, and the religious orders. The sermon was very appropriate for the occasion, and was well delivered; it was preached by Father Francisco Pinelo, of the Order of St. Dominic. His text was very opportune, taken from Job 12, verse 6: Abundant tabernacula pradonum, et audacter provocant Deum cum ipse dederit omnia [in manus eorum] — "The dwellings of pirates are full of riches; they become haughty and bold at their strength; they scorn and provoke God; but it is He who gives them success, in order to punish and correct the Christians."9 All this has happened in the present case; for the Moros insolently ill-treated God and His saints in their holy images, cutting off the arms of the crucified Christ, and saying that they had taken captive the God of the Christians. The preacher added this from verse 13, which says: Apud ipsum est sapientia et fortitudo, ipse habet consilium et intelligentiam,10 etc. — "The wretched ones do not know that God unites in Himself a council of state and one of war; in the former He decrees their ruin, and by the latter He carries it out," as has been clearly seen in this expedition.

The thanksgiving fiesta was held on the seventh of June, in the cathedral, on account of the great concourse of people to hear it; but even that had not room for them. The procession started from the cathedral and passed through the same streets as it does on Corpus Christi day. These streets were all adorned with handsome arches and green branches, and many altars laden with decorations and rich ornaments. The final touch was given by the citizens, who adorned the streets with hangings. It is generally affirmed that never have there been seen in Manila so many and so rich draperies, so that, even after seeing them, people hardly believed that the city contained so many of them, and so elegant and valuable — besides those which hung from the balconies, which latter were those that ordinarily have been displayed. From the balconies upward was erected an awning of bamboo, and that also was filled with hangings, and ribbons, and pieces of silk.

In the procession marched a body of pikemen in two files, their pikes held aloft. Between these files came first the captives who escaped from Corralat's power; they were well dressed and marched thus, three soldiers, and then six captives, and so on, observing always the same order. Then followed the citizens, and, after them, all the religious orders. The procession was enlivened by a great variety of dances and similar exhibitions, accompanied by various musical instruments and two portable organs. Toward the end of the procession came four floats, so made as to form a sort of doubly-sloping roof. On the float were placed [the sacred things] which the Mindanaos had plundered: on each slope lay the chasuble, choristers' mantles, frontals, and other sacred ornaments; on the ridge stood the chalices, monstrances and patens; and at the edge were hung the chrismatories and small bells. This sight moved the people to pity, and many tears were shed. The students in our college of San José carried three of these floats on their shoulders, and the fourth was carried by our brothers who were students, clad in surplices. Immediately after the floats came Father Marcelo Mastril, with the banner which he carried when the town of Cachil Corralat was taken; he had also borne it in another procession, which was made there in thanksgiving after the surrender. On this banner were depicted, standing back to back, that figure of Christ which had been stabbed and insulted by the enemy, and our father San Francisco Javier, the patron saint of the whole expedition, whose eyes were bent upon the blessed sacrament. Then followed the royal standard, which was carried at first by the governor, and then in turn by the gentlemen of the royal Audiencia and the alcaldes-in-ordinary. These were followed by the city magistrates, who carried the poles of a canopy under which advanced a stately car directed by robed priests, and bearing the blessed sacrament. When this car was seen entering the street, the blessed sacrament received a joyous salute from the nine ladled cannon and the twenty-seven culverins and falcons which stood in the Plaza de Armas. All these weapons, except three large pieces that were left in the fort of Samboangan, had been taken from Corralat. Not less solemn and magnificent was the salute made by the corps formed of eight companies of arquebusiers in the city square. Mass was celebrated by the ecclesiastical chapter, and sung with great solemnity; and Father Juan de Bueras preached a very appropriate sermon in three quarters of an hour. The text on which the sermon was based was taken from Genesis 14, verse 14 — when Abraham with three hundred and eighteen of his servants defeated the hostile kings who had taken captive his nephew Lot; and took from them all the plunder and the captives, together with all the precious and valuable things they possessed. For this victory Melchisedec, priest of the Most High, in thanksgiving offered a sacrifice of bread and wine; and it is to be noticed that Abraham asked nothing of the plunder for himself, content to give God the thanks for so great a victory.

In order that there might not be lacking a pleasant interlude to so grave a drama, I shall relate what happened in this port of Cavite on the same day, June seventh. On Saturday afternoon, June sixth, the children, having been dismissed early from the two schools, went to play at the fort which has been begun at the outer edge of the town, and there began a game, some being Moros and others Christians — one party defending the fort, and the other rushing on to capture it. Not satisfied with this, they made arrangements to carry on the game in a more fitting manner the next day. In the meantime they provided themselves with flags and with wooden and bamboo swords. He who played Cachil Corralat hoisted his flag on the fort, incited his men to defend it, and even insulted the Christians by calling them "Spanish blusterers," and "hens." The latter, eager to assault, boldly attacked them, but were so bravely repelled by the Moros that some were wounded and roughly handled. This threw the Christians into such rage that they furiously attacked the fort again, desisting only when they had gained entrance to it. Cachil Corralat, who fell into their hands, was flung down from the wall, and was badly hurt on the head, so much so that it required five stitches in dressing the wound; but now I see him walking the streets, but with his head bandaged.

Finally a very agreeable drama on the conquest of Mindanao, written by Father Hieronimo Perez, was presented in the evening of July fifteenth, in our church.11 The play told the story of the campaign as it occurred — not, however, without certain devices in which was displayed the holy zeal, faith, and piety of the Society of Jesus. These kindled in Don Sebastian's mind the purpose to take vengeance for the insults offered to God, and to put a stop to the injuries which the Christians of these islands, and especially our missions in Pintados, are suffering. The play ended with a tourney-dance, for which prizes were given. Thus everything was as well and splendidly performed as one could desire.

The crowning touch was given to the pleasure of the audience by the news, which was brought to the governor while the prologue was being spoken, that the ships from Castilla had arrived.

Laus Deo Virginis Mariae (sic)

1 It is the copy of a letter written by Father Juan Lopez at Cavite. — Barrantes.

2 Bobadilla's version of this letter (see his "Glorious victories against the Moros," post) says that they landed "at the beach of Santiago de Bagumbaya, a settlement in front of Manila, an arquebus-shot distant." Some additional details given by Bobadilla will be used, like this, as annotations to Lopez's own letter.

3 Francisco de Roa was born in 1592, in the City of Mexico. At the age of fourteen, he went to Manila, and became a student at the Jesuit college of San José. On May 18, 1609, he became a Jesuit novice there, and after his ordination as a priest he was sent to the missions of Pintados. Afterward summoned to Manila, he was a teacher in San José for five years; he was twice rector of the Manila house, and three times (1644, 1648, and 1659) was chosen provincial. Going on an official visit to Mindanao, the ship which carried him was lost, with all on board (January, 1660). See Murillo Velarde's Hist. Philipinas, fol. 267, 268.

4 Bobadilla says of these natives: "They are a brave people, very faithful, and excellent Christians, and handle their weapons very skilfully. They drill in companies in the camp at Manila, among the Spanish companies. In all the garrisons and expeditions they perform military duty well."

5 "Our college is very near the gate, in the second square" (Bobadilla).

6 "A young and very handsome gentleman, a son of his Majesty's accountant, Martin Ruyz de Salaçar" (Bobadilla).

7 Barrantes adds (pp. 310–317) copies of these verses, and of others which were evidently used on the arch above mentioned; and states that Father Lopez, at the end, informs his correspondent that these stanzas were composed, the scrolls lettered, and the address committed to memory, between seven o'clock at night and seven the next morning, on account of the short time available before the entry of the governor.

8 An abridgment of Lopez's letter to this point is found in the Ventura del Arco MSS. (Ayer library). The following additional remarks are presumably added by the compiler of that collection: "The relation nevertheless neglects to mention the reception by the city or municipal council, which apparently

must have been very cold; for neither the Audiencia nor the regidors awaited the governor at the gates of the city, although they should have gone out to the Puerta Real ["royal gate"]. Neither does the relation state whether the city council paid the bills for any function in honor of Corcuera and of the Spanish arms. The only ones who celebrated these were the Jesuits, the soldiers, the Indians, and some private persons—a matter which demands attention."

9 A paraphrase, rather than a translation of the Latin. The Douay version reads: "The tabernacles of robbers abound, and they provoke God boldly, whereas it is he that hath given all into their hands."

10 In the Douay version: "With him is wisdom, and strength, he hath counsel and understanding."

11 "Among the spectators, and greatly enjoying the play, were the governor, the royal Audiencia, the archbishop, and the principal persons of the city of Manila" (Bobadilla).

Royal Aid Requested by the Jesuits at Manila

Most potent Sir:

I, Father Francisco Colin, rector of the residence of the Society of Jesus of this city, declare that his Majesty was pleased to order the issue of the royal decree which I present directed to this royal Audiencia—ordering that it inform him of the condition of the work on the said my residence, what is still to be done, and whether the said my residence has enough funds to enable it to continue the said work without his Majesty granting the ten thousand ducados payable in unassigned Indians, which was asked from him on the part of the said my residence. In that work have been spent the ten thousand ducados which his Majesty granted to the said my residence in the year one thousand six hundred and twenty-five; and besides the said ten thousand ducados have been spent forty thousand six hundred and eighty-one pesos. In order to be enabled to meet the said expense, because of the great need in which the order stood of a house and church, and because it had no money with which to do this, it obtained a loan of twenty thousand two hundred, pesos, for which it pays one thousand and ten pesos interest annually. The other twenty thousand four hundred and eighty-one pesos this residence owes to various persons, who, because they wish us well, have lent those amounts to the said residence. Besides that, all the legacies and alms that have fallen to it in the course of fourteen years have been spent, as appears more in detail in the certification which I present. As is evident and well known, the said work is yet to be finished. There still are lacking the construction of the porter's lodge, the principal stairway of the house, the school, and the infirmary, with which the said work will be preserved and extended. It is in danger of ruin from earthquakes, for a part of the said building is now open for lack of connecting walls, as appears more in detail from the certification of Miguel Sanchez Marufo, architect of this city, which I present. Therefore, I petition and beseech your Highness to be pleased to make the said report, so that it may be despatched in this patache, paying heed to the fact that all the aforesaid in this writing is accurate and true. Thereby will this residence receive grace and alms.

Francisco Colin

Manila, at the meeting of August three, one thousand six hundred and thirty-seven. Let his Majesty be informed according to the royal decree.

[The certification presented was as follows:]

I, Father Francisco Colin, rector of the residence of the Society of Jesus of this city of Manila, certify that it appears, from the account-books for the work of the church and house of the said residence, that there has been spent on the works the ten thousand ducados which his Majesty granted it in the year one thousand six hundred and twenty-five, and which were collected in the time of Governor Don Juan Niño de Tavora. In addition to the said sum, it also appears that there has been spent in the same work, forty thousand six hundred and eighty-one pesos, which this residence now owes: twenty thousand two hundred of borrowed money, on which it pays one thousand and ten pesos interest; and the other twenty thousand four hundred and eighty-one in coin, which are due to various persons, who lent them to this residence because they favor us; besides, the legacies and alms that have fallen to it, in the course of fourteen years since the first stone was laid, have also been consumed in the same work. All the above is apparent to me, both by the account-books of this residence, and because most of them were in my time and partly by my authority. And, inasmuch as this is true, I affixed my signature to the same in this residence of Manila, July twenty-eight, one thousand six hundred and thirty-seven.

Juan [sic; sc. Francisco] Colin

[The certification of the architect is as follows:]

I, Miguel Sanchez Marrufo, architect of this city, having examined at the petition of Father Francisco Colin, rector of the residence of the Society of Jesus of this city, the work on the said residence, find that, although that part of the building which contains most of the residence-quarters of the religious is now finished, there is still another part yet to be constructed — namely, the porter's lodge, the principal stairway of the house, the schools, and the infirmaries, with which the quadrangle of buildings will be completed, and the said work will be extended and continued. What is finished is in danger of ruin from earthquakes, for, by lack of connecting walls, one part of the building finished is still open. This will cause greater injury if it be not remedied, making the edifice secure by completing the quadrangle of the said house. Inasmuch as this is true, I affixed my signature to the same. Manila, today, July twenty-eight, one thousand six hundred and thirty-seven.

Miguel Sanchez Marrufo

[The archbishop, Hernando Guerrero, wrote the following letter in regard to the matter:]

Sire:

By a decree of July ten, one thousand six hundred and thirty-five, your Majesty orders me to inform you on the first opportunity, and to send my opinion, in regard to an alms of ten thousand ducados in unassigned Indians which is asked for in behalf of the residence of the Society of Jesus in this city of Manila, for the work on the said residence and church, in addition to another of like sum which your Majesty was pleased to grant it in June, one thousand six hundred and twenty-five, for the same purpose. Having made the investigations in fulfilment of the mandate of your Majesty, I find that the first ten thousand ducados have been consumed in the said work, as well as another large sum which citizens of this city have given as alms and loans. Although the principal part of the building is finished, it is in danger because the fourth arch is wanting, which will join together what has been built. This ten thousand additional ducados which is now petitioned will be very necessary; and although the said residence has some revenues, I am informed that these do not cover the expense of their ordinary support, because it is the seminary for study, the infirmary, and the hospitium of all the province. Consequently, I opine that it will be a work very proper for the royal kindness of your Majesty, and for the service of the Divine Majesty, to grant the residence the alms of the said sum — or greater, if your Majesty be so pleased. Its being in unassigned Indians, with which grant the soldiers are rewarded, is not a [mere] favor to the said fathers, since they embark with the soldiers on all the occasions demanding a fleet, and are employed in the rearing of the youth of this community, and all their ministers are engaged in the service of the community, gaining much fruit, and signalizing themselves among the other orders. With them and with me the said fathers are now in excellent harmony, and are the instrument of the peace between the tribunals, of which I am giving your Majesty a special account, so that you might have in your royal Council an account of the dissensions which, as I advised you, we had last year. May our Lord preserve the Catholic and royal person of your Majesty as He can, and as is necessary to Christendom. Manila, August six, one thousand six hundred and thirty-seven.

Fray Hernando, archbishop of Manila.

Letters from Corcuera to Felipe IV

Sire:

When your Majesty, through your grace and condescension, sent me to serve you in these Filipinas Islands, you were pleased to give me your commands in one of your royal decrees, dated at Madrid, on the sixteenth of February in the past year, one thousand six hundred and thirty-five—issued on account of the information which you had from this royal Audiencia of the losses which these islands have suffered, during the past thirty years and more, from Cachil Corralat, king of the great island of Mindanao, from the kings of Jolo and Burney, and from the Camucones. They have plundered the islands, and taken captive the poor Christian Indians, selling them as their slaves from one country to another, seizing the religious and the ministers of the holy gospel, burning the villages, and devastating everything. The royal Audiencia has given your Majesty but scant information of the great and excessive injuries which these poor islands have experienced from these Moro enemies. For in the year when I arrived here, they did not content themselves with taking captive more than twenty-five or thirty thousand vassals of your Majesty; at this time which I mention they seized and carried away captive from the island of Calamianes Don Diego de Alabez, your Majesty's alcalde-mayor in that island and province, together with three religious, Recollects of the Order of St. Augustine, who in various places were furnishing instruction to the vassals of your Majesty. At the same time when they made this notable seizure, they sacked the churches, and afterward burned them, carrying away the monstrances with the most holy sacrament, the chalices, and other sacred vessels, with all the ornaments that they could find—even taking the bells. All together, this booty was worth more than two or three thousand pesos—which for churches so poor, and for poor Indians, was a considerable loss.

Having made inquiries as to what measures had been taken by my predecessors in so many years to check such lawless acts, I was assured by this royal Audiencia, and by all the oldest and most experienced residents of this colony, that in the past thirty-four years there had been expended from your Majesty's royal exchequer more than two hundred thousand pesos, in equipping fleets in Cebu, Oton, this city, and other places, against these enemies. But these fleets were never able to come up with the pirates because of the swiftness of the Moro vessels, and because of the negligence of the commanders who were sent on these expeditions; consequently, all that was accomplished was to go to the islands where these enemies had been, and to live on the tender chickens and other supplies which the poor Indians had carried away to the hills. All these things, and the commands that your Majesty was pleased to lay upon me in your royal decree above mentioned, constrained me to summon a council of war. It included all the old soldiers who are in this city, not only those in active service, but those on half-pay; also the royal Audiencia, and the royal officials of your Majesty. I told them how important it was to put an end to these raids, as your Majesty had commanded, and proposed to go in person to punish these Moros. All the members of the council uttered opinions contrary to mine, deeming it to be of greater importance that I should remain in this city. Only one thought that I should go to render this service, and that was my nephew, Captain and Sargento-mayor Don Pedro Hurtado de Corcuera; and some one among them said that your Majesty's power was not sufficient to conquer the height of Mindanao, where the king Cachil Corralat was.

Considering what your Majesty had commanded me in your royal decree, and the blasphemies which these Moros had uttered—saying that by carrying away the monstrances with the most holy sacrament they were carrying the God of the Christians captive, trampling upon them, and mocking them in other ways; spitting in the chalices; and using the patens as receptacles for the saliva from their buyo-chewing—all these things obliged me, Sire, [to go on this quest]. After having sent to Terrenate two galleons well armed, two pataches, and six champans, with two hundred infantry and two hundred mariners, to carry supplies to those forts, together with one new galley which the governor of those forts, Don Pedro de Mendiola, had requested from me that it might accompany the one which he maintained there (of which enterprise and of those islands I will give your Majesty an account in a separate letter), I embarked with eleven champans—vessels which were indeed frail and weak, but the other galley had not been completed. I had my own company of infantry, of one hundred and fifty soldiers; another, of a hundred Pampango Indians; and that of Captain Lorenco de Orella y Ugalde, containing another hundred men, mariners. With these two hundred and fifty Spaniards and one hundred Pampango Indians, I sailed as far as the fort of Camboanga, which (as I wrote to your Majesty last year) Don Juan Cereco de Salamanca had begun, or had ordered to be built, in that very island of Mindanao; by way of this port sail the ships which go to Terrenate for the relief of those forts. I made the decision which I have stated to your Majesty, in order to see if that port was of so much importance as they were all assuring me it was, and whether the expenses which that fort has caused your Majesty were being checked; I also went in order to visit the rest of the islands, which lie on that route, and to repair the wrongs which certain persons are inflicting on the poor Indians. A few months before, I had sent to that fort a new governor and a new commander, judging that those officers who had until then been stationed there had accomplished nothing of importance with their flotilla. After Sargento-mayor Bartolome Diaz Barrera arrived as governor, and Sargento-mayor Nicolas Gomez as captain of both companies, those Moros withdrawing [to their own country] with the rich prize of those religious and the consecrated vessels which I have mentioned to your Majesty, and a friendly Moro having informed us that the pirates had passed, two leguas from there, by the island of Basilan (or Taguima, for the island has both names), Bartolome Diaz Barrera sent Sargento-mayor [Gomez] with five caracoas and his company of soldiers. They encountered the Moros in the middle of their voyage, with their booty, and fought with them. One of our own balls, strangely, struck one of the missionary fathers, who tried to see how the Spaniards were fighting; and he was killed. Out of seven caracoas which were conveying the enemy with their spoils, the said sargento-mayor captured four and burned one; and he rescued more than one hundred and twenty Christian captives, the rest being killed by our bullets. There were also some Moros who, as those people are so stubborn, would not stop killing our men, and perished by drowning. As soon as our men captured two of the caracoas, the rest took to flight, and by hard rowing reached their own lands, with the two priests and the greater part of the sacred vessels which they were carrying away as plunder.

In the province of Camarines there was another piece of good-fortune; for Don Pedro Mena, alcalde-mayor of that province, burned eighteen of the Moro caracoas; and of the rest more than ten were wrecked by a storm, in which were drowned the Moros and the Christian captives whom they were carrying away. In the island of Leite, two other officers, half-pay alférezes, sailed out in different vessels after the rest of the Moro horde; and they captured from the pirates a caracoa, and slew many of their men. With these two successes, then, I arrived, Sire, at Camboanga with the troops whom I have mentioned; and from that fort I took Sargento-mayor Nicolas Gomez, with his company. With these, I had a force of three hundred and fifty Spaniards and one hundred and fifty Pampangos, and with them proceeded to Lamitan, the principal village of the king, Cachil Corralat; but only four caracoas and two champans could arrive at the same time with me, on account of stormy weather. Confiding more in the goodness and mercy of God than in the number of my soldiers, and having left those vessels well guarded, I landed with about seventy Spaniards and two small field-pieces (which they themselves fired). They engaged the enemy, in both the village and the fort; and God was pleased to give your Majesty a great victory, although by the means of forces so weak and so few soldiers. The village and fort were gained in less than half an hour; in them were two pieces of bronze artillery, for six- and eight-libra balls respectively; thirteen bronze versos, and some forty or fifty muskets and arquebuses; and in the mosque were found two bells. In the river were more than three hundred barks and other vessels; four of these, belonging to some merchants, were laden with wax, oil, and other goods, which made rich booty for the soldiers. I reserved for your Majesty only the wax and oil, and the arms. If I had had more men, I would have followed the king to the top of the height; and it might be that before he reached the height he would have fallen into the hands of your Majesty's soldiers. I thought it best to give thanks to God for what had been accomplished, and to content myself with that until the rest of the men should arrive. This was Friday, the thirteenth of the month; on the sixteenth the rest of the vessels arrived. Having made all the soldiers confess and receive communion, I distributed among them ammunition, and biscuit and cheese for four days. I sent Nicolas Gomez with one hundred and fifty Spaniards by way of the rear of the hill, two hours before daybreak, and fifty Pampangos, and some Indians to carry the supplies. I myself set out with about two hundred Spaniards, fifty Pampangos, and as many more Indians, by the route in front, and arrived at the foot of the hill, a distance of about a long legua. I found a large village built below, and abandoned by the Moros, who had retreated up the hill. I set out over the rugged slopes, and although the Moros uttered many shouts and outcries, they did not interrupt my progress until we were at a musket-shot from their fortification. I had given orders to the captains who were leading the vanguard, Lorenzo de Ugalde and Don Rodrigo de Guillestigui, and to my nephew the sargento-mayor, to make observations and reconnoiter when they reached the fort, instructing them to win the fight, with hearts all the more courageous since they had seen that in the assault on the village not one man had been killed, and no more than two or three wounded. They laid siege to the hill before I could reach the scene of conflict, to which I proceeded with your Majesty's colors. The Moros awaited us with a good supply of muskets and versos; at the first volley they killed some of the more daring soldiers, and wounded others. Our men reached the stockade, shouting "Santiago!" and asking for more men from the detachment which was still ascending the hill, by one of slopes and paths as rugged and narrow as any which I ever saw in the Alarbes or the Pirineos, or in any places where I have served your Majesty. On account of the haste with which he had tried to reach me, Captain Ugalde had lost an arm; and Captain Don Rodrigo de Guillestegui, alférez in my company, had been several times struck by stones, so that he could hardly move. My nephew Don Pedro had received a musket-shot in the right leg, across the shin-bone. There were twenty-three killed, officers and men, and more than fifty wounded. Although your Majesty's soldiers fought with great valor, the enemy could not have received much damage, even from our musketry, on account of the great strength of their stockades, which were everywhere pierced with holes from our musket-balls; and, because we were unable to carry up the hill our two small field-pieces (which carry two-libra balls), the musketry could not accomplish much. Seeing that we could not carry the fort, and the number of men I had lost, so that there were hardly a hundred effective men left, and knowing that on the hill the Moros numbered four thousand, well armed, I took command of the rearguard, ordered that the wounded be carried away, and went down from the hill, uniting my troops with the guard of Pampangos whom I had left with the cannon. Although I desired to hold that post, I had not men for this; on that account, and in order that the Moros should not harass me by cutting off the heads of the wounded men, I had to escort them as far as the fort of San Francisco Xabiel, which had been gained below. I reached it at night, with the troops discouraged, and reduced to the small number that I have mentioned to your Majesty. On this occasion I had not the support of Sargento-mayor Nicolas Gomez and his men—who went as the rearguard, on account of pains in his legs—although he had not more than three leguas to go from four o'clock in the morning to eleven, when the battle commenced. They were reconnoitering, carrying Nicolas Gomez in a hammock because he could not, on account of his foot, climb paths so rugged. He did not come back until the morning of the next day, when I had sent eighty men who survived from the vanguard, to which Nicolas Gomez had to go, setting out as soon as the men had heard mass. They went at that time because the enemy had not fortified the rear of the hill. Captain Gastelu, who led Nicolas Gomez's vanguard, gained a good position, and killed some Moros who were defending a passage across which they had only felled a tree. Captain Gastelu passed this obstruction, and gained the top of the hill and the rear of the king's main stronghold, where he had his house, and four pieces of artillery. Of these, one was bronze, with your Majesty's arms on it, carrying an eight-libra ball; the three others were of cast iron, for six- and eight-libra balls. They were loaded up to the mouth with balls, chains, and spikes, in order [to destroy us] if we had gone up the hill by that route, on which the guide whom I took with me had already started us. But God influenced my choice, in order that we should go by the other road; for although I did not get off very cheaply, yet by this road it would have cost me far more dear. At the time when we were fighting above on the seventeenth of March, the eve of St. Joseph's day, the eighty men whom I sent with Captain Rodrigo de Guillestigui, my alférez, arrived at the foot of the hill on this other side; and, as a result of the pious haste which Father Marcelo Mastrilo used in saying mass in order that we might pursue our march, the news was soon brought to me that the Moros had flung themselves down from their heights in flight, and that your Majesty's banners were flying over their three forts and our chaplains singing the Te Deum laudamus. Other arms were secured there—twelve or thirteen versos, and more than a hundred arquebuses and muskets; everything else was given to the soldiers as booty, as a reward for their labors. Thus your Majesty gained a victory, as others will write you. As the king, Cachil Corralat, is very influential in those regions, I have made public an offer to give three thousand pesos for his head. The captives and his wife's servants tell me that the king was wounded in an arm by a musket-ball; with that, I understand, he will not be able to keep up his people's courage; and, if he does not go away into those rugged mountains, he will not escape me. His wife threw herself from the walls, with a little child in her arms; and many other women belonging to the leading families were sold here on your Majesty's account—fifty of them, besides as many more men; while more than two hundred Christian captives were set free. Of the two Augustinian fathers, one had been slain in revenge because we had killed, in the assault from below, the commander of that fort, who was a nephew of the king, and two others of their chiefs. On the day when the height was carried by our men, the Moros, when they took to flight, inflicted so many wounds on the other father that, although they brought him to me alive, he had seventeen mortal wounds, so that within thirteen hours he died, in my quarters. His death left us all as envious as compassionate of his fate. Thus all the three fathers, Sire, have died, at various times. I brought away the ornaments and sacred vessels, and returned them to their owners, after having displayed them in a procession which was made as a thank-offering to the most holy sacrament—from which, as I firmly believe, your Majesty received this favor [of the victory], on account of the fiestas which had been celebrated a few months before, in accordance with your royal decree. I send an official statement of this, in order that your Majesty may know in what manner your commands were obeyed. I had intended to make this relation more concise, but I have not been able to do so. Others will give a more detailed account of the campaign; but I am telling your Majesty only the substance of the service that has been rendered to you.

I returned to Çamboanga, after I had sent Sargento-mayor Pedro Palomino with five caracoas to the king of Buayen, to reduce him to a vassal of your Majesty, and to make him pay tribute, or else wage war against him as we had done to Corralat. He yielded what was demanded from him, and became tributary to your Majesty. He and all his vassals pay the annual tribute: every married man, three eight-real pesos; and each single man, a peso and a half. To some persons it has seemed that I have imposed a heavy tax on them; but they do not consider the great expenses which these Moros have caused to your Majesty's treasury, nor my granting them the favor, in your Majesty's royal name, of remitting half the tribute to those who shall become Christians. I doubt much whether they will do so; for they are a fierce and obstinate people. The king of Buayen will allow the fathers of the Society to supply instruction, under the condition that they baptize only children, and do not annoy or urge the adults; I granted this, as being so in accord with the holy gospel, since God does not bring any one by force to His holy law; and gradually both the children and their grandparents will become Christians. I have therefore brought to settle and live in the fort of Camboanga nearly four hundred Moros; and I hope that within a year all that island (which is larger than the whole of España) will pay tribute to your Majesty.

I sent Captain Juan Nicolas with eighty Spaniards and twenty Pampangos, with a thousand fighting Indians from among your Majesty's Christian vassals; and he harried all the coast of more than half of the island—burning villages and grain-fields, and destroying the trees, and cutting off more than seventy heads—until he reached the fort of Caraga in the same island. That fort (which I have now finished) is built of stone, without any expense from the royal treasury of your Majesty; and that at Çamboanga will cost very little. Thus, between Juan Nicolas and myself, we made the entire circuit of the island.

This coming year I will go, or I will send some one, to explore the country inland to the lake of Manala [i.e., Malanao], around which there are more than seventy houses, I mean villages, containing many people. They are not supplied with firearms, although the Moros are well provided with long arrows and other missile weapons. I hope in God to carry on that enterprise as promptly and easily as this other one; and even to bring down from his lofty stronghold the king of Jolo, and reduce him to obedience to your Majesty. And I will try to send an expedition—if not next year, then the year after—against the king of Burney, who shelters and favors the Camucones, who by themselves and alone are of no account. When that is done, in all this archipelago there will remain no enemy except the Dutch. God knows that if I had a thousand more Spaniards, I would give them enough in which to earn reward; but I have so much territory to guard, and in so many posts, that, with the small forces that there are in these islands, one thousand five hundred men, I cannot attempt to render your Majesty this service.

Although your Majesty has not authorized me to grant extra pay, when I saw how your soldiers fought in my presence, and how at the cost of their blood and their lives they won credit for your Majesty's arms, I granted in your royal name an increase of pay to the wounded, to each one a peso more than his usual wages; and to some I gave two pesos. This will be, in all, ninety-seven pesos of extra pay. In order to compensate for this new expenditure from your Majesty's revenues, I placed in the royal treasury two hundred and fifty pesos which will be vacant at this time in every year, in order that from this sum may be paid the twenty-one and thirty pesos which an adjutant had who died in the campaign; these amounts also will remain on the half-pay list. Accordingly, the only extra expense thus incurred from your Majesty's revenues is the other forty-six pesos; and from that I have cut out more than twenty pesos, by means of offices which I have given to those soldiers—while within a year, or sooner, I will have given offices to the rest of them, and thus will have canceled all the extra pay which I granted them.

The royal official judges made objections to doing this, alleging their obligations. I replied that nevertheless they must confirm these grants, and that I would give account of them to your Majesty; and that, in case you were not pleased to approve them, I would pay them from my own salary. For I consider it a grievous thing to see before me your soldiers fighting, and being crippled in your Majesty's service, and I not able to encourage them with the reward of a peso of extra pay, which is very little gain for them. I entreat your Majesty to be pleased to command that this be examined and approved; and, in case objection is made, to be pleased to let me know of it, so that—although in like cases I may grant other favors to the soldiers in your royal name—I may not give them extra pay; and so that the royal official judges may pay this amount from my salary, deducting from it what shall have been thus spent. May our Lord protect the Catholic person of your Majesty, as Christendom has need. Manila, August 20, 1637. Sire, your vassal kisses your Majesty's feet.

Sebastian Hurtado de Corcuera
Sire:

Master-of-camp Pedro de Heredia has by your Majesty's grace governed the forts of Terrenate for twelve years, and you have commanded that his residencia be taken; but he has ingenuity and shrewdness, and always has been able to make gifts to my predecessors. It is reported that he is accustomed to say among the soldiers that he has 30,000 pesos to close one eye of any governor who shall send to take his residencia, and, if it should be necessary, as many more pesos to close the other eye; but he has found the door to this shut. He is availing himself of his ingenuity, as he has done before, to make the residencia which I have taken of his government suit his wishes. After I came here (or before), a Portuguese resident in Malaca demanded from him 60,000 pesos, which Don Pedro had seized from his property. I appointed Auditor Don Antonio Alvarez de Castro as judge in this suit. The sentence having been pronounced, on sufficient evidence, that he must repay 12,000 pesos to this Portuguese, Simon Texeira, Don Pedro appealed to your Majesty's royal Council of the Indias; but as you have here your royal Audiencia, the affair was placed in its hands. He challenged Auditor Marcos Çapata and all the lawyers of this city; his plea was that in Terrenate he had brought to trial Sargento-mayor Don Marcos Çapata, son of the auditor, because he had punished with the cudgel a subordinate of his for a certain shameless act, and because officially, without having complained to any one, he upbraided him for holding illicit relations with a married woman, without having corrected or punished him. This might be true, because, in order to cover up his own evil proceedings, there was not a captain, nor a commander of the relief ships, nor a private soldier, with whom he did not pick a quarrel, in order to keep that man under guard during his term there, defending himself by saying that they were his enemies, on account of his quarrel with them. Besides this, Sire, is the money which has come into his hands and those of the accountant during these twelve years, together with the military supplies of all kinds which are carried to him every year. The provisions he distributed among the soldiers, without charging these against their pay; and he has, according to assertions made to me, charged large quantities of supplies to many men who had fled to the enemy on account of the bad treatment that they experienced, and to others who had died of sickness; it cannot be known, therefore, whether these men actually received them. All these things are made public by the soldiers whom I have had exchanged from those forts, which have held these men as slaves for twenty or twenty-four years, without their being allowed to come to this city. On account of all these things, I have ordered that all the papers of the accountancy for those forts shall be brought here, so that it may be seen how so great an amount of your Majesty's properly has been spent. Since the old soldiers have come back, there is no end to the petitions against him—for having taken away from some of them honor, from others their possessions.

As I found last year your Majesty's royal treasury in a needy condition, and the citizens not only had no money to lend it, but instead had asked me for more than 60,000 pesos from the Sangley licenses in order to relieve their own needs, I managed through an intermediary person to inform Don Pedro that he could make a donation to your Majesty of 100,000 pesos, which would adjust his residencia and his affairs, rendering satisfaction to the parties concerned, so that his reputation might be saved and that he might have opportunity to receive grace from your Majesty; for the universal opinion is that he possesses wealth amounting to 400,000 pesos. Not only did he refuse to do this, but he even undertook to offer only 15,000 pesos; so I ordered that nothing more be said in this matter. This man is so subtle that if your Majesty does not send an official to take his residencia, he will come out from it with everything just as he desires, as every one says. I assert that it is necessary for your Majesty to send some one, because with all the officials here Don Pedro is so shrewd and crafty and suave that he sways every one at his will, and will attain all his desires. I have fulfilled my duty in placing this before your Majesty; now you will be pleased to command what is most expedient to your royal service. May our Lord protect the Catholic person of your Majesty, as Christendom has need. Manila, August 20, in the year 637. Sire, your vassal kisses your Majesty's feet.

Sebastian Hurtado de Corcuera

[Endorsed: "Manila; to his Majesty; 1637. Don Sebastian Hurtado de Corcuera, August 20; contains particulars regarding the master-of-camp Pedro de Heredia." "February 5, 1639; hand to the fiscal." "The fiscal says that this letter comes alone, and without any accompanying proofs of the allegations. This residencia could be awaited, if an account of it comes in the fleet; and if it is delayed in the Audiencia it can be entrusted to the auditor whom the Council shall be pleased to appoint, so that the residencia may be taken in a thoroughly satisfactory manner and referred to the Council for its decision. Let the governor be informed that he must endeavor most carefully to administer justice in such cases, without giving any opportunity for composition of offences, which is so injurious to justice, which should be administered with the utmost equity and uprightness to all persons. Madrid, February 22, 1639." "February 28; wait for the coming of the fleet, to see what information about this matter shall arrive; and if any comes, let it be brought with this letter."]

Bibliographical Data

The following documents are obtained from MSS.
in the Archivo general de Indias, Sevilla:

Letter by Corcuera, June 30, 1636. — "Simancas — Secular;
Audiencia de Filipinas; cartas y espedientes del gobernador
vistos en el Consejo; años de 1629 á 1639; est. 67, caj. 6, leg. 8."

Royal decrees. — The first of these is in "Audiencia de
Filipinas; registros de oficio, reales ordenes dirigidas
á las autoridades y particulares del distrito de la
Audiencia; años 1605 á 1645; est. 105, caj. 2, leg. 12."

Auditorship of accounts. — "Simancas — Secular; cartas
y expedientes de los oficiales reales de Manila vistos en
el Consejo; años 1623 á 1641; est. 67, caj. 6, leg. 30."

Letters by Corcuer, 1637. — The same as No. 1.

The following documents are obtained from
the Academia Real de la Historia, Madrid (the first
being a printed book, the others original MSS.):

Informatory memorial to king. — This is collated with
the MS. copy in the Biblioteca Nacional, Madrid —
pressmark, "MSS. 8990, Aa 47, fol. 273–350."

Defeat of Moro pirates. — In "Papeles de
los Jesuitas; tomo 84, n°. 31."

Conquest of Mindanao. — The same as No. 6, save "n°. 24."

Events in Filipinas. — The same as No. 6, save "n°. 26."

The following documents are taken from the "Cedulario Indico," in the Archivo Historico Nacional, Madrid:

Letter to Corcuera. — In "tomo 39, fol. 219b, n°. 210."
2. *Royal Decrees.* — The second and third decrees, "tomo 39, fol. 226b, and 225," respectively.

The following document is taken from Barrantes's *Guerras piraticas*:

Corcuera's entry. — pp. 303–310.

The following document is taken from Pastells's edition of Colin's *Labor evangélica*:

Aid requested by Jesuits. — Vol. iii, pp. 757, 758.